Sicher im

Abi

Oberstufen-Wissen

Englisch

Landeskunde
Great Britain/United States of America

Ekkehard Spann

Klett Lerntraining

Ihre Meinung zählt!

**Hallo, wir sind das Redaktions-Team.
Unser Ziel ist es, die besten Abi-Lernhilfen zu machen.**

Helfen Sie uns dabei!

SIND SIE ZUFRIEDEN MIT DIESEM BUCH?

Dann freuen wir uns über Ihre **Weiterempfehlung**. Erzählen Sie es Ihrem Freundeskreis, dem Buchhändler Ihres Vertrauens oder schreiben Sie eine **Rezension** bei Onlinekauf.
Das hilft nicht nur uns, sondern auch anderen Kunden bei der Suche nach einer passenden Lernhilfe für das Abitur.

SIE HABEN FRAGEN BZW. KRITIK ZU DIESEM BUCH?

Wir freuen uns über Ihre Anregungen.
Schreiben Sie uns eine Nachricht an **kundenservice@klett-lerntraining.de**.

So können wir mit Ihrem Feedback in Zukunft noch bessere Bücher anbieten.

Vielen Dank und viel Erfolg im Abitur!

Ihre Redaktion von Klett Lerntraining

Social Welfare in Britain and the United States

The British and American Economies

Education in Britain and the United States

The Mass Media in Britain and the United States

Religion in Britain and the United States

British Empire and the Commonwealth

Britain and Europe

The United States and the World

Anglo-Irish Relations

Liebe Abiturientin, lieber Abiturient,

dieses Buch bietet Ihnen das **ausführliche** und **komplette Wissen** zur **Landeskunde Großbritanniens** und der **USA**. Es ist der **ideale Begleiter** für die gesamte Oberstufenzeit und bestens geeignet für eine gründliche Wiederholung der Lerninhalte. Schaffen Sie mit diesem Buch die Basis für eine **gute Note** und gehen Sie **sicher** durch jede Klausur und die Abiturprüfung!

Hilfreiche **Elemente** strukturieren den Lernstoff. Sie machen das Lernen mit diesem Buch komfortabel und sorgen für einen **optimalen**, **nachhaltigen Lernerfolg**.

OVERVIEW Diese Doppelseiten vor jedem Kapitel dienen dem raschen Einstieg, indem sie die wesentlichen Lerninhalte des Kapitels optisch übersichtlich und in gegliederter Form präsentieren.

IN BRIEF Jedes Kapitel beginnt mit einer kurzen, stichpunktartigen Zusammenfassung. Sie führt ins Thema ein und nennt das Wichtigste.

REVIEW bringt am Kapitel-Ende das Grundwissen auf den Punkt.

RANDSPALTENTEXTE helfen, das Wissen zu strukturieren und durch Schlüsselbegriffe den Überblick zu behalten. Vokabelangaben, im Text grau hinterlegt, erklären schwierige oder neue Begriffe.

GLOSSARY Zentrale Begriffe sind blau hervorgehoben und werden im Begriffsverzeichnis/Glossary ab S. 200 erläutert.

Zusätzlich können Sie sich kostenlos passende Lernvideos ansehen. Sie stützen den nachhaltigen Lernerfolg durch die visuelle Aufbereitung. Zum Ansehen der Videos scannen Sie einfach mit einer QR-Code-App den Code. Sie gelangen dann zur Video-Übersicht. Alternativ können Sie auch die Seite www.abitur.klett-lerntraining.de aufrufen und in der Reihe „Oberstufen-Wissen" Ihr Buch anklicken. Sie sehen die Video-Übersicht und können dann per Klick ein Video starten.

Viel Erfolg im Abitur wünscht Ihnen
Ihr Team von Klett Lerntraining

OVERVIEW

Queen Elizabeth II

The Sovereign

"reigns, but does not rule"

- no political power
- only representative role
- acts on the advice of the Prime Minister
- Head of State of the UK
- symbol of unity
- summons, prorogues and dissolves Parliament
- Head of State of the Church of England
- must be a Protestant

Palace of Westminster, London Parliament (House of Lords and House of Commons)

House of Commons

Sovereign power

- Her Majesty's Government
- makes laws
- 659 Members of Parliament
- elected by the people

The British System of Government

Prime Minister

- head of Her Majesty's Government
- leader of the strongest party in the House of Commons (at the moment: Conservative Party)
- elected by the people

Gordon Brown (2007–2010)

David Cameron (2010–2016)

Theresa May (2016–2019)

Boris Johnson (since 2019)

1 Political Life in Great Britain and in the United States

Legislative Branch

Congress (House of Representatives / Senate)
- makes and passes laws
- can override President's veto with ⅔ majority
- can impeach the President
- elected by the people

Capitol, Washington

The American System of Government:
System of Checks and Balances

Judicial Branch

Supreme Court
- interprets laws
- chief justice and 8 other justices appointed for life
- can determine that laws are unconstitutional
- In July 2009 the first Hispanic was appointed Supreme Court justice

Supreme Court

Executive Branch

President
- carries out laws
- can veto bills passed by Congress
- elected for four years and by an electoral college

Barack Obama (2009-2017)

Donald J. Trump (2017–2021)

Jo Biden (since 2021)

IN BRIEF

1.1 Political Life in Great Britain

- There is no written Constitution.
- Britain is a hereditary constitutional monarchy.
- The Sovereign (Queen) has mainly a representative function as head of state.
- Parliament consists of two chambers, the House of Commons and the House of Lords.
- The government is led by the Prime Minister and the Cabinet.
- Devolution involves power sharing between the Westminster Parliament and parliaments or assemblies in Scotland, Wales and Northern Ireland.
- Britain has developed a classical two-party system (Labour Party, Conservatives).
- The electoral system is a majority vote.
- Since June 2010 the Conservative Party has been in power. It is led by Boris Johnson since 2019.

The **British Constitution** is not written, but consists of **individual laws** (Acts of Parliament) and **conventions** (unwritten rules, customs, precedents). Therefore there is no need for a "constitutional court".

Major documents of British constitutional history are e.g.
- Magna Carta (1215)
- Bill of Rights (1689)

trial: legal process

franchise: right to vote in an election

The British Constitution

The constitution of a country is a system of principles governing the affairs of a nation.

Britain's Constitution (→ p. 24) is basically unwritten. It is not contained in any single document as that of the United States, but consists of **1. laws** and **2. conventions** that have evolved in the course of time.

1. The **constitutional law** consists of individual historical treaties or declarations (sometimes going back as far as the Middle Ages), which define the rights of the individual and restrict the power of the Sovereign, and of **Acts of Parliament** (statutes) which serve to define certain aspects of the Constitution.

Important documents of the British Constitution	
Magna Carta (1215) Petition of Rights (1628) Habeas Corpus Act (1679)	These illustrate the development of the principles of parliamentary control in legislation (no imprisonment without a fair trial) and taxation.
Bill of Rights (1689)	This states that the King rules by approval of Parliament, not by Divine Right.
First, Second and Third Reform Bills of 1832, 1867 and 1884	These extend franchise to men in the upper middle class, lower middle class and the working class respectively.
Equal Franchise Act (1928)	Both men and women who are 21 years of age can vote.

2. **Constitutional conventions** are unwritten rules or customs that are acknowledged by the citizens. They have evolved over time and are part of the British Common Law, a legal system that is based on precedents. As normal Acts of Parliament can change constitutional conventions (Common Law), the British Constitution is always evolving. In Britain there is no "constitutional court", such as the Supreme Court (→ pp. 30 ff) in the USA, to protect the Constitution.

precedent: a former case that may be used as a rule for taking a similar decision

Despite the tradition of freedom of speech and other rights in the UK, until recently there was no modern document that stated clearly the **rights of the citizens**. This has changed, in recent years, with the adoption of European Union law and the European Convention on Human Rights, which formally guarantees specific rights not provided in UK law. These provisions are enacted in the **European Communities Act 1972** and the **Human Rights Act 1998**.

With British EU membership, European law was introduced which guarantees basic human rights.

The Sovereign

Great Britain is a **hereditary constitutional monarchy**. The Sovereign must be a Protestant (Church of England).
In the course of history the Crown was deprived of all its real political power, so that the Queen, in practice, has little personal influence. Yet **formally** and **symbolically** the powers of the Crown remain very great, because all government actions are carried out in its name.

hereditary: A position in society that is hereditary is passed on as a right from parents to their children.

Representative Role of the Sovereign

- head of state of the United Kingdom;
- head and symbol of unity of the Commonwealth;
- head of state of a number of Commonwealth states (e.g. Australia, Canada, Jamaica, New Zealand);
- head of the Church of England;
- Commander-in-Chief of the British Armed Forces.

Britain is a **hereditary constitutional monarchy**. The Queen has no real political power. Her role is more representative as e.g. head of state and a symbol of unity. She holds only a limited number of rights (royal prerogatives). She "reigns, but does not rule".

Royal Prerogatives

The Royal Prerogative is the right of the Sovereign to act independently of Parliament. Constitutional convention has reserved certain political functions for the Queen to fulfil, which are often no more than ritual play-acting:

- she summons, prorogues and dissolves Parliament;
- she delivers her annual Speech from the Throne (drawn up by the Prime Minister) at the opening of Parliament;
- she gives royal assent to bills passed by Parliament;

to summon: to order members to assemble

to prorogue: to bring a session of Parliament to an end without dissolving it *(vertagen)*

assent: agreement

- she has regular talks with the Prime Minister about the political situation of the country;
- she appoints the Prime Minister and the Cabinet on the Prime Minister's advice;
- she creates peers and knights;
- she makes state visits and fulfils good-will tours to create interest in Britain and her industrial products;
- she takes part in important national celebrations and ceremonies.

In carrying out this role, the Queen always acts according to the policies and wishes of the government at that time. In other words: **"The Queen reigns, but she does not rule."**

After more than 50 years on the throne, Elizabeth II is still very popular and well-respected by the people. On the other hand, the Royal Family is increasingly criticized, and there are some doubts about the future. This is because they are seen as costly, remote from ordinary people and failing to set a good example in their personal life.

Parliament

The **British Parliament** has developed for more than 700 years into a model of democracy. It is the highest legislative assembly and comprises the House of Commons and the House of Lords. Its main tasks are to pass new laws, to control government policy and to debate political issues.

The British Parliament has gradually evolved over more than 700 years. In the 13th century it began as literally a place for the **Sovereign to talk to his people.** Through the 17th century it struggled to gain **supremacy over the Crown**, and by the 19th century it represented the increasingly **democratic** voice of the nation. The present-day structure has a **dominant Prime Minister**, an executive Cabinet, and a political party system which can form an effective opposition. The next big challenge for Parliament is the increasing involvement of the **European Union** in all aspects of governance.

Parliament is the most important **law-making body** of the British people. It has full legislative and executive powers and is neither restricted by a written constitution nor by a special court as in the USA. It consists of two chambers: the **House of Commons** and the **House of Lords**. The main functions of Parliament are:

- to pass laws;
- to control government policy;
- to debate the controversial political topics of the day.

suffrage: the right to vote in national elections

constituency: town or district that sends a representative to Parliament

The **House of Commons** now consists of 650 Members of Parliament (MPs), who are elected by universal suffrage in individual constituencies for five years. 533 seats are for England, 40 for Wales, 59 for Scotland and 18 for Northern Ireland. The Scottish Parliament (Constituencies) Act 2004 reorganized most Scottish constituencies cutting their number by 13 to bring their size, in terms of population, in line with those in England.

The **seating plan** of the House of Commons illustrates the de facto **two-party system**. The Prime Minister and the Cabinet occupy the front bench facing the Opposition, which is led by the Leader of the Opposition and his Shadow Cabinet. Less important MPs of each party have their seats on the back benches and are therefore called "backbenchers".

Individual MPs, their political parties and the government all depend on each other: MPs need the support of their party; parties need the loyalty of their members; the government needs the support of MPs to pass legislation. The exact balance between these political groupings is constantly shifting, with the personality of the Prime Minister being the most important single factor. Party discipline is exercised by the so-called "whips", who ensure that members keep to the party line, that the government can complete its legislative programme and that the Prime Minister keeps his/her majority. The most dramatic part of the business of the Commons is Question Time, when government ministers have to account to the House for their actions; MPs have the ultimate power of passing a vote of no confidence to bring down the government.

The **House of Lords** has 744 members (Oct 2010) of whom 627 are Life Peers, 91 Hereditary Peers and 26 Bishops. They receive no salary for their parliamentary work but can claim expenses. Following a series of reforms the number of hereditary peers was reduced from originally over 750 to only 91. The number of members of the House of Lords is not fixed; new life peers can be created at any time, and the number of hereditary peers reduces as they die.

The **Church of England** is represented by the two archbishops and 24 other senior bishops.

Like the Crown, the Lords nowadays have very little direct political power. They can

- make amendments to a bill and return it to the Commons;
- delay bills for a year (except Money Bills);
- initiate non-controversial bills.

The Constitutional Reform Act 2005 made provision to create a **Supreme Court** of the UK to take over the judicial function of the House of Lords. This reform was completed in October 2009. The 12 former Law Lords are no longer peers, but have become Justices of the Supreme Court of the UK. The Supreme Court is the final court of appeal in the whole of the UK for civil cases, and also for criminal cases except in Scotland. It hears cases of the greatest public or constitutional importance affecting the whole population.

The House of Commons consists of 650 Members of Parliament who are elected by local constituencies for five years. It also includes seats for Scotland, Wales and Northern Ireland.

whips: functionaries that are appointed to ensure that party members vote

The **House of Lords** has 744 (2010) members, hereditary peers and life peers. It has very little direct political power, but only a consultative function. It can propose amendments to bills but cannot veto them.

amendment: alteration

to initiate: to introduce

For and Against the House of Lords

For

- Party discipline is much less important than it is in the Commons, so members are able to speak freely.
- When opposition in the Commons is weak, the Lords can be effective by inflicting defeats on the government.
- It is of great value as a revising chamber.
- It can be an effective moderator against rash decisions.

Against

- It is out of place in a democracy, as it is not elected.
- The House of Commons always wins in the end, so the House of Lords is a waste of time and money.
- It preserves class distinction.

Her Majesty's Government

The British Government is a **parliamentary monarchy**. It is led by the Prime Minister and the Cabinet.

The British Government is formed by the body of ministers who take responsibility for the administration of political affairs. It is led by the **Prime Minister** (by convention the leader of the political party which enjoys a majority of votes in the House of Commons) and his/her **Cabinet**.

The Prime Minister

The Prime Minister is the head of the British Government. He / she determines the principles of government policy and appoints his / her Cabinet members.

- presides over the Cabinet;
- chooses and dismisses Cabinet members;
- is responsible for the distribution of functions among members;
- determines the principles of government policy;
- may request the Queen to dissolve Parliament and call a general election at any time during the five-year parliamentary term;
- informs Parliament of the activities of government;
- informs the Queen of the government's policy;
- recommends appointments to the Queen (e.g. Church of England, civil appointments).

The Cabinet

unanimous: When a group of people are unanimous, they all agree about sth.

It is composed of about 20 members chosen by the Prime Minister. Ministers in charge of the governmental departments are called "Secretaries of State" or "Ministers". They are responsible not only for their own departments, but also jointly for governmental policy. The Cabinet acts unanimously, even when

Cabinet ministers do not agree (collective responsibility). Each minister is expected to support the government's policy or to resign.
British governmental policy is the result of collective decisions made by the Cabinet, with the Prime Minister as Chairman of the Cabinet. However, many people claim that, in practice, the Prime Minister may have too much power, especially at a time when Parliament or Cabinet rarely refuse to support strong Prime Ministers who tend to pay more attention to the news media than to Parliament. In his ten years in power, Tony Blair was just such a dominant figure, modelling himself on former US President Clinton and relying on short announcements in the media to maintain public support. His successor from 2007, Gordon Brown, found it difficult to continue this style of government through a series of crises, and failed to win the next General Election in May 2010.

The **Cabinet** consists of some 20 members chosen by the Prime Minister. These Secretaries of State work together with the Prime Minister to support the government's policy (collective responsibility). In practice the Prime Minister may have too much power.

Devolution

By devolution we understand the **transfer of power** from the Westminster Parliament to Assemblies in Scotland, Wales, and Northern Ireland (→ pp. 192 ff). The idea is to end the demands of the nationalist parties in Scotland (Scottish Nationalist Party) and Wales (Plaid Cymru) and to strengthen the union of the United Kingdom.
Devolution started in the UK in 1920, when the Northern Irish Parliament took control of many aspects of life in the Province. This power was, however, suspended in 1972 after outbreaks of violence between the Protestant majority and the Catholics. Eventually, devolution ("Home Rule") was restored in 2007.
In 1979 referenda in Scotland and Wales rejected the proposal for devolution, but 20 years later 75 % of the Scottish people voted for a "Parliament" of their own. This has 129 members, and is responsible not only for health, education, housing, transport, and law and order, but also has the power to make laws and raise income tax. Foreign affairs, defence, and economic policy continue to be the responsibility of Westminster. The Welsh Assembly, consisting of 60 members, has only limited powers, such as local government, social services, education, language, and environmental protection.
A more fundamental move towards full independence led to another referendum in Scotland in 2014. This was narrowly rejected, but led Westminster to promise further devolved powers for the "Parliament", and also to demand in England for Scottish MPs to be excluded from votes on purely English matters. After the UK's vote in 2016 to leave the EU, the Scots - 62% of whom had voted for remaining within the EU - demanded to be given the right to negotiate on the terms of Brexit.

Devolution means the transfer of powers from the central government in London to regional assemblies.

A first transfer of legislative power from Westminster to a regional government in Northern Ireland failed because of the Northern Irish conflict in 1972.

It was only at the end of the 20th century that directly elected regional assemblies for Scotland and Wales were set up. Powers devolved were limited: they were increased following the referendum on Scottish independence in 2014, which suffered only a narrow defeat.

The Party System

Britain has developed a **two-party system**. The two parties are the Conservatives (Tories) and the Labour (Socialist) Party.

Britain provides the classic example of a **two-party system**. From the middle of the 17th century, political parties represented different aspects of contemporary society, such as aristocrats, middle class, landowners, businessmen, or the Church. Sometimes these groups united against the Crown, sometimes they opposed each other. By the early 20th century, the two main parties were the **Conservatives** (Tories) and the **Liberals** (Whigs). With the rise of the working class, the **Labour** (Socialist) Party replaced the Liberals, who became a small opposition party.

Since 1945, power has alternated eight times between Labour and Conservatives, sometimes very closely balanced and at other times with one party dominant (1980s Margaret Thatcher's Conservatives; 1997–2007 Tony Blair's "New" Labour).

- The parties are not organic wholes, as they often have opposing tendencies within them. The party programme is nothing but the common denominator of these divergent viewpoints. Shifts in political programmes reflect the "take-over" of certain groups, especially after an electoral defeat.
- Splits of parties are a common phenomenon.

common denominator: *gemeinsamer Nenner*

divergent: different

The Conservatives

The **Conservatives**, traditionally representing the upper and middle classes, landowners and businessmen, are mainly concentrated in the rich South. They favour a free market economy without government interference and a strong foreign and defence policy.

They are traditionally the party of the **upper and middle classes**, of landowners and businessmen. Tory strongholds are the middle-class residential areas of the big towns and country areas. Today they have become the party of the rich South with its high-tech and service industries. The party is composed of two divergent tendencies, reflecting different views on social policies and on European integration. Those on the left of the party, i.e. closer to the central position in the political spectrum, are inclined to a paternalistic view of social support and gradual economic reform; they are regarded as European enthusiasts, while those on the right tend to be Eurosceptics and strong supporters of the free market and individual responsibility.

The Conservatives under David Cameron pursue the following aims:

- monetary policy: belief in a free market without government interference;
- an economic policy of low inflation to create an atmosphere in which business can flourish;
- privatization of nationalized industries and promotion of a property-owning democracy (share-holding);
- firmness in foreign policy (e.g. Falklands conflict) and defence (nuclear weapons, deployment of missiles in Britain, belief in a strong Western Alliance);
- limitation of the power of trade unions;
- better targeting of government expenditure (education, welfare, health).

paternalistic: behaving like a father

share-holding: A shareholder is a person who owns shares in a company. Shares can be bought by people as an investment.

deployment: *Stationierung*

targeting: *gezieltere Verteilung*

The Labour Party

Labour is traditionally the party of **industrial workers** and **union members**. It is composed of two main opposing interest groups, which are:

- unionists, Marxists and socialists with a strong left-wing bias, who demand the redistribution of private property, state control, and the nationalization of major industries;
- social reformers who support the welfare state, but prefer a mixed economy policy.

This second group is strongly in the ascendency since the mid-90s; under Tony Blair the whole centre of gravity of the Labour Party moved towards the centre. In his first two years as PM, Gordon Brown has not yet established his priorities. Traditional regions of support of the party are the mining and industrial areas in the Midlands and the North of England, along with Scotland and Wales. Today it is even more concentrated in the North, where the population has been worst hit by unemployment and cuts in subsidies. Labour is also predominantly voted for by Britain's coloured population.

Some of the most significant changes in British society were the introduction of the **Welfare State** (→ p. 82 ff) and the **National Health Service** (→ p. 84 ff) as well as the nationalization of important industries by the Labour Government (1945–1951). It introduced full-blooded socialism in Britain which was only replaced in the 80s by the Conservatives.

The divergent views of political factions within the Labour Party resulted, in 1981, in a split which weakened the party. This occurred when trade union influence on the structure of the party grew, and a number of discontented MPs formed the moderate Social Democratic Party (SDP). The SDP never established itself, however, and ceased to exist in 1990.

The party programme of present-day Labour:

- policy of full employment;
- improvement of social welfare and the National Health Service;
- government support for manufacturing industries;
- modernization of transport, especially public services;
- reduction of defence expenditures;
- a better system of education;
- devolution in Scotland, Wales, and Northern Ireland.

The **Labour Party** mainly represents the interests of industrial workers and trade union members. Its main regions of support are the industrial areas of the Midlands and the North. The party advocates a mixed economy, strong trade unions, full employment and a well developed welfare system.

bias: tendency of mind, inclination

ascendency: *Aufstieg*

cuts in subsidies: reduction in money paid by the government

The Labour Party is responsible for some of the most significant changes in British society:

- the introduction of the Welfare State
- the National Health Service.

The Liberal Democrats

A small third party, the **Liberal Democrats** are in favour of free trade, civil liberties and proportional representation.

proportional representation: a system of voting in elections by which each political party is represented in proportion to the actual number of votes it receives.

to merge: to combine, to become part of each other

Formerly one of the two great British parties, the Liberals declined after a split in the party in the 1920s from which they never recovered. They were traditionally the party of the middle classes, tradesmen, businessmen, and left-wing intellectuals and had their stronghold in Celtic areas, especially in Scotland. They favour in particular:

- Britain's EU membership, free trade, and industrial prosperity;
- the development of social services;
- the expansion of civil liberties;
- proportional representation in Britain;
- greater autonomy of Scotland, Wales, and Northern Ireland.

In the 80s the party worked closely with the SDP, finally merging to become known as the Liberal Democrats. Their hopes of being an effective force were raised by the decline of the Conservatives since 1997, but recent developments have pushed them firmly back into third place.

The Electoral System

The British electoral system is a "first-past-the-post system" or **simple majority vote**. The candidate with the most votes in a constituency is elected. The votes for the losing candidates are disregarded.

One big advantage of this voting system is that in most cases there is a clear majority. On the other hand, smaller parties have hardly any chance to win a seat in Parliament which they would have in the proportional representation system.

Britain operates the first-past-the-post system or **majority vote**. This means that the candidate who gets the most votes in a constituency is elected. The votes for the other candidates are lost, in contrast to the proportional representation system which guarantees seats also to smaller parties in proportion to the total of votes.

Here are some of the arguments for and against the majority vote system.

For

- There is usually a clear majority and coalition governments are avoided.
- Smaller parties cannot determine who forms the government (like the German FDP).
- There is no chance whatsoever that one of the extreme right- or left-wing parties wins a seat in Parliament.

Against

- The system is terribly unfair to the smaller parties like the Liberal Democrats, because votes for the unsuccessful candidates are simply disregarded.
- The winning candidate of a constituency may represent a majority of voters who voted against him; theoretically a 34:33:33 result would suffice to represent a constituency.
- No government, since 1945, has had an absolute majority of over 50% of votes cast.
- The electoral system favours a polarized Parliament of two parties alternating in power. The result is a discontinuity in British politics.

Commentary on the 2019 General Election in the UK

Results

Party	% Votes	Seats (650)	% Seats
Conservative	43.6	365	56.2
Labour	32.2	203	31.2
Liberal Democrats	11.5	11	11.5
Scottish National Party	3.9	48	7.4
Green	2.7	1	2.7
Others	5.4	22	3.6

Comments

The 2019 Election was a vote on Brexit. The Conservatives under Prime Minister Boris Johnson witnessed a landslide victory for their consequential way out of the European Union. They gained an absolute majority by winning 33 additional seats. For Labour it was the worst result since 1935.

Further points to note

The effect of the first-past-the-post electoral system is visible in this result:

- The winners of the election, the Conservatives, got more than half (i. e. 56.2%) of the seats with a minority of the vote (43.6%), while Labour´s seats were in balance with their percentage in the popular vote.
- The great regional divide is shown by the fact that there are only six Conservative seats in Scotland and 14 seats (35.0% of the total) in Wales.
- The Conservatives remained strongest party in England, gaining seats in the „red wall“ district, i.e. the Midlands which used to be Labour strongholds.
- On the other hand, the Scottish National Party (SNP) received 81.4% in Scotland and gained 48 out of 59 seats for the House of Commons. However, they received only 3.9% of the national vote.
- The anti-European UK Independence Party (UKIP), which had scored high numbers of votes across the whole country in previous elections, lost its importance.

Britain since the 1990s

poll tax: tax of a fixed amount collected from every citizen, especially before he / she could vote

For 18 years the **Conservative Party** under **Margaret Thatcher** and **John Major** had formed the British Government.

They suffered a heavy defeat in the 1997 election when the **Labour Party ("New Labour")** with their leader **Tony Blair** came to power. New Labour had moved to the centre, thus becoming more attractive for the middle classes. Blair repeated his victory in 2001 and 2005, but the low turnout illustrated the discontent of the British voters. Consequently Tony Blair stepped back in 2007 being replaced by his Chancellor of the Exchequer (Finanzminister) **Gordon Brown**.

The 2010 election ended 13 years of Labour rule, resulting in a Conservative/ Lib Dem coalition. Its main aim was to bring the finances under control, but it ran out of time. The 2015 election returned a Conservative majority government with the task of reuniting the country and plans to hold an EU 'Brexit' referendum and to bring the finances under control.

Divisions over Europe, the introduction of a poll tax and other reasons led the Conservative Party to remove **Margaret Thatcher** in 1990. However, a deep economic depression soon began as inflated property values collapsed. The Conservatives unexpectedly won the 1992 election, albeit with a very small majority, which made government rule almost impossible. Indeed, by 1997 **John Major** was heading a minority government.

In spite of a favourable economic climate, the Conservatives suffered a massive defeat in 1997. This was a classic example of "time for a change": the Conservatives had been in power for 18 years, while the **Labour Party** reinvented itself with a new leader (**Tony Blair**), an abandonment of traditional socialist policies (e.g. State planning, nationalization of industries), and a move to the centre of the political spectrum which attracted many new voters from the middle classes. The New Labour Government spent the next four years telling everyone that they were improving the three main priority areas as promised: health, education and transport. However, few people felt any real improvement, dispite of low unemployment and rising affluence, and Europe, especially the Euro currency, remained very controversial.

The threat and reality of terrorist activity in the UK continued, with the bomb attacks in London in July 2005 killing more than 50 people. The government responded with tougher anti-terrorist laws.

The 2005 election gave Labour a reduced majority, and in June 2007 **Gordon Brown** succeeded Tony Blair as Prime Minister, just as the world financial crisis began. The collapse of a bank and other political problems gave Brown a difficult job. The new Conservative leader David Cameron was well established and enjoyed a good rate of approval, but not enough to gain an overall majority in the 2010 election. This led to the formation of a coalition with the Liberal Democrats.

The focus of the new government was to deal with the massive financial crisis. The previous Labour government spent much more money than it received in taxes. The coalition proposed to bring the finances under control over its 5-year term, but this target slipped, in spite of a reduction in people's incomes and spending power, leading to the threat of strikes and a return to recession. The political and financial crisis in the Eurozone was also a concern for the UK, and there was growing pressure to move from debt reduction to economic growth.

The move towards full independence for Scotland was rejected by a referendum in September 2014, but the landslide success of the Scottish National Party (SNP) in the 2015 general election showed that it had not gone away. All in all, many people in the UK had lost confidence in politicians of all parties, and were more interested in their own situation in terms of jobs, social conditions and financial outlook. The rise of UKIP, which scored 12.6% of the national vote but only gained one seat, due to the effect of the first-past-the-post system, led Cameron to offer an in/out **"Brexit"** (**British exit**) referendum before the end of 2017 following negotiations for reform of the EU/UK relationship (→ pp. 173 f). The results of the 2016 referendum (a 52% majority for leaving the EU) surprised almost everyone. People in England and Wales voted strongly for Britain's exit from the EU, the Scots and Northern Irish against it; people in the big cities and the younger generation were more pro-European, the older generation and people in the countryside more anti-European. Cameron's government and leaders in industry, commerce and finance had made no plans for taking the Brexit forward; it was assumed that a 'leave' result would cause the economy to collapse.

The 2016 referendum decision had an unexpected result, as 52% of the population voted to leave the EU. A new government under the leadership of Theresa May was formed, to negotiate terms with the EU over the next 2 years. The expected immediate collapse, however, did not happen.

Cameron resigned as Prime Minister, to be replaced by **Theresa May**, who had been Home Secretary in his Government. The shock caused the currency to lose value, and some panic was seen in the business sector. After a few weeks, however, the situation was back to normal. The actual process for leaving the EU started in March 2017, when a letter from the UK government was handed to the European Council to trigger Article 50 of the Lisbon Treaty; this process was expected to take two years to the final exit. The long term effects on both the UK and the EU will take years, possibly decades to become clear.

In April 2017 Mrs May called for a general election to be held in June 2017. The reason for this early election was that she only had a thin majority in Parliament and that other parties were opposed to her Brexit plans. Thus she intended to strengthen her position in the complicated negotiations with the EU. Polls pointed to a comfortable lead for the Conservative Party right up to the day of the election. However, a very good Labour campaign and some serious errors by the Conservatives led to a late surge in support for Labour. The final result was a hung parliament, but Mrs May was able to form a government with support from the Democratic Unionist Party of Northern Ireland.

Mrs May's plans went badly wrong and left the UK in a weaker Brexit position rather than a stronger one.

hung parliament: situation when a general election results in no single political party winning an overall majority in the House of Commons

However, they did not support the Prime Minister in her dealing with the Irish question (i.e. border between Britain and the EU), a decisive hurdle in the Brexit negotiations. Additionally, proponents of a different Brexit course within the governing Conservative Party caused a historic defeat of a prime minister in parliament. With an overwhelming majority the House of Commons rejected May's deal with the EU three times in a row. Most MPs feared an endless bond to the EU without any seat in the European Parliament or other international committees.

After this revolt in her own party, May resigned and was followed by Brexit-hardliner **Boris Johnson**. In order to secure a majority within the Conservatives he called for a snap election in December 2019, the third general election in five years. Opponents in the Conservative Party were expelled. With his uncompromising manner and the slogan "Get Brexit done" he triumphed in a landslide victory. After Brexit had been postponed twice, Britain formally left the EU on 31 January 2020.

Under Brexit-hardliner Boris Johnson (PM since 2019) Britain formally left the EU in January 2020.

Political Life in Great Britain

The Constitution
- Britain's Constitution is basically unwritten.
- It consists of laws and conventions that have evolved in the course of time.

The Sovereign
- has a representative role as head of state, head of the Commonwealth, head of the Church of England, and Commander-in-Chief of the British Forces;
- has certain royal prerogatives: summons and dissolves Parliament, delivers his/her annual speech from the Throne;
- appoints the Prime Minister and the Cabinet, signs Acts of Parliament;
- "reigns but does not rule", has no real political power, but acts according to the policies of the Government.

Parliament
- has been the model for most modern democracies;
- is the most important law-making body of the British people;
- consists of two chambers: the House of Commons and the House of Lords.

The House of Commons
- consists of 650 Members of Parliament (MPs).
- Its main functions are to pass laws, to control government policy, and to debate controversial topics.

The House of Lords
- has about 740 members (mainly life peers; hereditary peers are about to be abolished);
- has nowadays little direct power;
- makes amendments to bills coming from the House of Commons;
- can delay a bill for a year;
- its former judicial function as the highest court of appeal was transferred to the newly created UK Supreme Court.

Government
is formed by the Prime Minister and his/her Cabinet.

The Prime Minister
is the leader of the majority party. His/her tasks are
- to choose and to preside over the Cabinet;
- to determine the principles of Government policy;
- to inform the Sovereign and Parliament of the Government's policy;
- to request the Sovereign to dissolve Parliament and call a general election at any time.

The Cabinet

is chosen by the Prime Minister and is composed of about 20 Ministers ("Secretaries of State") who are in charge of the governmental departments.

Devolution

means the transfer of power from the Westminster Parliament to Assemblies in Scotland, Wales, and Northern Ireland.

- In the late 1990s the Labour Government offered a referendum to Scotland and Wales to end the demands of the nationalist parties and to strengthen the union of the UK.
- The Scottish and the Welsh voted "yes" and now have a Parliament of their own.
- The Scottish Parliament is responsible not only for health, education, housing etc, but also has the power to make laws and raise income tax.
- The Welsh Assembly has only limited powers, such as local government, social services, language etc.

Political Parties

- Today Britain has basically a two-party system: the Labour Party and the Conservatives.
- The Labour Party was traditionally the party of industrial workers and union members, with socialist ideas of state control and the ideal of a welfare state; New Labour (under Blair) has moved more towards the centre.
- The Conservatives, traditionally the party of the upper and middle classes and landowners, believe in a free market without government interference, limitation of the power of the trade unions, and encouragement of a property-owning democracy.
- A less important third party, the Liberal Democrats, emphasizes free trade and the expansion of civil liberties.

The Electoral System

is a first-past-the-post system or majority vote.

- The candidate with the most votes in a constituency is elected.
- Votes for the other candidates are lost.

IN BRIEF

1.2 Political Life in the United States

- The US Constitution is the world's oldest written constitution still working successfully.
- The Bill of Rights guarantees the rights of the individual.
- The System of Checks and Balances makes sure that no branch of the government becomes too powerful.
- The US President (the executive) is the world's most powerful politician.
- Congress (the legislative) is made up of the Senate and the House of Representatives.
- The Supreme Court is the highest US court of law.
- The main political parties are the Republicans and the Democrats.
- The electoral system is an indirect majority vote (Electoral College).

The American Constitution

Origins

The American Constitution (1787) is a **single written document**. Its principle is that a government must receive all its powers from the people.

The American Constitution is the oldest written constitution still in force. It reflects influences of the British parliamentary system (two chambers) and of English Common Law (principles of the Bill of Rights). Moreover, it has served as a model for the constitutions of many other nations.
The Constitution of 1787 replaced the "Articles of Confederation" of 1781, a loose agreement of the 13 states, which gave the central power too little authority over the individual states. The original 13 states were: Delaware, New Hampshire, Massachusetts, Rhode Island, Connecticut, New York, Pennsylvania, New Jersey, Maryland, Virginia, North Carolina, South Carolina, and Georgia.

The basic ideas of the Constitution

inalienable: which cannot be taken away *(unveräußerlich)*

- government by agreement of the governed; final authority belongs to the people;
- belief in the fundamental rights of the people as expressed in the Bill of Rights (cf Declaration of Independence: "certain inalienable rights" (→ p. 59));
- a representative democracy; representatives are elected by the people to run the governments;
- the federal system; power is divided between the national government and state governments;
- separation of powers into three branches: legislative (Congress), executive (President), and judicial (Courts);

- system of checks and balances of the three branches; governmental power limited by constitutional law;
- flexibility of the Constitution; it can change through amendment and judicial reinterpretation.

The basic idea of the Constitution is that a government must receive all its powers from the people. Great ideals in the Constitution are also a representative democracy and the separation of powers.

Common consent of states of different size to the Constitution was only possible with the help of compromise:

- The "Great Compromise" provided for a Congress of two houses: the **Senate** with two delegates from each state and the **House of Representatives** with representation proportionate to the population of each state, in 1787 one delegate for every 30,000 people. Nowadays one delegate represents 500,000 people.
- A second compromise concerned slavery (→ p. 66). The Constitution does not mention the word "slaves" but speaks of "other persons" and "persons held in service". The question was whether slaves should be counted in the population in deciding on the number of representatives from each state in the House of Representatives or not. The compromise on slavery settled the North-South controversy: three-fifths of all slaves were to be counted in the population of a state.

The Basic Rights and Freedoms of Americans

The **Bill of Rights** (the first ten Amendments to the Constitution) was added in 1791 to state the rights of the individual against governmental powers.
Later amendments (11–27) concerned e.g. the rights of citizenship and the voting rights of the Blacks (1865–1870) and women's suffrage (1920).

The **Bill of Rights** (1791) are ten Amendments (additions) to the Constitution protecting the rights and freedoms of Americans.

Freedoms Guaranteed by the Bill of Rights	
Freedom of religion	Freedom of worship. Freedom to belong to any religon or to none. No official religion may be established.
Freedom of the press	Freedom to print books, newspapers and magazines. No one may print falsehoods or writings that harm our citizens.
Freedom of petition	Freedom to urge our governments to pass laws. Freedom to ask our governments to take certain actions.
Rights to equal justice	All persons accused of a crime must receive fair and equal treatment in a court of law.
Freedom of speech	Freedom to express ideas and opinions. No one may use this freedom to speak falsely in order to harm or to injure other citizens.
Freedom of assembly	Freedom to hold meetings. Meetings must be peaceful and obey local laws.
Freedom and security of citizens	No unlawful search may be made of our homes. Right to bear arms to protect ourselves. No troops may be stationed in our homes.

Freedoms guaranteed by the Bill of Rights:
- Freedom of religion
- Freedom of the press
- Freedom of petition
- Rights to equal justice
- Freedom of speech
- Freedom of assembly
- Freedom and security of citizens

An **amendment** to the US Constitution can be initiated by Congress (two-thirds vote of both houses), or by the legislatures of two-thirds of the states, and becomes effective upon ratification by three-fourths of the states. In Britain, on the contrary, a simple majority decision in the House of Commons can bring about a change in the British Constitution.

The importance of the Constitution for Americans:

heritage: *Erbe*

- The document, as a source of patriotism and self-identification, has greatly contributed to the making of the American nation.
- It set forth the legal heritage upon which the US is built.
- It has become a symbol of stability and continuity, as it has been in force for over 200 years without any basic changes.
- The great ideals and basic values expressed in the Constitution have served as a model for the free world:
  - a government elected to serve, not to rule the people, and based on the consent of the governed;
  - equality of all citizens under the "supreme law of the land";
  - guarantee of basic human freedoms.

The System of Checks and Balances

The System of Checks and Balances makes sure that each branch (the executive, the legislative and the judicial branch) has the powers to control those of the two other branches.

One characteristic feature of the Constitution was (and still is) the establishment of a system of checks and balances. Each of the three branches of government serves to control (to check) and to equally divide (balance) the power of the others, thus avoiding a misuse of power.

The Separation of Powers
Checks and Balances

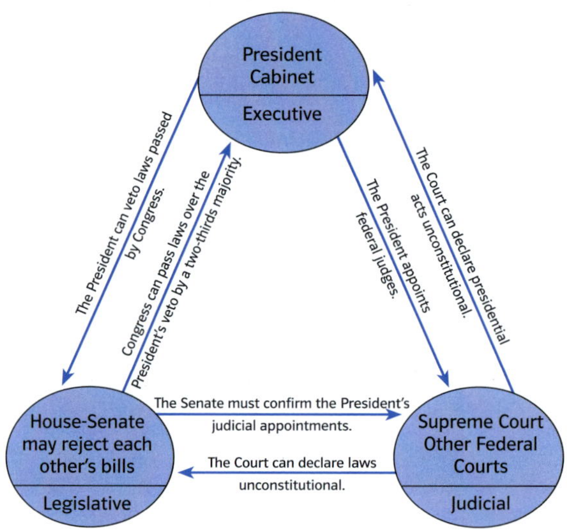

The President

Election and Functions of the American President

The President is the head of the executive branch. He must be
- a native-born American citizen;
- at least 35 years of age;
- a resident of the USA for at least 14 years.

Any native-born American citizen can become President of the United States. The President can be elected twice, each time for a four-year term. He is elected indirectly through the Electoral College.

Up to 2008, Presidents of the USA had usually been white male Protestants. Neither Blacks, Jews nor women had so far become presidential candidates of one of the major parties. John F. Kennedy (1960) was the first Roman Catholic to become President. Candidates are often Vice Presidents (Johnson, George H. Bush) or state governors (e.g. Carter, Reagan, Clinton, George W. Bush). The President is elected every four years, but can hold office for two terms only (22nd Amendment of 1951).

The President is elected by the voters through the **Electoral College**, not by the strongest party in Congress (Senate or House of Representatives). Therefore the President is not necessarily from the majority party of Congress, where elections take place every two years. After two years' Presidency of the Democrat Clinton for instance, the Republican Party captured control of both Houses of Congress in the November 8th 1994 elections.

The President is elected every four years by the voters through the **Electoral College** (name given to the group of 538 Presidential electors) who cast the official votes for President (electoral votes).

The United States is a **presidential democracy**. The chief functions of the President are:
- **head of state** (ceremonial duties);
- **head of government** or Chief Executive:
  - proposes laws and government programmes to Congress;
  - appoints federal judges with the consent of Congress;
  - keeps Congress informed about the state of the nation and the economy;
  - prepares the federal government's budget;
  - must approve of all bills passed by Congress, but can veto legislation; presidential veto can only be overruled by a two-thirds majority of Congress;
  - conducts America's foreign policy;
- **Commander-in-Chief of the armed forces**:
  - can send US forces into any part of the world, which sometimes involves the risk of war, but only Congress has the power to declare war. The President's power has been restricted since 1973 by the War Powers Act.
- **Leader of his own party**.

The **American President** combines the roles of **head of state** (ceremonial duties) and of **head of government** (numerous political functions). He is only responsible to the Constitution, but not to Congress.

The American President and the System of Government

As opposed to the British parliamentary system, the US system has special characteristics:

- The **President** is head of state and head of government.
- The **executive branch** is formed by the President alone.
- The **US Cabinet** (the 14 Heads of Departments) is not responsible to Congress, but individually to the President. It consists of a group of "advisors" who can be removed at will.
- The President is only **responsible to the Constitution**; he cannot be deposed by Congress by a vote of no confidence, but can only be removed by "impeachment". Congress carries out the impeachment process.
- **Secretaries of State** or other government officials cannot be members of Congress.
- There is no possibility to dissolve Congress.
- The US President cannot count upon the automatic support of Congress, even if his own party is in the majority.

to depose: If a leader is deposed, he is removed from his position by force.

impeachment: accusation of a crime brought against a high official

Current Issues concerning the Presidency

- US involvement in world affairs has increased real presidential power at the expense of Congress, thus threatening the balance of power in the US government. US commitment to the unpopular Vietnam War (→ pp. 183 ff) and the Watergate scandal (→ pp. 138, 185) in particular shook popular confidence in the Presidency. The Watergate scandal of the early 1970s exposed President Nixon's participation in illegally obtaining Democratic party documents. This led to a process of impeachment, and forced Nixon to resign.
- The executive branch entails a great number of offices. This leads to a distribution of tasks in federal executive departments and other executive agencies, which can result in a lack of coordination in administration and of control of state machinery.
- The complicated and lengthy presidential nomination system does not necessarily find the most competent candidates. It could even discourage the best from entering the race.
- Only candidates that can sell themselves in the media have a chance of winning office.
- Four years is a very short period of time for a term of office as it includes two years of preparation for the re-election and campaigning. Moreover, the re-election campaign causes delays in decision-making, as presidents are tempted to defer unpopular decisions until the second term. Therefore, many think that the four-year term with the possibility of re-election should be replaced by a single six-year term.

at the expense of: at the cost of

The American presidency tends to become too powerful at the expense of Congress. Other points of criticism concern e.g. the lengthy presidential nomination process, the influence of the media and the short period of a four-year term.

to defer: to put off, to postpone

Congress

The Congress of the United States

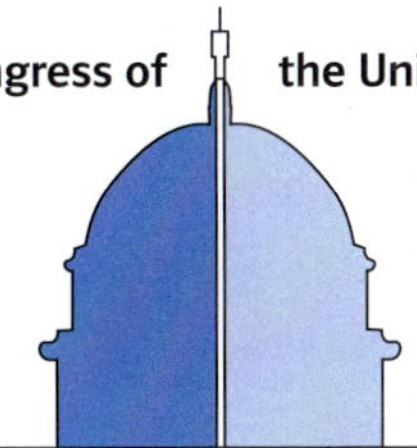

The Senate

100 Senators
2 from each state

The House of Representatives

435 Representatives based on state populations

	Length of term	When elected	Required age
Senators	6 years	One third of Senate elected every 2 years	At least 30 years old
Represen-tatives	2 years	Entire House elected every 2 years	At least 25 years old

Congress is the **legislative branch** of the US government. It is made up of the **Senate** and **the House of Representatives**. Senators (two for each state) are chosen in statewide elections by all voters. Members of the House of Representatives (altogether 435) are elected by voters of congressional districts within each state. About 500,000 constituents form a district and elect one Representative. Therefore the number of districts and consequently of Representatives is determined by the size of the population of a state (e.g. Alaska 1 Representative, California 52).

The **Congress** of the United States, the legislative, consists of two chambers, the Senate and the House of Representatives. Its main powers are:
- to propose bills
- to impeach
- to pass laws about immigration.

Both parties, the majority and the minority party, select their own party leadership. The majority party has certain privileges, such as selecting the leader of the House of Representatives. Most congressional work is done in committees and subcommittees which correspond to the main departments of the executive branch (e.g. defence, labour, commerce, finance). Membership of House and Senate committees is determined by party caucuses in the two Houses. The partisan composition in these committees corresponds roughly to the party ratio in the two Houses.

caucus: a group of people in a political party, who meet to discuss and decide on political plans

ratio: proportion

Each House has the power to **propose a bill**, but can also **veto a bill** passed by the other. Therefore, a bill must go through a long process, must be approved by both Houses, and signed by the President before it becomes a law. If the President vetoes legislation, Congress can pass it into law by a two-thirds majority of both Houses.

Laws must be passed by both Houses of Congress and signed by the President. Congress can override a presidential veto by a $^2/_3$ majority.

Advantages of a Bicameral Congress

- It helps to check and balance the work of the legislative branch.
- It is an obstacle against rash legislation.
- It reflects the historical Great Compromise between equal representation in the Senate and apportioned representation (one representative for approximately half a million persons) in the House of Representatives.

Congress and President

American policy is characterized by the struggle for power between Congress and President. More recently under Clinton and G.W. Bush war powers have been at issue in former Yugoslavia, Haiti and Iraq.

Historically, American policy is characterized by the struggle for power between the **executive (the President)** and the **legislative (Congress)**. In the past 40 years, Presidents Johnson, Nixon, Reagan, and George W. Bush have tended to dominate Congress, while Ford, Carter, the elder Bush, and Clinton have been less successful in achieving their aims against the will of Congress.

Examples of these struggles:

- **1973 War Powers Act** to restrict the power of the President to send troops abroad;
- Congress rejects budget demands of Ford and Carter, and refuses to ratify SALT **II**: Second strategic Arms Limitation Talks between the USA and the USSR;
- George H. Bush forced to raise taxes;
- Clinton's health care reforms blocked;
- impeachment of Clinton in the Monica Lewinsky affair;
- George W. Bush pushes through tax cuts;
- **2003 Iraq invasion** (→ pp. 40 f, 108, 183 ff) in spite of a reluctant Congress.

The Supreme Court

The Judicial Branch

The judiciary is made up of a federal court system and a state court system. The federal courts decide cases concerning the USA as a whole, the state courts handle civil suits between private persons, and between private persons and local or state governments.

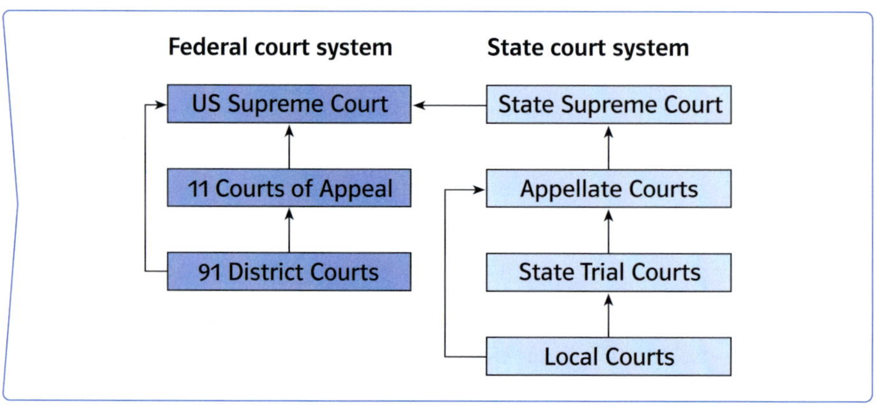

The US Supreme Court as a Court of Law

The Supreme Court is the **highest** court of the United States and the only court specifically provided for by Article III of the Constitution: "The judicial power of the United States shall be vested in one Supreme Court, and such inferior courts as the Congress may from time to time ordain and establish." It consists of nine justices (one Chief Justice and 8 Associate Justices) appointed for life by the President. Appointments must be confirmed by the Senate. The approval of the Senate is not automatic. As Presidents tend to nominate justices of their own political persuasion, appointment to the Court is of great political significance. Decisions of the Court need not be unanimous, a simple majority is sufficient. The Court usually publishes the majority decision and the dissenting opinion of the minority.

The Supreme Court is the **court of final appeal**. It is the highest court of **original and appellate jurisdiction**. Original jurisdiction means the Court acts in the first and last instance. Appellate jurisdiction means it reviews cases that are appealed to it from lower courts. It has original jurisdiction in cases between states and in cases involving foreign officials. All other cases reach the Court by appeal from the lower federal courts or the state supreme courts.

The **Supreme Court** is the highest court of the USA. It is made up of nine justices. Its decisions are final. It has the power to review a law passed by Congress and decide whether a law is constitutional or not (Judicial Review).

to be vested: to be given the lawful right to sb. to use power

to ordain: to decree *(anordnen, verfügen)*

The Supreme Court as a Policy-making Body

The US Supreme Court serves a double function: it is not only the highest court of law, but a **political institution** of great influence. Chief Justice John Marshall developed the instrument of the **Judicial Review** in 1803. The term describes the authority of the Supreme Court to declare laws passed by Congress unconstitutional, i.e. violating the principles of the Constitution. The most significant function of the Court, therefore, is to guard and interpret the Constitution.

It has the power to review a law passed by Congress (Judicial Review).

Current Issues concerning the Supreme Court

- The Court's problematic 5:4 ruling often raises questions because of the narrow margin of decision.
- The question of "original intent" and "judicial interpretation": Should the original meaning of the Constitution be strictly observed or should it be interpreted in the light of modern ideas ("constitutional flexibility")?
- The two opposing views of "judicial activism" (stressing the role of the court as a policy-maker) and "judicial restraint" (lack of the Court's involvement in political affairs).
- Judicial independence: the appointment of "liberal" or "conservative" judges influences Court ruling.

narrow margin of decision: *knappe Mehrheit*

The decisions of the Supreme Court (such as the interpretation of the Constitution) have not been free of controversy.

The Main Parties

For over 100 years the Republicans and the Democrats have been America's two major political parties. This **two-party system** has developed because of the majority vote.

The history of US political parties dates back to the late 18th century. From the very beginning, majority vote led to a concentration of the American party system, and a **two-party system** developed.

Origins

- At the time of the ratification of the new Constitution (1788), the **Federalists** (leader: Alexander Hamilton) opposed the **Anti-Federalists** (leader: Thomas Jefferson, US President from 1801 to 1809). The more conservative Federalists supported a strong government as opposed to the more liberal Anti-Federalists who tried to limit the power of the federal government.
- The Anti-Federalist Party developed after 1800 into the Democratic Republican Party. This split in 1824 into the more radical Democratic Republican Party of the common man (named the **Democratic Party** in 1828) and the more conservative National Republicans or "Whigs". Political groups who opposed the policy of the Democrats and the spread of slavery into the new territories founded the **Republican Party** in 1854. Its strength grew rapidly, particularly in the North, whereas the old Whig Party lost its significance.

During the Civil War the Democratic Party supported the policy of the South, whereas the victorious Republicans with Abraham Lincoln in the North opposed the spread of slavery.

Depression: Economic crisis of the 1930s brought about by the stock market crash in October 1929.

New Deal: New social and economic legislation proposed by Roosevelt and the Democratic Party to ameliorate conditions of unemployment and poverty.

During the 1930s the Democrats developed into the party of the left, establishing labour legislation and social welfare programmes.

Historical Development of the Democrats and the Republicans

In the 1860s the Democrats supported the losing side on the issue of slavery; they were also defeated in the 1860s elections in which Abraham Lincoln (US President from 1861 to 1865) led the Republican Party. In the **Civil War** that followed these elections, the North (mainly Republican) defeated the South (mainly Democrat), and the Republicans then held office for the remainder of the 19th century. The Union was strengthened and industrial progress was promoted in the North, while the Democrats' power base in the agricultural South was neglected. At this time the Republicans favoured strong central (federal) government, the Democrats supported State autonomy.

In the early part of the 20th century, the Democrats gained the support of the poor European immigrant workers and encouraged the emerging labour movement. During and following the **Depression** (1930s) the Democrats were in power for 20 years, with President **Franklin Roosevelt**'s (US President from 1933 to 1945) **New Deal** (→ p. 87) policy bringing in reform of labour legislation and social welfare, along with greater government interference in the economy.

The Democrats were now clearly the party of the left, yet the ultra-conservative South continued to vote for them until the 1960s, and it is only in the last 20 years that the Southerners have turned more to the Republicans.

In the last few years there has been growing discontent with the domination of a two-party system. This can clearly be seen from the 1992 Presidential Elections where Perot, an Independent, stood as a candidate alongside George H. Bush (Republican) and Clinton (Democrat), and won 19% of the votes.

Characteristic Features of the Party System

For European observers the American parties are very similar, and it is often difficult to distinguish between them. The reasons for this remarkable fact are:

- Both parties represent almost all groups of voters.
- The parties are not based on an ideology and are therefore more flexible.
- The diversity of each party paves the way for "middle-of-the-road" candidates.
- Due to the federal character of the parties, each state organization of a party is autonomous; there is no party leader and no identity of interest or conviction.
- There is no party loyalty like in Britain; members of Congress are free to serve the interests of their constituents even against the official policy of their party.
- The American parties tend to find a common party line for elections, but most of the time they are more preoccupied on a regional and local level.
- The American party landscape is characterized by the existence of a "geographical" vote (i.e. the tendency of a region to vote for a certain party).

It is difficult to distinguish between American parties. They tend to take a "centrist" position. Set party programmes, ideology or party loyalty do not play such a decisive role as in other countries.

American Parties in the 2010s

	Republicans (Grand Old Party / G.O.P.)	**Democrats**
Emblem	the elephant	the donkey
Regions of Support	rural areas of the Northeast, Midwest, Rocky Mountains states, suburbs, country	big cities, South
Votes	middle class, the wealthy, rich farmers, White Anglo-Saxon Protestants (WASPs), big business	the poor, working-class people, immigrants, minorities, Blacks, Jews, smallhold farmers, labour unions, intellectuals

The **Republicans** tend to be more conservative and traditional. They stress the responsibility of the individual and refrain from government interference.

The **Democrats** tend to be more liberal. They advocate social programmes for the needy and taxation of the rich.

	Republicans (Grand Old Party / G.O.P.)	Democrats
Party Stances Defence	• usually in support of strategic weapons and nuclear strength, • treaties only from a position of national strength, • favour a large military budget	• usually more in support of conventional forces and want to scale down nuclear weapons, • treaties through diplomacy and mutual understanding
Foreign Policy	• advocate sending troops abroad (Nicaragua, Grenada, Kosovo, Iraq), • staunch opponents of communism	• usually more cautious about international political interference, • not as hard-line about communism
Economy	• usually in support of big business, maybe offering tax breaks	• tend to support the poor and are more likely to heavily tax the rich
Crime and Social Issues	• do not favour gun control regulations, • support death penalty for violent crimes or drug barons, • usually against abortion, • have cut back on some social welfare programmes (Medicare (→ pp. 87 f), food stamp programme) and stress the responsibility of the individual, favour prayer in schools	• usually for stricter gun control, • usually oppose death penalty, • are more liberal regarding abortion, approve of more social welfare programmes, fewer cutbacks in e.g. Medicare, • favour the expansion of civil rights laws for minority groups
Environment	• have cut back spending for national parks and environmental protection, • sometimes not as strict with pollution standards (connected with big business)	• strengthen spending for parks and environmental protection

The Electoral System

The Presidential Election

The election of the President is a long and complex political process. Only people who register can go to the polls to vote. Most states have permanent **registration**, i.e. you need register only once in your life-time.

The **election campaign** begins at least a year before Election Day. Candidates travel throughout the country, raise funds, discuss important issues, establish contacts with party leaders, especially with those of the important states, and devote special attention to the media. Gradually they build their own campaign organization with media experts and public-relations specialists.

The election campaign of the presidential candidates takes a full year. During that period candidates try to establish contacts with influential people and to raise money. The media, too, play an important part in the campaign.

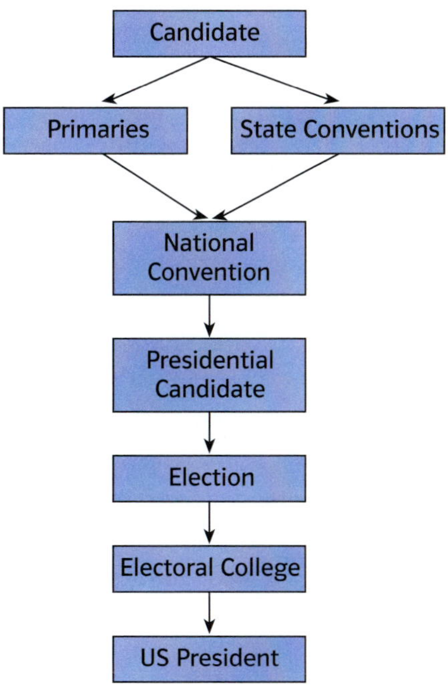

A candidate may take two routes to be elected presidential candidate at the **National Convention** of his party. Some states have **primaries**, others have **party conventions or caucuses**. In primary elections voters have a chance to choose candidates to run in a general election. **State conventions** or caucuses are meetings of party representatives who select their delegates to the National Convention. This is a meeting of party delegates who adopt the party platform and nominate the candidate for President.

Presidential Elections are an indirect majority vote.

Indirect election

voters
↓
electors
↓
President

The schedule of primary elections in the states has been significantly altered. Several states, including California, have chosen to have their primary elections earlier in the year because the people recognize that an earlier primary election means their state has more influence in the selection of their party's presidential candidate.

The Presidential elections constitutionally take place on the Tuesday following the first Monday in November.

The method of electing the American President is an indirect one. On Election Day, the voters cast their votes not for the candidate nominated for President, but for electors chosen by the candidate's political party. Each state has as many electors as it has Senators and Representatives in Congress **(Electoral College)**.

In a first stage the voters of each state vote for a list of electors of one of the two major parties. The winning party gets all the electoral votes of that state (majority vote).

In a second stage the electors who are bound by the voters' choice cast their votes for officially electing the President.

to be pledged to doing sth.: to be committed to doing sth. *(dazu verpflichtet, darauf eingeschworen sein, etwas zu tun)*

The election of the President takes place in two stages:

1. The people in each state choose the list of Presidential electors for that state (either the Democratic or the Republican list). However, the voters are really voting for the official Presidential candidates of the two parties, because the electors are already pledged to voting for the candidate of "their" party. The set of electors with the largest number of votes is the winner and therefore wins all the electoral votes of a state. The votes for the second list of candidates are all passed on to the winner. Thus the American electoral system is a **majority or winner-takes-all vote**.
2. The electors from all the states cast their votes for "their" Presidential candidate. In order to be elected President a **simple majority of 270 out of 538** electoral votes is needed.

Current Issues concerning the Electoral Process

The possible influence of special-interest groups, the role of the media during the electoral campaign and the present Electoral College system cause controversy.

- The candidate's fund-raising activities may bring him under the influence of special-interest groups. These groups and political lobbies tend to weaken the political parties and to modify their party platforms ("boss rule").
- Observers are worried about the important part played by the media in the presidential campaign. Media experts and public-relations specialists have gained great importance in the planning and carrying out of a campaign.
- The original idea of the Electoral College provided for in the Constitution was that inexperienced voters should vote for well-known personalities of their state, who, in their turn, would elect the President. But today presidential electors are mere party nominees who are pledged to a party's particular candidate. Direct election is, as supporters claim, more democratic, as the actual votes are counted. Under the present system it is possible to win more popular votes than the opponent and yet not win enough electoral votes to become President (e. g. Hillary Clinton in 2016).

The USA in the 2010s – The Obama Years

Barack Obama was elected in 2008 to be the first black president, with the slogan "Yes, we can", but a hostile Congress blocked many of his plans.

In 2008, after the Bush era, charismatic **Barack Obama** was elected America's first black president. In his presidential campaign Obama stressed with his slogan "Yes, we can" the need for social and political change, but created expectations that, in the end, he could only partially meet. In the midterm congressional elections of 2010 the Republicans seized control of the House of Representatives and in the 2014 midterm elections also of the Senate, which meant that Obama was more and more faced with a Congress that tried to block his policies.

When Obama took office the **US economy** was hit by the credit crisis and the longest economic **recession** (2008-2009) since the Great Depression in the 1930s. The bursting of the housing bubble led to falling property prices, immense losses by banks (bankruptcy of the fourth-largest US investment bank Lehman Brothers) and a rapidly increasing unemployment rate. In order to prevent another Wall Street crash as in 1929 the government and the Fed(eral Reserve System) responded to the financial crisis with various fiscal measures such as stimulus programmes and an extension of tax cuts. By the time Obama left office eight years later, the economy had fully recovered. The annual growth of the American GDP was at 2 to 3% and the unemployment rate stood at 5%. Obama had created a small economic miracle, an achievement often underappreciated by the American public.

The credit crisis in 2008 led to falling property prices and failing banks; an 8-year successful drive to stabilise the economy followed.

In **domestic policy** Obama's greatest legacy was his legislation to reform **healthcare** against the fierce resistance of the Republicans. With the passage of the Affordable Care Act (ACA, "Obamacare") 2009, he achieved something several Democratic presidents before him had failed to introduce. With this bill he reduced the uninsured rate of 18% to about 11%, which was a step towards the Democrats' ideal of healthcare for all.

Obama's greatest legacy was his healthcare reform. His attempt to control immigration was less successful. Moves towards gun control were blocked by Congress, and racial violence increased.

With regards to **immigration** liberal-minded Obama was less successful: his aim was to provide citizenship for immigrants illegally living in the US and to protect them from deportation, but an obstructive Congress prevented a new immigration reform.

During Obama's presidency, especially from 2012 onwards, several mass shootings took place. This caused Obama to call for new **gun control** legislation to regulate the sale and ownership of guns. But all these attempts were blocked by Congress, which maintained that the right to bear arms is guaranteed by the Constitution.

With the election of the first Black president in 2008 and the first nomination of a Hispanic judge to the Supreme Court in 2009 21st century America seemed to come to terms with multiculturalism and the motto of "E pluribus unum". But then, during the later Obama years, **racial tensions** rose again, when in a series of conflicts several unarmed young blacks were arrested, brutally treated and even fatally shot by white policemen.These cases sparked off nationwide unrest and blacks formed the new "Black Lives Matter" movement against racially driven police shootings.

Furthermore, the Obama administration engaged in a new **climate policy** which aimed at cutting carbon pollution in America and favoured the development of clean energy (wind power and solar energy). The Clean Power Plan aimed at reducing emissions from coal and gas-fired plants and to regulate the emissions of new power plants, cars and trucks. In 2016 Obama signed the Paris Climate Agreement together with 55 other countries, which pledged to decrease greenhouse gas emissions.

Developments in climate policy led to Obama signing the Paris agreement in 2016. It aims at decreasing greenhouse emissions.

His foreign policy sought to reduce commitments by withdrawal from the Middle East. He normalised relations with Cuba after 50 years, and struck a deal to limit Iran's nuclear programme, but failed to close the Guantanamo prison.

As to **foreign policy** Obama pursued the aim of reducing America's foreign commitment: he ended George W. Bush's war in Iraq (2011), eliminated the terrorist leader Osama bin Laden (2011) and reduced US troops in Afghanistan (2011). Obama's critics, however, maintain that the retreat of US troops from Iraq helped the terrorist IS to increase its influence in that area. In his second term Obama normalized relations with Cuba after more than 50 years of hostilities (2014/15) and together with other world powers struck a deal with Iran to limit its nuclear programme. The more negative results remaining from this presidency include the NSA's (National Security Agency's) surveillance programmes even among befriended nations, his broken promise about a shutdown of Guantanamo military prison and the US's indecisive role in Syria's civil war.

The Trump Era (2017–2021)

Donald J. Trump unexpectedly won the election to become the 45th US President. His "Make America Great Again" slogan appealed to disillusioned voters left behind by the political elite represented by **Hillary Clinton**.

After the most divisive and hard-fought electoral campaign ever in US history the Republican candidate **Donald Trump**, a well-known American businessman and television personality, achieved a stunning and unexpected victory and was elected 45th President of the United States. His opponent Hillary Clinton, former First Lady and Secretary of State, an experienced politician, who was about to become the United States' first female President, had to admit defeat after a long and bitter struggle.

President Trump mainly scored among a generation of disillusioned working and middle class voters who felt dissatisfied with the unequal distribution of America's wealth and felt left behind and forgotten in the world of the political establishment. So in spite of his apparent lack of political experience, his populist message, his outrageous campaign style of open xenophobia and his sexist behaviour, Trump achieved this remarkable result over an opponent who was identified with the ruling political class of the Clintons and Bushes, which had for so long decided about America's future. Furthermore Hillary Clinton was known to deliver highly paid political speeches and was involved in an FBI probe about using a private email server as Secretary of State, and thus appeared to be dishonest to the public.

Following his campaign slogans **"America first"** and **"Making America great again"**, President Trump redefined the role of the USA in the world and the country`s priorities. As a former businessman, economic interests dominated his policies:

- Trump did not believe in climate change, but regarded it as a Chinese invention. He withdrew from the Paris Climate Agreement which aimed at keeping the rise of global temperatures below 2 degrees Celsius. He supported fracking despite its environmental dangers.

- Like other Republican presidents, Trump was very strict with respect to illegal immigration. He built an unsurmountable wall out of concrete and metal at the US-Mexican border. Despite harsh criticism, he stopped the "Dreamer" program by which illegal minors were protected from deportation. Furthermore, he separated undocumented children from their parents after being caught at the border. He generally banned immigration from seven Muslim countries which he identified as a source for terrorism.
- The President tried to repeal Obama's health care reform, or replace it by a slimmer program, but failed.
- In order to strengthen the American economy Trump began a trade war with China and the European Union. Extra tariffs were put on foreign products (cf. steel, BMW) to ensure domestic growth. With regard to a major decrease in unemployment, his policy "Buy American, hire American" was successful.
- Trump called off Obama`s Iran deal to limit and control its nuclear program, although other western countries still believe in it.
- He expanded the military with the help of an increase in the defence budget.
- He tried to found new alliances with dictators like Kim Jongun (North Korea) and Putin whereas the relations with old partners like Germany severely deteriorated. When his call for higher financial contributions of European partners was not heard, he announced the withdrawal of American NATO troops from the European continent. It became clear that the architecture of post-war security by NATO was generally questioned by Trump.

His personality, his often inconsistent course and his overall political aims left the US a divided country. Internationally, after four years of the Trump administration, America seems to be more isolated than ever.

The Presidential Election of 2020

Joe Biden versus Donald Trump

Biden`s political career

The Democrats chose **Joe Biden**, former Vice President in the Obama administration, as their presidential candidate. Biden had been the youngest senator in American history. In contrast to Trump´s late entry into politics, he had taken over political responsibility for almost half a century. Two times Biden had tried to become the Democratic presidential nominee (1988, 2008) and failed.

Kamala Harris as an important sign for the African American community

As his running mate Biden picked the 56-year-old black **Kamala Harris**, daughter of an Indian biologist and a Jamaican-born professor. The choice of the Californian senator was a clear sign for the African American community and other minorities. While Trump and Mike Pence represented white America only, Biden and Harris reproduced multicultural society in the US.

Different personalities of the candidates

The personalities of the two presidential candidates could not have been more different. The narcissistic Trump, aggressive in his rhetoric and behaviour, which he showed in the TV debates, stood against, the emphatic, more well-tempered and decent Joe Biden.

Covid-19, the economy and racial issues

Covid-19 crisis fundamentally influenced the elections

The election campaigns were fundamentally influenced by the Covid-19 crisis. America was severely hit by the virus, hundreds of thousands had already died, among them disproportionally many African Americans. From the beginning, President Trump played down the danger of the virus, fearing to have a major impact on US economy. He did not trust in his scientific advisors and kept businesses and schools open. On the other hand, Biden continued to emphasize the mortality rate of Covid-19 and indicated that he would take action, even considering the option of a partial lockdown.

In contrast to Trump, who organized big rallies (usually without masks), Biden was more careful and often spoke to his supporters via video chat from his home. Trump mocked him as "Sleepy Joe" for his unspectacular campaign. For a long time it was unclear whether Biden would draw out voters to the polls with his strategy. However, surveys just before the elections showed that the majority believed the former Vice President had more competence in dealing with the Covid-19 crisis.

Economic competence, on the other side, was rather seen on Trump's side. He unified supporters with the false claim that Biden would aim at a socialist, state-run economy due to left-wing groups in his own party.

Racial issues played an important role in the election campaign, too, in particular after the African American George Floyd had been killed in an act of police brutality. Other instances of racially motivated police violence sparked off a renewal of the Black Lives Matter movement. Sometimes peaceful demonstrations turned into racial unrest.

Trump called for law and order, threatening to send federal troops into Portland, Chicago and other cities. He blamed incompetent Democratic leaders for the riots, even though similar upheavals occurred in Republican-run urban areas as well. Biden, on the other hand, admitted that there is a major problem of racial inequality in the US and sympathised with the non-violent protesters.

Results

Biden benefitted from the high turnout and got 50.5% of the popular vote

In the highest voters' turnout in a century Joe Biden received 50.5% of the popular vote, while Trump got only 47.7%. Due to the different perception of the Covid-19 virus, one could observe different voting patterns along the party lines.

Republicans went to the polls on election-day, whereas Democrats preferred personal early voting before November 3, 2020 or used Absentee ballots.
Although the Democrats had hoped for a landslide victory, turnout on election-day in the crucial swing states gave President Trump a massive lead. As a consequence he prematurely declared himself the winner of the presidential elections. Absentee ballots, however, were only allowed to be counted afterwards. In a dramatic turn over several days these legally cast votes paved the path for Biden to become the 46th President of the United States. In the end, he won in the decisive states of the "Rust Belt" like Pennsylvania, Michigan, Wisconsin, securing him the majority of 306 to 232 in the Electoral College.

Importance of mail-in ballots

Biden`s majority in the crucial swing states of Pennsylvania, Michigan and Wisconsin

Margins of less than 1% between the two candicates in several states resulted in recounts. Trump believed in a widespread fraud and blamed the Democrats that they would "steal the elections", without presenting any evidence for his claim.
As expected, Trump had mainly been voted in the Midwest and in rural areas by white males with an average age of 45 years. However, the media talked about a suburban, referring to the fact that a lot of the traditionally Republican suburbs had voted for Biden. Educated white women in particular in these areas went to the Democrats. Biden`s stronghold were the densely populated metropolitan areas. He was also favoured by African Americans and the millennials who were allowed to vote for the first time.

African Americans and first-time voters for Biden

With the age of 78, Joe Biden is the oldest president in American history. Kamala Harris is the first black and the first woman to serve as vice president.

The 2020 United States presidential election
(status 11/24/2020)

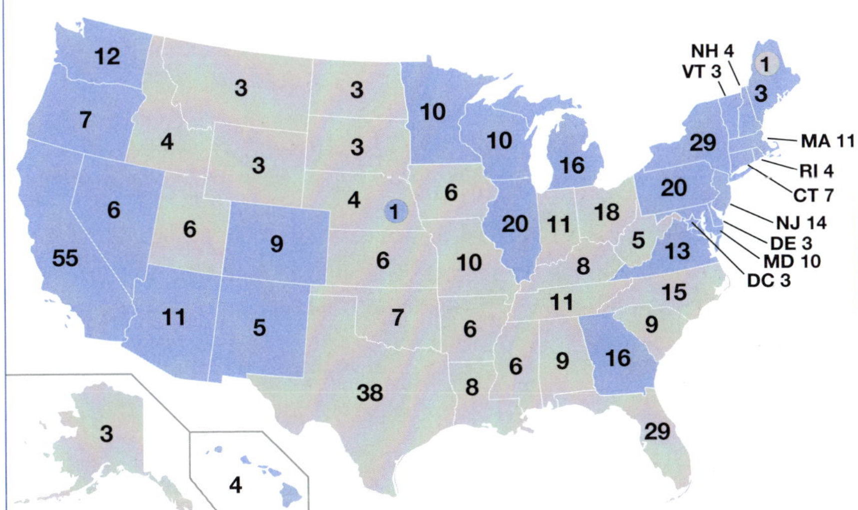

states projected for Biden/Harris
states projected for Trump/Pence
Numbers indicate allotted electoral votes.

Map of U.S. Election 2020 (status 11/24/2020)

We offer this page as an update pdf on our homepage, depending on political developments in the USA.

Political Life in the United States

The Constitution (1787)

is the oldest written Constitution still in force. Its basic ideas:

- government by agreement of the governed;
- belief in the fundamental rights of the people;
- a representative democracy;
- the federal system;
- separation of powers;
- flexibility of the Constitution.

The Bill of Rights (1791)

is a document containing the first 10 Amendments to the Constitution. It states the rights of the individual against governmental powers:

- freedom of religion, of the press, of speech, of assembly; rights to equal justice.

Branches of Government

- The executive branch (the President) carries out laws;
- the legislative branch (Congress) makes laws;
- the judicial branch (Supreme Court) interprets laws.

The President (Executive Branch)

is elected for four years, but can hold office for two terms. He combines the powers of a German President or the British Queen and a Prime Minister:

- head of state (ceremonial function);
- head of government;
- proposes laws to Congress;
- appoints federal judges with the consent of Congress;
- keeps Congress informed about the state of the nation;
- must approve of all bills passed in Congress, but can veto legislation;
- Commander-in-Chief;
- leader of his own party.

The Cabinet

The US Cabinet (the 14 Heads of Departments) is responsible to the President.

Congress (Legislative Branch)

is made up of two chambers:

- Senate (100 Senators, two from each state; elected for 6 years);
- House of Representatives (435 Representatives, each representing about 500,000 constituents elected for two years).

The powers of Congress are: to declare war and peace, to raise armed forces, to raise taxes, to propose bills, to impeach.

The Judicial Branch
is made up of a federal court system and a state court system.

The Supreme Court
is the highest court of the USA. It
- consists of nine justices appointed for life by the President (appointments must be confirmed by the Senate);
- is the court of final appeal;
- guards and interprets the Constitution;
- has the power of Judicial Review (i.e. can declare laws passed by Congress as unconstitutional).

The Separation of Powers
is guaranteed through a System of Checks and Balances:
Each of the three branches serves to control (check) and to equally divide (balance) the power of the other two.

Political Parties
There are two main parties, the Democrats and the Republicans.
- Both parties represent almost all groups of voters.
- The Democrats tend to be more liberal, more in favour of welfare programmes, of the poor and minorities.
- The Republicans represent more the interests of big business, favour a large military budget and stress the responsibility of the individual.

Presidential Elections
are indirect: voters → electors → President.
- Voters cast their votes not for the candidates nominated for President, but for electors (the Electoral College) chosen by the candidate's political party.
- The set of electors with the most votes wins all the electoral votes of a state; thus the voting system is a majority vote or a winner-takes-all vote.
- A simple majority (270 of 538 electoral votes) is needed to be elected President.

OVERVIEW

- social class as an important factor of British society
- class differences by birth, education, occupation and language

- upper class – middle class – working class
- the "us gainst them" attitude of the working class

Anti-cuts rally on March 26, 2011 in London

Social Structure of Britain

- after 1945 development into a multi-ethnic society
- immigrants from Asia, the West Indies and Africa
- reasons for immigration: Commonwealth citizenship, labour shortage in British industries, persecution in their home countries
- minority problems: mostly unskilled and underpaid jobs; unemployment, racial discrimination
- the Government's Immigration Acts and the Commission for Racial Equality

2 Social Structure of Britain and of the United States

- the ideal of the American Dream
- the "salad bowl" concept
- structure of contemporary US population: Whites form about 62%, major minorities are Indians, Blacks, Hispanics, Asians
- struggle for Civil Rights
- US immigration policy

The sonnet "The New Colossus" of the American writer Emma Lazarus (1849 – 1887) is graven on a tablet within the pedestal on which the Statue of Liberty stands.

The United States: A nation of immigrants

Emma Lazarus: The New Colossus

" … Give me your tired, your poor,
Your huddled masses yearning to breathe free,
The wretched refuse of your teeming shore.
Send these, the homeless, tempest-tost to me,
I lift my lamp beside the golden door! "

Übersetzung:

» … Gebt mir eure Müden, eure Armen,
Eure geknechteten Massen, die frei zu atmen begehren,
den elenden Unrat eurer gedrängten Küsten;
Schickt sie mir, die Heimatlosen, vom Sturme Getriebenen,
hoch halt' ich mein Licht am gold'nen Tore! «

The US coin commemorates Ellis Island as the "Gateway to America"; the reverse shows two lines from the sonnet "The New Colossus" by Emma Lazarus.

2.1 Social Structure of Britain

IN BRIEF

- Social class is an important factor in British society.
- British society is divided into three groups, known as upper class, middle class and working class.
- In spoken English, a speaker's social class and regional origin may be revealed by his or her accent.
- Britain developed into a multi-ethnic society after WW II.
- Immigrants to Britain show different characteristics, depending on their origin, their motives for migration and the areas where they settled.
- Integration into white society has not been easily achieved.

The Importance of Class

Distinctions between capitalists, professionals and industrial workers formed the class system in the 19th century **(Industrial Revolution)**.

WW II made class differences less obvious due to shared experiences. Other factors were e.g. the foundation of the **Welfare State** and the introduction of the **Comprehensive School** system.

In spite of this development class distinctions have remained essential in British society. This is reflected for instance in the existence of a **separate medical service**, the importance of **private education** and the **gap between rich and poor**.

stratum, pl. strata: A stratum of society is a group of people who are similar in their education, income, or social class.

Class distinctions and **class consciousness** have always played a great part in British society. The reasons can be traced back to the 19th century, when Britain became the first industrial nation in the world. The **Industrial Revolution** split up 18th century society into capitalists (landowners and factory-owners), a mercantile middle class, and the proletariat (an industrial working class). **World War II** marked a decisive cut in this traditional concept of society. The common war experience, the mingling of classes in the army and rationing of food after the war paved the way for a more egalitarian view of society. As a result, class differences in post-war Britain have become less obvious, and **social mobility** – the movement from one class to another – has become a characteristic aspect of contemporary Britain.

Different factors have contributed to this development:

- The creation of a **mass society** with uniform customs, manners and tastes has been encouraged by the increasing influence of the mass media, and the lifestyles of the British have become less varied. (Cf the common "teenage" pop culture.)
- The foundation of the **Welfare State** (→ pp. 82 ff) and the extension of social and medical services helped to bring about a new concept of social security and thus lessened the gap between rich and poor.
- The abolition of the tripartite school system in favour of the **Comprehensive School** (→ pp. 114 ff) as the generally acknowledged type of state school has been a means of mixing children of different social strata from an early age. Even so, 7% of all pupils still attend private independent schools.

However, in spite of more **social flexibility** and levelling of class distinctions, "class" has not disappeared, but has remained fundamental to stratification in Britain.

In practice, class redistribution has been limited. Slow economic growth or even decline, rising unemployment, separate medical services for the well-to-do ("private patients"), and a dual educational system of state and private education ("Public Schools") have prevented a move towards a fairer distribution of property and income and the mingling of classes.

class redistribution: *Umverteilung der gesellschaftlichen Schicht*

Today, many question the assumption that Britain is evolving into a more homogeneous society and that the gap between rich and poor is closing. In contemporary Britain there is little evidence of shared values and feelings, of identification across social boundaries. A new prosperity on the one hand, and life on welfare on the other, show that Britain remains two nations – separate and unequal.

In practice, the gap between rich and poor is not closing (main reason is the bad economic situation).

Social Class in Britain Today

There is no general agreement on how the lines between different social groups should be drawn, and statistics vary a great deal. Traditionally, sociologists identify three main classes in **capitalist industrial societies**:

upper class – middle class – working class

A more differentiated class model distinguishes five or even more social groups:

upper – upper middle – lower middle – working – lower

2 models of social groups

The government uses a 5-point scale to keep records on population and occupations: 1. professionals, 2. lower professionals, 3. skilled workers, 4. semi-skilled workers, 5. unskilled workers.

The most important factors which determine class and preserve social inequality are birth (hereditary titles and estates), education, occupation, income, housing, lifestyle, prestige, and language. The current convention in Britain to determine social class in official census reports is the separation of people into groups based on their **occupations**. The advertising industry, for example, divides the population into social grades using occupation as a basis.

In Britain the separation of people into different social groups is based on their **occupations**.

The occupational structure of Britain shows a trend away from the proletarian society. As in all modern industrial nations the number of workers has sharply declined. Simultaneously, the **middle classes** have grown considerably due to the increase of white-collar workers and of those who work in the so-called tertiary sector, the **service industry**. There has been a strong rise in professional and managerial grades and increases in the number of women in higher occupations, especially in the skilled non-manual group.

Post-war social trends show that the **middle class** is growing ever bigger, with sharp declines in the nobility in the upper class and industrial labour in the lower class.

white-collar worker: office worker

The expression "status group" describes a group sharing a common lifestyle and valued collective identity.

Class depends on more than occupation alone, namely on **power, prestige, wealth, income, and lifestyle**. The following outline of social strata in Britain is therefore based on the traditional class model.

The **upper class** (about 4000 people) consists of the aristocracy and of landowners.

The aristocracy consists of the nobility and the landed gentry.

The **upper class** is a status group consisting mainly of the aristocracy and of landowners. It comprises only about 4000 people and therefore is not considered to be a class of its own but part of the upper middle class. The aristocracy consists of 1. the nobility and 2. the landed gentry.

The National Trust is an organization founded to protect and preserve historic buildings and countryside areas of natural beauty in the UK.

1. For centuries, the **nobility** has been politically represented in the House of Lords (→ pp. 12 f). The hereditary peers are now being phased out and replaced by life peers appointed (not elected) from all classes. Meanwhile, many of the great landowners have been forced by heavy taxation and social change to hand over their houses and estates to the National Trust.

2. The **landed gentry** (lower aristocracy), made up of "baronets" and "knights", has provided British society with the ideal of the "country gentleman", who owns and administers his land and draws part of his income from farming. This figure has survived every change and is still an ideal of the upper classes. Formerly the "governing class", the aristocracy has lost its legal and economic privileges, but survives as a social and political force of British society.

civil servant: *Beamter, Beamtin*

The **upper middle class** has become a very important stratum of society and has partly replaced the aristocracy in politics, administration, and the civil service.

The **upper middle class** is formed by managers, civil servants, the professional classes, businessmen and businesswomen. They have become a very important stratum of society and have partly replaced the aristocracy in politics, administration, and the civil service. Notable of the **middle classes** is their recent expansion. These social groupings profited most from the Thatcherite "enterprise culture", in which self-employment, small business, share-holding and house ownership were encouraged. Women make up $\frac{2}{5}$ of the workforce today. The growth of part-time and flexible working patterns, training and retraining schemes has enabled more women to become employed. The Sex Discrimination Acts 1975 and 1986 make discrimination between men and women illegal.

The **lower middle class** is the biggest stratum of British society.

The **lower middle class** consists of lesser officials, owners of small business, non-manual white-collar office workers, and skilled manual workers, such as builders and electricians. The lower middle class is the biggest stratum of British society.

The **working class** is hardest hit by the decline of major industries. Many of them are the real poor of the country; they are dependent on state benefits.

The **working class** is basically formed by semi-skilled and unskilled manual workers. Typical of the working class are close family and community ties, union membership, and an "us-and-them" attitude (workers against the "Establishment"). Today this stratum is hardest hit by the decline of major industries like steel, textile, shipbuilding, and coal mining. The unemployed, the elderly, the disabled, unsupported mothers, casual labourers, the low-paid, among them many West Indians, are the real poor of the country. These groups are to a great extent dependent on state benefits. Britain's working and **lower classes** are those who suffer from widening inequality.

Unemployed claimants: by age and sex, May-Jul 2016		
Age	Males	Females
16 – 17 18 – 24 25 – 49 50 – 64 (M) / 59 (F)	34.0% 13.8% 3.3% 3.5%	23.3% 9.6% 4.1% 2.8%
All aged 16 and over	5.1%	4.7%

Labour Force Survey

Today, family background and social status have lost much of their former importance, and are being replaced by efficiency and **merit** ("meritocracy"). These qualities are rewarded by different levels of income. Everything is available if you can afford it.

merit: personal wealth *(Verdienst, Einkommen)*
„meritocracy": *Leistungsgesellschaft*

Factors preserving the class system	Factors favouring a more democratic society
„Thatcherism" (→ p. 98) economy, politics	**Welfare State** social legislation
education (→ pp. 114 ff) private schools Oxbridge old-boy network language	**education** Comprehensive Schools "meritocracy"
aristocracy hereditary titles	**influence of the mass media** (→ pp. 132 ff)
House of Lords	**pop culture**

Social Class and Language

According to **R. C. Shaw** "speech is the last remaining rampart of class in Britain. And it's unassailable." In the 2000s this class distinction is still evident, although today an increasing number of accents are heard through the media. The upper class has preserved its own kind of speech, and some middle-class people, wanting to imitate them, send their children to public schools, where they might pick up the distinctive **"upper class" accent**. The „real" upper class accent is more exaggerated than the accepted standard British accent, the so-called **Oxford English**, Queen's English, BBC English, or „Received Pronunciation". In Britain you may be classified by your accent, and speaking a local dialect suggests you lack educational and social background and are thus disqualified from a successful career. Language is said to mirror social status and education. The speaker's grammar, vocabulary, and pronunciation may be "vulgar", "colloquial", or "refined", thus classifying him/her in the social hierarchy. The social acceptability of **regional accents** depends largely on geography. Southern accents are more acceptable in Britain than accents from regions like the North or Wales that are connected with heavy industry. The Scottish accent, on the other hand, is more recognized, as Scotland has developed a much respected educational system of its own. **Cockney**, the standard London dialect, is mainly spoken by the lower classes and is therefore considered as a mark of inferior education and of low social status.

received: accepted in high society

Historically, spoken English varied according to geographical region and educational differences. These accents (e.g. the famous upper class accent) still exist, but modern media influences are making them much less important.

Britain: A Multi-ethnic Society

The most decisive change to have taken place in British society in the last five decades has been its transformation from an Anglo-Saxon into a **multiracial** or **multi-ethnic society**. Up to the 1950s, "class" was the decisive code word of Britain's social structure. Since then, "ethnicity" has become a second dominant factor.

Before World War II Britain had experienced comparatively small immigration waves. The black population of the 18th and 19th centuries was as easily assimilated as the Irish immigrants and the Jewish and Eastern European refugees in the first half of the 20th century were. It was only after World War II that **mass immigration** of coloured people from the former colonies started, a reflection of Britain's imperial past. The following ethnic groups can be distinguished among the four million immigrants:

- **Black immigrants** from the **West Indies**, mainly from Jamaica. They are the descendants of former slaves that were transported to the Caribbean Islands and the American colonies.

Before WW II British society was almost 100 % Anglo-Saxon. Since the 1950s very large numbers of Asians and West Indians have migrated to the UK.

The main ethnic groups among the 4 million immigrants:

- black immigrants
- Indians
- Pakistanis and Bangladeshis.

- **Indians** from their native country and from **Kenya**. After Kenya's independence, the Indian and Pakistani minority of about 200,000 people began to suffer persecution by African nationalists, and decided to emigrate to Britain, as they were British citizens.
- **Pakistanis** and **Bangladeshis**.
- Minor immigration groups are from Africa, the Mediterranean (Cyprus, Malta, Gibraltar), and Hong Kong.

Motives for Immigration

- Some were found employment by British job centre officials because of a labour shortage in the basic industries (textiles, coal, shipbuilding), public transport, and the services. Employers began to recruit the labour force from overseas Commonwealth countries for menial, badly-paid jobs.
- Some came because they were attracted by a higher standard of living, in search of a better job or any job at all. As citizens from Commonwealth countries they were, moreover, entitled to all the advantages of the British welfare system.
- Some, like the West Indians, thought of themselves as British with Britain as their home country: they had been educated by white teachers from Britain and did not have any language problems.
- Some came because of racial discrimination and persecution in their own countries, like the Indians and Pakistanis from Kenya.
- A substantial number of Coloureds, for example Indians, had served during World War II in the British army and, after the end of the war, settled in Britain.

There were many reasons for immigration. As citizens of the Commonwealth the immigrants had the right to live in the UK; there were jobs on offer, mainly in basic industries; living conditions at home were often poor; and many suffered persecution in their own countries.

Ethnic groups in the United Kingdom, 2011	Numbers (thousands)*	%*
White: Total	55,073.5	87.2
All non-white minorities	8,108.6	12.8
Mixed: Total	1,250.3	2.0
Asian or Asian British: total	4,373.3	7.0
Indian	1,451.8	2.3
Pakistani	1,173.8	1.9
Bangladeshi	451.5	0.7
Chinese	433.1	0.7
Other Asian groups	861.8	1.4
Black or Black British	1,904.6	3.0
Other Ethnic group: Total	580.3	0.9
Total	63,182.1	100

Source: 2011 Census

* Figures may not sum due to rounding

Preferred Areas of Settlement

foundry: *Gießerei*

midwifery: *Geburtshilfe*

Most immigrant groups are nowadays concentrated in and around London.

Pakistanis settled predominantly in Yorkshire/Humberside and the North of the country and found work in the shipbuilding, vehicles and textile industries. In the Yorkshire city of Bradford the number of Asian immigrants stands at 15% so that racial tensions sometimes turn to violence, as in 2001. **Indians** settled largely in the Midlands, worked in foundries and for public transport in the bigger cities or engaged themselves in the distributive trades. The **West Indians** live mostly in the Southeast, Greater London, and the Midlands. They originally worked in the public service industries (British Rail, London Underground, buses, hospital and midwifery services). Most immigrant groups are nowadays highly concentrated in and around London, but few coloured people live in the rich "Home Counties", e.g. in Hampshire, Kent, and Surrey.

Characteristics of British Immigrants

The majority of British immigrants came from different continents with different cultures, religions and languages. This often leads to racial discrimination and also explains why they are not a homogeneous group, but disunited.

Unemployment rates by ethnic group, Apr – Jun 2016	per cent
Total	4.9
White	4.4
All non-white minorities	8.6
Mixed	11.5
Indian	5.3
Pakistani	11.8
Bangladeshi	8.3
Black	11.5
Chinese	6.1
Other	6.2

Labour Market Statistics

- Compared to the German "guestworkers" who have chiefly emigrated from Southern European countries, most British immigrants came from different continents, often with completely different cultures and religions, and therefore their integration poses a racial problem, which has often led to racial discrimination.
- The immigrants are not a homogeneous, cohesive group, but differ in religion (Hindus, Sikhs, Muslims, Rastafarians, Christians of different denominations), in language (e.g. Hindi, West Indian English), in cultural background, in education, and in social habits. The fact that they are of different origin explains why they are disunited and seldom take action on common ground. On the contrary, there are sometimes street fights among the different immigrant groups.
- Three fifths of the new arrivals (Indians and Pakistanis) had language problems which cut them off from social contacts with the rest of the community. Nowadays the problem has been alleviated somewhat, but many immigrant families still speak their own language at home.

to alleviate: to make pain or suffering less or easier to bear

Britain's Coloured Population and its Problems

The situation of Britain's coloured population has changed since the 1950s, when large-scale immigration first started. Yet not every group of immigrants has been equally successful in coping with the new living conditions. Whilst Indians and Pakistanis adapted rather well to their new surroundings, it seems that the black immigrants have formed a new British lower or under class. However, Britain's coloured population still has some common problems. They are more likely to be unemployed, more likely to live in inferior housing, and often discriminated against.

Britain's coloured population still has some common problems. They are more likely to be unemployed, more likely to live in inferior housing, and are often discriminated against. Typical jobs of coloured immigrants are **unskilled jobs** with **low wages** (e.g. factory worker, street cleaner).

In general, immigrants filled the vacancies in **unskilled jobs** that were abandoned by Englishmen in the 60s for more profitable jobs in the expanding, booming industries of an affluent consumer society; jobs that demanded know-how in modern technology and electrical engineering. Typical jobs of coloured immigrants are manual jobs, unskilled or semi-skilled, e.g. the factory worker, the street cleaner, the dustman, the nurse, the postman, the bus conductor, the ticket collector, the shop assistant, or the waiter. These jobs are characterized by **low wages**, long or unattractive working hours, bad working conditions, and heavy or monotonous work on the assembly line.

affluent: prosperous

When the economic situation of Britain deteriorated in the late 60s and 70s, the coloured population suffered disproportionately from **unemployment**, as the mostly unskilled immigrants were the first to be dismissed, and vacancies were filled with better qualified British workers.

to deteriorate: to become worse

Over the last 10 years there have been **some advances in racial equality** regarding work. Immigrants and their children are now getting better jobs and more professional advancement. In particular **African Asians** and **Indians** have settled as businessmen, shop-keepers or traders as well as doctors of the NHS (National Health Service (→ pp. 84 f)). Extended family ties and hard work have helped this group to advance in society. There has been an expansion of commercial enterprise and numerous self-help projects in ethnic communities. The proportion of ethnic minority members with professional and managerial positions is increasing. In 2015 there were 41 ethnic minority MPs. Black competitors represent Britain in international sporting events. In sports like athletics, almost all the top-class British athletes are black. Many are also in football at highest level. Ethnic minority talents in the arts and in entertainment have gained growing recognition.

On the other hand, as new generations born in the UK grow up, there has been progress. Many have succeeded in business and in the professions, and many of the top British sportsmen and women are now of immigrant origin.

West Indians (Black Caribbeans), on the other hand, are still the most disadvantaged group. They still have the greatest percentage of under-achievers, alienated young people, and youth unemployment. Moreover, single-parent families are highest among West Indians. Low pay and the desire to live in close communities forced many Blacks to live in overcrowded, unsatisfactory accommodation. They are, in particular, concentrated in run-down inner city

council house: house or flat in Britain that is provided by the local council for a very low rent

areas, and often live in council houses or flats in insanitary slum conditions. Most of the Blacks came in the immigration surge of the late 50s and early 60s, when job opportunities were good. At first they were officially welcomed and generally accepted, and it was supposed that they would soon assimilate. But gradually, as the number of immigrants increased and the economic situation of the country deteriorated, a deeper resentment and a more open hostility towards the presence of the Blacks was felt.

harassment: behaviour which is intended to trouble or annoy sb. *(Schikane, Belästigung)*

Racial discrimination and **intolerance** intensified unemployment and housing problems. Racial prejudice by the white population and **harassment** by the police, especially towards unemployed youths, caused a lot of trouble and consequently led to riots like those in the London areas of Notting Hill in 1958 and Brixton in 1981.

statutory: controlled by law

liaison: cooperation, exchange of information

Harassment through „sus" laws (the right of the police to arrest sb. on "suspicion") is controversial. As an attempt to alleviate tensions between police and ethnic minorities, there is statutory consultation between the police and the community. Liaison work is also done with children in schools.

Responses of White Society

The British government has tried through the years to deal with the problems of immigration by passing laws. The most recent Act in 2006 **(Asylum, Immigration and Nationality Act)** aims to control new immigration and make the integration of those who are already in the UK more effective.

White society has reacted to racial integration in different ways. The British Government's attempt to deal with minority problems has been based on legislation, with six Acts passed between 1981 and 2006. The most recent of these Acts, the **Asylum, Immigration and Nationality Act** 2006, brings together all the provisions of the earlier Acts. In particular it

- aims to tighten controls;
- improves the speed and efficiency of handling appeals (e.g. against asylum or immigration decisions of the British government) and deportations;
- makes integration of those immigrants who are accepted into the country easier;
- deals with criminal activity such as people trafficking and drug abuse;
- makes it possible to take away a person's right to British citizenship if found guilty of terrorism.

people trafficking: *Menschenhandel*

A second response by the Government has been the attempt to stop racial discrimination and to promote good relations between immigrants and native British. It has founded various institutions, the most significant being **The Commission for Racial Equality** (1967) which can carry out formal investigations not only in individual cases, but into whole areas of public life and whole organizations. These moves have had a positive effect, although problems remain. The right-wing extremist National Front (a small extreme right-wing party founded in 1966) has very little support in the country.

Asylum and Migration

From the 1990s the annual number of asylum seekers in the UK increased rapidly, peaking in 2002 at 84,000 before falling gradually to about 25,000-30,000 per year. Since 2008 the number of applicants has stayed relatively stable compared to European trends. Of those who apply, 90% are already in the UK, and about one third are accepted at their first attempt.

Most would-be immigrants today are asylum-seekers from the world's trouble-spots (the Balkans, the Middle East, East Africa, Asia).

Most applicants come from the trouble spots of the Balkans, the Middle East, East Africa and Asia. Added to these are economic migrants which are seeking a better life style rather than fearing for their lives as genuine refugees.

Of a total of 34,687 **asylum applicants** in March 2016, the top nationalities came from Iran (4,305), Eritrea (3,321), Iraq (2,805), Sudan (2,769), Pakistan (3,254) and Syria (2,669). Due to the civil war in Syria the number of Syrian refugees has increased steeply in recent years.

With the accession to the EU in 2008 of a number of Eastern European countries, migration from e.g. Poland and Romania rose sharply. Polish people especially came in such big numbers that this caused from time to time a hostile reaction from the British. In the 2016 referendum on whether to stay within the EU or to leave it, the large influx of Eastern European people was a strong argument for a certain part of the population to vote against Europe.

A sharp increase in EU migrants led to a hostile reaction from some Britons, and to more referendum votes for Brexit.

In order to come to terms with immigration, the British government introduced two Immigration Acts (2014/2016) which both aim at tightening the UK's immigration law. Thus the Acts foresee a tighter control of undocumented migrants and illegal working, stronger action against worker exploitation and a requirement for language fluency in a number of jobs. All these measures are intended to discourage foreigners from coming to Britain by creating a less welcoming environment.

New laws aim to stop illegal entry and to improve integration of legal migrants.

This does not of course mean a total exclusion of all EU citizens from the UK after Brexit is achieved; many of those already in Britain will stay indefinitely, and many employers will continue to recruit people with particular skills that are in short supply – at one extreme highly qualified engineers, technologists and medical specialists, at the other extreme seasonal agricultural workers willing to work long hours in all weathers to harvest crops such as strawberries and daffodils.

The future will probably see some control of borders, but not total exclusion of all EU citizens from visiting, living and working in the UK.

In 2015 the top countries whose nationals received settlement grants were India (18,741), Pakistan (10,564), Zimbabwe (4,847), Nigeria (4,397) and China (3,728).

Grants of Settlement (UK, 2015)	
All regions	118,035
Asia	50,528
Africa	31,690
Europe	18,250
Americas	8,850
Middle East	4,617
Oceania	3,413
Others	705

Home Office 2016

Social Structure of Britain

Britain: A Class-ridden Society

Class distinction and class consciousness have always played a dominant part in Britain. Three main classes can be distinguished: upper class – middle class – working class.

Upper Class

- consists mainly of the aristocracy and of landowners some of whom are politically represented in the House of Lords as hereditary and life peers;
- has provided for the ideal of the "country gentleman";
- enjoys considerable prestige in social and cultural life;
- is not necessarily the richest part of the population.

Middle Class

- has grown enormously in recent years;
- consists mainly of the upper middle class (managers, civil servants, the professionals, businessmen and businesswomen) who have partly replaced the old aristocracy in politics, administration, and the civil service; the lower middle class (lesser officials, owners of small businesses, non-manual white-collar workers, and skilled manual workers) which nowadays forms the biggest stratum of British society.

Working Class

- is basically formed by
  a) semi-skilled (factory workers, shop assistants) and
  b) unskilled (cleaners, farmlabourers) manual workers;
- big gap to the other classes, solidarity to fellow-workers, "us-and-them" attitude (workers against the "Establishment");
- many of them form the lower class of the unemployed, the elderly, the low-paid (unsupported mothers, casual workers, among them many immigrants).

Preservation of Class Distinction through

- language (e.g. "upper class accent", Cockney);
- education (e.g. private schools, Oxbridge universities);
- hereditary titles (e.g. "Lord");
- membership of the House of Lords.

Britain: A Multi-ethnic Society

After 1945 Britain has developed into a multicultural and multi-ethnic society.
The main immigration groups are:

- Black immigrants from the West Indies (Black Caribbeans);
- Indians from Africa and India;
- Pakistanis and Bangladeshis.

Motives for Immigration

- labour shortage in Britain in the 1950s;
- higher British living standard;
- British citizens from (former) colonies;
- soldiers of the British Army in World War II;
- asylum.

Characteristics and Problems

- no homogeneous group (different ethnic origins);
- of different religion (Christians, Hindus, Muslims, Sikhs);
- language problems;
- racial discrimination in jobs and housing; private harassment.

London Fashion Week, February 18, 2014 in London

Homeless man in the city centre of London

2.2 Social Structure of the United States

IN BRIEF

- The USA is a nation of immigrants.
- They have had many different motives for leaving their native lands to follow the ideal of the American Dream.
- The "melting-pot" concept of a new society has proved difficult to achieve, and has given way to other terms such as "salad bowl".
- The settlement of America involved a continuous westward movement, as new lands became part of the USA.
- The population of the USA is about 63% white, of European descent.
- The basic human rights of minorities have not always been respected by the white majority.
- Immigration was practically unrestricted until 1880; since then it has become more and more limited.
- Class structure in the USA is based on a five-point scale model, depending on social, economic and ethnic factors.

Historical Development of US Society

The overwhelming majority of the US population can trace their descent from immigrants.

influx: the arrival of large numbers *(Strom, Zustrom)*

The United States is commonly called **"a nation of immigrants"**. The country was not only settled and shaped by immigrants, but has accepted more immigrants than any other country in the world. That is why the study of immigration, the influx of some **50 million people** over more than three centuries, is fundamental to the study of contemporary American society.
To describe the social structure of the United States, therefore, means

- to outline the historical development of US society, to discuss the **basic values** and **beliefs of the immigrants** and to compare ideals with reality;
- to give a survey of the present-day population structure of America and to point out the **significance of racial and ethnic origin** in one of the most heterogeneous societies in the world;
- to examine the **importance of social class** in American society.

Among the forces that have shaped modern America are such basic values and beliefs as

- the ideal of the American Dream;
- the "melting-pot theory";
- the frontier spirit.

According to John F. Kennedy religious persecution, political oppression, and economic hardship were the chief motives for the mass migration to America

("A Nation of Immigrants", 1964). Edward N. Kearny et al., "The American Ways" (1997), distinguishes the following three reasons why immigrants have been drawn to America:

- individual freedom,
- equality of opportunity,
- material wealth.

The price they had to pay for these advantages was:

- self-reliance,
- competition,
- hard work.

The Ideal of the American Dream

The United States is a country that is strongly committed to **egalitarian ideals**. This is due to the fact that America is a nation of immigrants, and all its citizens, apart from the Indians, are immigrants or the descendants of immigrants.
The motives for immigration to America have been manifold:

- They have come as **religious refugees**, seeking a land where they can practise their faith (e.g. the Puritan settlers of the first colony in Massachusetts in 1620, called the "Pilgrim Fathers", and the first German Mennonites).
- Suffering from **political persecution** in their native countries, they have emigrated in the hope of finding political freedom.
- They have come for **economic reasons** and in search of better living conditions.

The immigrants have moved to America because of religious persecution, political oppression and/or economic hardship in their native lands.

What they have all had in common is the **dream of a new classless society**, where one is free to develop one's innate abilities, and to realize one's potential. This ideal of the American Dream existed for more than a century before it was formulated and written down by Thomas Jefferson in the Declaration of Independence (1776).
The **"inalienable rights"**, the fundamental principles of American democracy, are:

They were drawn to America by the dream of a new society based on **individual freedom**, **equal opportunity** and **material wealth**.

- **Equality**: equality of opportunity (each individual should have an equal chance for success); political equality (allowing everyone the right to vote); racial and social equality.
- **Liberty**: individual freedom (to be free of controls); religious, political and economic freedom.
- **Pursuit of happiness**: personal fulfilment; to live according to one's abilities; the right to exercise an appropriate profession, and in a more modern sense: the belief that you can make it "from the log cabin to the White House", that you can rise from "rags to riches"; the ideal of the self-made man and America as the land of unlimited possibilities.

A closer examination of American history and the development of the nation shows the discrepancy between America's historical reality and the American ideal of equality, liberty, and the chance of personal fulfilment.

Reality also involves racialism, poverty, social prejudice and economic pressures.

The **concept of a classless society** has been **handicapped** from the very beginning: by the existence of a **native population** that resisted white lifestyle, by the introduction of the **slave trade** and the long history of racial discrimination, by the exploitation of many immigrants as cheap labourers. Until today the noble principles of the founding fathers have only been realized to a very limited extent. In American society racial discrimination often prevails. Instead of leading a life in dignity, some minorities scrape a living in **slum areas**. And, above all, the pursuit of happiness has for many people turned into a **blind pursuit of material wealth** and economic success, with the result that rivalry and competition put psychological and social pressure on the individual. American society has become obsessed with an upward mobility to reach the top.

to scrape a living: to get just enough food to stay alive

The "Melting-pot Theory"

The "melting-pot" theory means that foreign immigrants give up their old identities, languages and loyalties to form a new nation.

From the very start, the early settlers were filled with the idea of forming, with the help of God, a new society consisting of a new race of men: God's "chosen people". The main idea of the "melting-pot theory" was to create a new nation with mixed origins.

- In a **literal sense**, the term is used to describe a vessel in which different elements, e.g. metals, are fused together to form a new product, with the result that the former parts, the ingredients, are absorbed and transformed into something entirely different and, in general, more valuable.
- In a **figurative sense**, the metaphor implies that the foreign immigrants ideally give up their national identity, way of life, culture, language and become a new nation, i.e. become true Americans.
- The American people have demonstrated in recent years a growing eagerness to "get in touch with their roots". This has meant the organization throughout the country of ethnic "clubs" or groupings.

Limits of the melting-pot myth

In reality this ideal has had only limited success. Factors such as race, religion, language and culture have led to separate ways of life persisting.

Only few aspects of the "melting-pot concept" have ever been realized: a **common language** has been adopted, a **national identity** has been achieved and the specific "American Way of Life" has evolved. But a common **immigrant assimilation** and transformation into "true" Americans has not taken place. The following items show why the term "melting pot" is misleading:

- A **biological fusion of races** has never taken place. From the very beginning the term "melting pot" was only applied to Whites, the Indians being disregarded and the Blacks legally being considered as chattels in the Constitution.
- In the **religious sector** at least three different melting pots (Protestants, Catholics, Jews) can be distinguished, each with different cultural backgrounds

chattel: something that belongs to you, your belonging (*bewegliches Eigentum, Habe*; cf goods and chattels: *Hab und Gut*)

and accordingly different attitudes. As religious affiliation is a strong element in US society, cultural and religious differences continued.

- **The melting pot worked among Whites** (colonists and "old" immigrants [1800–1880]), as long as they were predominantly of Northern and Western European origins: English, Dutch, French, Germans, Scandinavians, although the British elements grew dominant in a one-way absorption with the result of "Anglo-conformity".

affiliation: *Zugehörigkeit*

From 1880 onwards, however, **a new type of immigrant** arrived: people from the **Mediterranean** (Italians, Greeks) and **Slavs** (Russians). These groups kept more to themselves and stuck together in their quarters, clinging to the traditions of their countries. The "new" immigrants were looked down upon by the Americans (i.e. the "old" immigrants) as being inferior in status and culturally less adaptable. The melting pot of the Whites had come to an end, too. The Western European Americans saw their position threatened because of the shift in ethnic origins, and as the influx of immigration was ever increasing, demands for **forceful immigration restrictions** (→ pp. 72 f) were put forward. The land of unlimited possibilities began to limit itself.

The "Salad bowl"

Quite a number of years passed, however, before the Americans became aware of the questionability of values incorporated by the "melting-pot theory". The turbulent sixties, the growing self-confidence of the minorities to fight for their emancipation, and the influx of even more aliens (Hispanics, Orientals) made American historians and sociologists look for a more suitable metaphor to mirror or symbolize American society.

The American historian Carl Degler suggested the term **"salad bowl"** (in: *Out of Our Past*, 1970) as a more accurate metaphor, the salad being the whole in which the different ingredients remain distinguishable elements. Others use the image of an **"orchestra"**, a **"mosaic"**, or a **"pizza"**. What all these metaphors have in common is that the parts have become vital to the whole; the whole is incomplete and imperfect without the respective elements. It is a concept that admits that American civilization is **multicultural, diverse and pluralistic**. This modern alternative to the "melting-pot theory" is a concept similar to that of a multi-ethnic society in Britain.

An alternative metaphor, the "salad bowl", has been adopted in which the different parts remain visible. All the parts are vital to the whole, but continue to have their separate identities.

The Frontier Spirit

Settlement in America, the conquest of the continent, was characterized by a continuous **westward movement**, by a constant **geographical shifting of the frontier**, as new lands were conquered or acquired by the Americans from

England, Spain, and France. This westward movement has made an impact on American society and the American character.

The **westward movement of settlers**, as new lands were opened up and became part of the USA, still symbolizes the American dream. It is seen as a new start in life, with the promise of freedom and opportunity, but also with the risk of isolation and violence.

"Going west" now connotes a new start in life, a new beginning in simplicity and peace as opposed to the hectic life in overcrowded eastern cities. It implies the promise of leading a freer and wilder life that offers greater satisfaction to the individual. In short, it promises to fulfil the American Dream.

This **idealized American way of life** has positive and negative effects. On the one hand, Americans value independence, self-reliance and persistence; they are full of energy and "can-do spirit", enjoying freedom of opportunity and the outdoor life. The other side of the coin is that these virtues can lead to lack of cooperation, poor social development, selfishness and violence, as seen in their attitude to the ownership and use of guns.

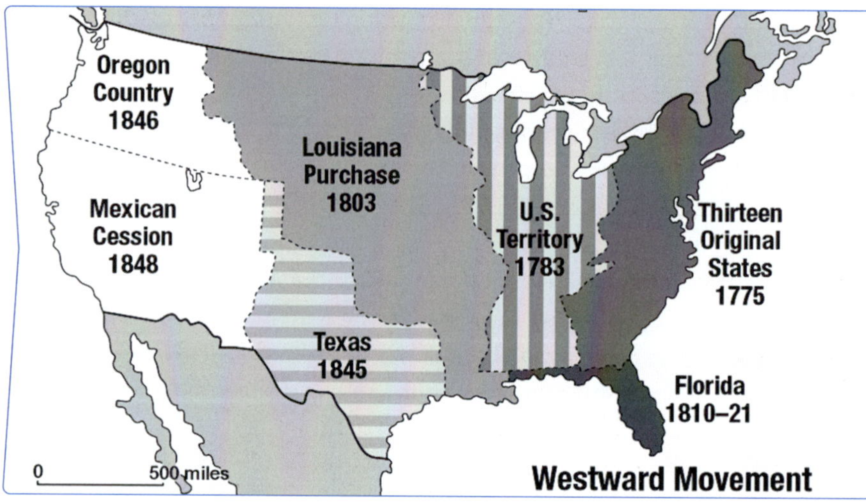

US Population Structure

America's current population is made up of immigrants or their descendants from virtually every country in the world.

Europeans

Ancestry (2014) in millions			
German	46,874	Scottish	5,401
Irish	33,918	Norwegian	4,452
English	25,181	Dutch	4,388
Italian	17,330	Swedish	3,984
Polish	9,452	Scottish-Irish	3,102
French	8,432	Russian	2,896

Infoplease.com

Europe has been the **major source of US immigration**, so that today Whites constitute about 75 % of America's total population.

For more than four centuries immigrants came from Europe.

The **colonists** (1607 – 1776) and "old" immigrants (1800 – 1880) were mainly of **Germanic** (Northern, Western and Central European) descent. Only after 1880 was there a noticeable shift in the ethnic origins, when great masses of "new" immigrants, mainly from **Southern and Eastern Europe**, arrived. With the exception of the Blacks, who were brought to America as slaves between 1609 and 1808, the United States remained a predominantly white country until the 1960s. Americans of European descent have formed the American way of life and control the politics and the economy of the country.

During the last 40 years, however, immigration from **non-European nations** has sharply increased. Today, legal and illegal immigrants from **Asia** and **Latin America** are increasingly changing the population structure of the country, and the so-called European heritage of America is undergoing a change. The rise of ethnic self-awareness among minorities has paved the way for ethnic diversity and cultural pluralism.

In recent decades origins have become much more varied, leading to ethnic and cultural diversity. This threatens the European-based way of life of the majority.

The overwhelming majority of the white population identifies with the American way of life and is integrated into mainstream America. This does not imply that Whites form a classless society and that they all enjoy equal opportunities. But the real problem groups are the ethnic minorities whose situation has led to conflict and controversy in US society. That is why these groups are more extensively dealt with in the following.

U.S. Resident Population, Decennial Censuses, 1790 – 2010

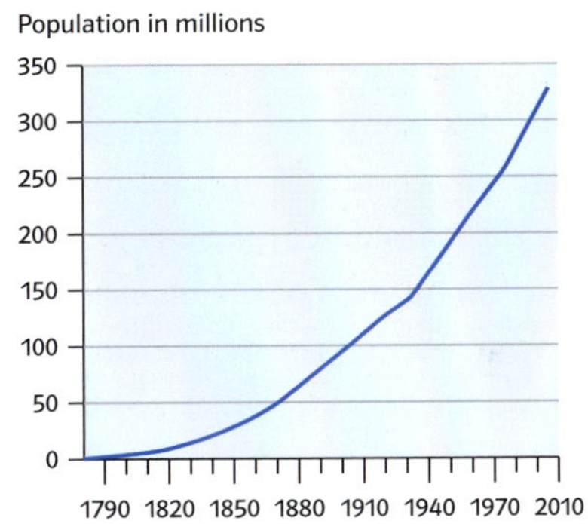

nach: U.S. Census Bureau

Minorities

The fate of minorities has become a major factor in the evaluation of US society. A country that has set up such high democratic values as principles of its society must be judged according to the application of these principles to the whole of its population, including the minorities. In the following paragraphs the question must be examined as to whether the basic human rights written down in the **Declaration of Independence** (1776) and guaranteed in the **Bill of Rights** (1791) as Amendments to the Constitution have been applied to these minority groups, and whether the Non-whites have been allowed to enter the mainstream of American life.

The basic human rights of minorities have not always been respected by the majority.

Indians

Indian population in the USA	
1600	1-2,5 million (estimated)
1900	240,000
1960	520,000
1980	1,500,000
2000	2,475,956
2015	4,010,885 (single race)
2015	6,623,941 (combined race)

States with the largest Indian population, combined race (2015)	
California	1,078,98
Oklahoma	532,016
Texas	452,905
Arizona	429,351
New York	315,526
New Mexico	246,716

U.S. Census Bureau 2016

The American Indians were diverse, widely scattered across the lands and with separate cultures and languages, which made effective resistance to the advance of settlers impossible.

villain: wrongdoer, wicked person

Today, most American Indians live in urban or rural non-reservation areas in the West, less than a quarter of the Indian population on more than 250 federal reservations which constitute about 4% of the total land area of the USA. Most of them are west of the Mississippi in the states of Oklahoma, Arizona, New Mexico, and Utah. Navajo is the largest reservation. Even today, the Indians suffer from a false or one-sided depiction of their lifestyle, as presented in fiction and film. This has the Indians as the villains, and the white cowboy as the romantic hero. In reality, the Indians or **"Native Americans"**, as they prefer to be named, represented, at the time of European contact, completely different cultures, such as woodsmen (East), hunters (Plains), fishermen (Northwest), seed-gatherers, shepherds, and desert dwellers (Southwest). They were separated by culture and language and split up into small tribal communities. Thus they could not take any joint action when confronted with the white man. It was the hunters of the Plains, provided with horses and firearms by the Spanish, who resisted the Whites as they pushed the frontier ever westward.

The world seen by an Indian:

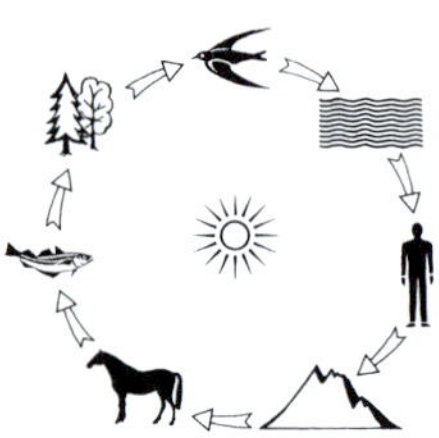

Indian society is characterized by the following items:

- The idea of **cosmic entity**: The earth is the mother of all living beings and man is only one member of a chain consisting also of animals, plants, and the soil. Therefore, any exploitation of mineral resources or the excessive killing of animals means a sacrilegious act against the creation.
- The idea of **common property** means that the tribe, not the individual or the family as among Whites, constitutes the final authority.

The world seen by a white man:

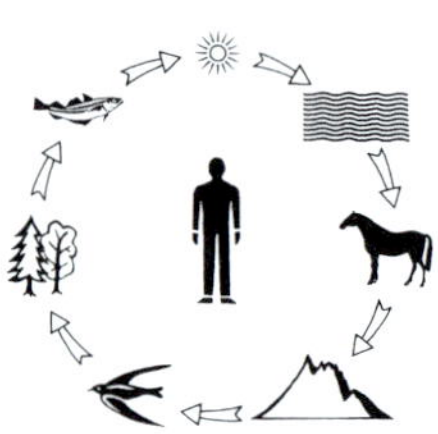

The opposing basic principles of private and common or tribal property led the Europeans and Indians to an inevitable conflict. The Indians were expelled from their traditional territories and herded together in isolated areas, called **"reservations"** ("reserved" for Indians). With their hunting and fishing grounds gone, the **decline of Indian cultures** was predestined. Many hundreds of thousands of Native Indians involved in warfare against the Whites died, or they were exterminated by European diseases. By the turn of the century only some 200,000 native Americans were left.

19th century Indian history	
1834	All Indians had to settle west of the Mississippi, the "permanent frontier", which the Whites were not allowed to cross.
1848	A new surge of immigrants and the discovery of gold led to the colonization of Indian lands west of the Mississippi; buffalo almost became extinct.
1860–1890	Phase of military action between Indians and US troops.
1876	The combined forces of the Sioux and Cheyenne defeated the federal troops under General Custer in the Battle of Little Bighorn.
1890	The massacre at Wounded Knee (300 Indians were killed) put an end to Indian resistance.

The government's policy to integrate the Indians has been disastrous. No solution to the conflict has yet been found.

The long-term objective of US policy towards the native Americans was one of **integration** and **assimilation**, with the aim of bringing them into the mainstream of American life. This policy was the very opposite of the policy of exclusion and rejection being practised against black Americans. The slogan of Indian resistance is "integrity, not integration" in contrast to the aims of the black Americans. The different attitude was due to the fact that Indians had never been the white man's slaves, and that they were in possession of valuable lands. For all of the 19th century and up to 1960, the US Government tried to integrate and assimilate the Indians, with disastrous results. The reaction of the Indians ranged from open warfare (1860s to 1890) to alcoholism, drug-abuse, unemployment, and isolation up to the mid-20th century. Stimulated by the Civil Rights Movement of the Blacks, the native Americans formed, in the late 60s, the **Red Power Movement**. By some spectacular protest actions, the Indians drew attention to their plight and their demands:

- self-determination on the reservations, without government interference;
- the preservation of their culture ("true Indianness") and rejection of "American uniformity" and the lifestyle of the Whites.

It will be the task of the Indians of tomorrow to find a solution to their conflict, namely to preserve their traditional cultural and national identity in a contrasting modern world of which they are a part.

Blacks (→ pp. 25, 60, 151)

The first African slaves were transported to America in 1619.

The history of the American Blacks is closely connected with the historical development of the United States. In 1513 the first Spaniards set foot on American soil; in 1607, Jamestown (Virginia), the first permanent English settlement, was founded, and **in 1619 the first African slaves** were transported to America, one year before the Pilgrim Fathers landed at Cape Cod, New England. Until 1808 African slaves were imported to America, mainly to the Southern colonies (Virginia, N. and S. Carolina, Maryland), where they were needed as cheap labourers on the huge plantations (cotton, tobacco). Slavery became an integral part of the economic system of the agricultural South. Between 1790 and 1860 the number of Blacks rose from 700,000 to 3,5 million. From 1833 onwards an **anti-slavery movement** in the North developed ("abolitionism": an organized movement in the 1830s and 1840s aiming at the abolition of slavery in the United States). In 1808 the slave trade was declared illegal in the United States.

By 1860 there were 3.5 million slaves in the Southern states.

The Civil War (1861–1865)

Disagreement over slavery was a major cause of the Civil War (1861–65). This was won by the North, and slavery was abolished.

Reasons:

- The contrasting economic systems of the industrial North and the rural South, in particular the economic dependence of the financially weak South on the North. Moreover, Northerners introduced protective tariffs on their manufactured goods which the Southern states badly needed, and thus put economic pressure on the South.
- The existence of two different social systems (free versus slave-holding states) and political clashes about the extension of the cotton-slavery system to new territories.
- The Secession of the Southern states and the establishment of the Confederate States of America threatened the union of the nation.

Results:

- In 1863 Lincoln proclaimed that all slaves in the USA were free (Emancipation Proclamation).
- After the victory of the Union (the North), slavery was abolished (13th Amendment to the Constitution in 1865).
- Citizenship was given to black Americans (14th Amendment in 1868).
- The right to vote (right of suffrage) was guaranteed to all male citizens of the USA (15th Amendment in 1870).

From Civil War to Civil Rights Movement

After the Civil War Blacks turned to politics and education, supported black politicians and founded black schools. They tried to achieve economic security, but were too poor to buy land and remained largely dependent on their former masters.

Development in the South

With the withdrawal of the Unionist troops from the South, Southerners started the "white backlash" to restore white political power.

- The Ku Klux Klan, a fanatical racist society that practised lynching, was formed.
- Legal means were introduced to eliminate Blacks as a political force (e.g. high poll taxes, literacy tests).
- The "Jim Crow laws" (system of unfair treatment of black Americans; "Jim Crow": contemptuous name for a black American) were passed, barring Blacks from public buildings (schools, trains, hotels, cemeteries) and introducing legal segregation.

backlash: sudden strong reaction against a recent development in society or politics *(heftige Reaktion)*

literacy: ability to read and write

After the Civil War segregation and discrimination of Blacks, especially in the South, continued.

In 1896, the Supreme Court supported this legislation by its "separate, but equal" doctrine. The Court ruled that **state segregation laws** did not violate the 14th Amendment. Around 1910, black migration to the industrial centres of the North set in.

Although Blacks were given US citizenship, the Supreme Court supported segregation in 1896.

Development in the North

After the Civil War the Northerners lost interest in the so-called "Negro question" and let the South handle the race matters in its own way. The North had fought for the end of slavery, but not for social equality. Thus, even in the North, a de facto discrimination existed regarding housing, education, and income.

The Civil Rights Movement

In 1954, the United States Supreme Court announced a **history-making decision:** In the case of the 11-year-old schoolgirl Linda Brown from Topeka, Kansas ("Brown v. Board of Education") it declared that segregated schools were contrary to the Constitution. This meant a rejection of the "separate, but equal" decision of 1896, and encouraged the Blacks in the movement for desegregation. Here are some of the most important groups that wanted to end discrimination and inequality in all sectors of public life and to achieve civil rights (**"Civil Rights Movement"**) for Blacks:

In a landmark judgement (1954) the Supreme Court overturned the "separate but equal" doctrine and declared **segregation unconstitutional**. This decision led to the Civil Rights Movement.

- **The National Association for the Advancement of Coloured People** (NAACP), founded 1909. Encouraged legal defence for black Americans. Won 1954 Supreme Court decision.
- **The Congress of Racial Equality** (CORE), founded 1942. Nationally prominent in the freedom rides of the 1960s. After 1965 moved away from integration and favoured violence.

Political groups were founded to fight for equal rights. They were united in their drive to end racial discrimination, but differed in their methods. Some demonstrated peacefully like **M. L. King** and his followers, while others used violent means like the Black Muslims or the **Black Panthers**.

- **The Southern Christian Leadership Conference** (SCLC), founded 1957. Mainly black Protestant ministers inspired by Christian ethics. Most famous leader, Dr. Martin Luther King, advocated non-violent action (sit-ins, boycotts, protest marches) similar to Gandhi's "passive resistance" in India. Aimed for the emancipation and integration of black Americans.
- **The "Black Muslims"** (formed 1930s). Blacks who had converted to Islam. Maintained that Christianity supported the Whites; most famous speaker Malcolm X, who demanded a separate nation of Blacks within the USA. Stressed African culture and rejected integration. Assassinated 1965. Present leader Louis Farrakhan.
- **The Black Panther Party** (1960). The most militant group. Demanded weapons to defend those areas of cities preferred by Blacks. Determined to fight against white police. Motto: "violence against violence".

The Civil Rights Movement	
1955	Bus boycott in Montgomery, Alabama.
1957	Use of federal troops in Little Rock, Arkansas, to protect black students on their way to school.
1962	The first black student enrolled in the University of Mississippi, escorted by federal troops.
1963	March on Washington, DC; King's famous speech "I Have a Dream".
1963	Race riots in Birmingham, Alabama.
1964	Civil Rights Act: announced equal status for Blacks in all social matters.
1965	Voting Rights Act: abolished poll tax in elections and made it easier for black voters to register.
1968	Martin Luther King assassinated.
1971	"Busing" was introduced to provide equal opportunities in education; some of the black children of a certain area were brought to "white" schools, and a certain percentage of the white children to schools in black areas; compulsory "busing" caused resistance among Whites and Blacks, and was dropped after an experimental phase in 1976.
1972	Equal Opportunity and Employment Act encouraged preferential hiring and promotion of ethnic minorities.
1983	Martin Luther King's birthday designated a federal public holiday. Martin Luther King Day is the third Monday in January.

The situation of the Blacks since the Civil Rights Movement

The different government decisions of the 1950s and 60s began to engage **Blacks in politics**, mostly at local levels. Jesse Jackson, first black candidate for the Democratic Party in the 1984 and 1988 electoral campaigns, raised the ethnic minority movement up to national prominence in the 80s, since when it has become an important factor in US politics: there are now black mayors of major cities and black governors of states. Colin Powell (2001–2004) and Condoleezza Rice (2005–2008) even became members of George W. Bush's Cabinet, and Barack Obama's (→ pp. 36 ff, 89) presidency (2009) so far marks the climax of this development for emancipation. However, socially and economically the Blacks are still disadvantaged and underprivileged in many areas, although the situation on the job front, in housing and school facilities is slowly progressing.

In the 1950s and 60s progress was made towards desegregation. The law now treats Blacks as equals, but they still suffer social and economic disadvantage.

Blacks on the jobs ladder

An increasing number of Blacks have been appointed to leading positions in the federal services, the universities and the US Army. The number of black office holders in elective positions is almost equal to their percentage of the population. **The Equal Opportunity and Employment Act** of 1972 established preferential hiring of ethnic minorities and thus put pressure on business leaders to recruit more Blacks, but the unemployment statistics show that lack of training and schooling as well as racial prejudice are still dominant factors in the professional life of the Blacks. "Affirmative action" is the special term for government programmes for employing a certain number of Blacks or other minorities in a business. It was designed to eliminate discrimination against minorities and give them increased opportunities. It is seen as having achieved some success, but is now being criticized by many as resulting in "reverse discrimination" and as unfair to white male persons.

Unemployment Rates by Race and Sex, June 2016 (%) (U.S. Dept. of Labor)

Race	Men	Women
All	4.8	4.8
White	4.1	4.2
Black	9.1	7.6
Hispanic	4.9	6.6
Asian	3.7	3.8

Today Blacks are found at the highest levels in the military, universities and government, right up to the President. On the other hand they still form much of the underclass, being unemployed and living in urban ghettos.

In 1968, Congress passed a new Civil Rights Act to end **discrimination in housing**, in an attempt to overcome the split into white and black neighbourhoods and to end school segregation.

On the whole, the integration of residential neighbourhoods has not made much progress. The migration of the Blacks from agricultural areas has aggravated the **ghetto situation** of the black Americans, all the more as the Whites have continued to move to the suburbs. In housing, and consequently also in schooling, de facto segregation is practised.

The over-all picture of the Blacks of today is ambiguous: middle class, higher education, well-paid jobs, suburban homes on the one hand, and underclass, urban ghettos, unemployment on the other.

The history of the black Americans mirrors the difficult and painful process of emancipation and integration of a people that accepted and wanted to adopt the American way of life, but was for so long denied the basic human rights, the foundations of American democracy.

Median Family Income ($)

	1985	1990	2000	2015
White	35,410	36,915	44,226	60,101
Black	20,390	21,423	30,439	37,211
Hispanic	23,112	23,431	33,447	45,148
Asian	–	–	–	73,166

In 2016 the official poverty line was a yearly income of $24,300 for a family of four persons.

Percentage below Poverty Level

	1980	1990	2000	2015
All	13.0	13.5	11.3	13.5
White	10.2	10.7	9.4	9.1
Black	32.2	31.9	22.1	24.1
Hispanic	25.7	28.1	21.2	21.4

Population by Origin in Percentage (one race)

Race	1990	2000	2015
All persons	248,7	281,4	321,4
Whites (not Hispanic)	80.3%	75.1%	61.6%
Blacks	12.1%	12.3%	13.2%
American Indians	0.8%	0.8%	1.2%
Asian-Pacific Islanders	2.9%	3.7%	5.6%
Hispanics	9.0%	12.5%	17.4%
Other/Mixed	3.9%	5.4%	3.0%

(The combined percentage of the whole population totals over 100% because persons of Hispanic origin may be of any race.)

Hispanics in the US 2015 (in millions)

Mexican	Puerto Rican	Cuban	Other	All
35,8	5,8	2,1	13,3	57,0

Hispanics (→ pp. 39 f, 61, 70, 76 f, 124 f)

The Hispanics make up the **largest ethnic minority** and are still increasing rapidly.

The Hispanics or Spanish-speaking Americans make up the largest ethnic immigration group and their numbers are still rapidly increasing today. This increase is not only due to immigration, but also to the fact that the Hispanic residents are a very young population group.

They are divided up into the following groups:

- The **Hispanos** are the descendants of former Spanish settlers that, from 1513 onwards, started to colonize the southern territories at the Mexican border (e.g. Florida, Texas, California). Today they are culturally assimilated and have adopted the English language.

They mostly come from Mexico, Cuba and Puerto Rico.

- The **Chicanos** or Mexican-Americans constitute nearly two thirds of the 57 million Hispanics. They leave their home country for economic reasons and enter the USA legally or illegally. Most of them settle in the border states. Originally, they came as seasonal or migrant agricultural workers; nowadays they are more concentrated in urban areas, especially of California. They share the same fate as the Puerto Ricans: both groups are economically deprived, have a low level of schooling and training, a High School dropout rate of 40 % and a low social status.
- The **Puerto Ricans** have US citizenship, although the island of Puerto Rico is not a state of the USA. Taken over by the USA as a result of the Spanish-American War in 1898, the island chose a "commonwealth" status with internal sovereignty in 1952. This immigration group is mainly concentrated in New York, often in similar conditions to the Blacks in the slums.
- The **Cubans** were mainly political refugees and chiefly belonged to the well-to-do. The Cuban exodus began after the rebellion of 1959, when Fidel Castro had established Communism. On the whole, the Cubans have managed within a short time to take advantage of opportunities and to get on in life. Many of them are well-established middle-class Americans. Their high concentration in Florida has, however, led to racial tension with the poorer blacks, who often lost their jobs. Today they are strongly opposed to a normalization of relations between the US and Cuba.

The Hispanics share a common language, Spanish, which now poses a threat to one of the unifying factors of the USA, namely the English language.

Chicanos, Puerto Ricans, and Cubans have one particular aspect in common that presents a serious problem to American society and to the unity of the population: for the first time in American history the greater part of all immigrants **speak just one language**, namely Spanish (→ pp. 76, 125), and the majority lives in **ethnic enclaves**, unwilling or unable to assimilate. (The US Constitution does not provide for an official language, so English is only the common language by use, not by law.) In order to integrate children of Hispanic origin, the Federal Office of Education established bilingual education for non-English-speaking children, a decision that met the strong criticism of those who fear for the unilingual school system, and who believe that the Spanish-speaking immigrants pose a grave threat to national unity.

Asians

The number of Asians migrating to the USA is small (4.8%), but is growing rapidly and achieving high standards.

Although the Hispanics are the largest immigration group making up 16.3% of the entire population, there has been a great increase in the number of Asians seeking a new home. They constitute only 4.8% of the total population, yet the number has more than doubled in the last 25 years. In comparison to other ethnic groups, the Asians achieve the highest academic standards and are often in good positions.

Growth of the different ethnic groups in US (in percents)

	2000–2010
All persons in the USA	9.7%
Whites	5.7%
Blacks	12.3%
American Indians	18.4%
Asian-Pacific Islanders	43.3%
Hispanics	33.0%

U.S. Census Bureau

US Immigration Policy

US policy allowed practically unrestricted immigration until the 1880s. Since then the laws have become ever stricter. The current threat of terrorism has led to the most recent legislation.

Up to the 1880s immigration was unrestricted. Then immigration laws were passed to limit the entry of special groups on the basis of national origin.

1882: The Chinese Exclusion Act banned all Chinese labourers. Later legislation (1907) banned most Oriental immigrants from entering the country.

1924: The Immigration Act introduced a quota system for Europeans based on the "national origins" principle, under which immigrants from Northern European countries enjoyed a favourable position. It limited the annual quota for European immigrants to 2% of the 1890 census of the US population and thus restricted the number of "new" immigrants from Eastern and Southern Europe.

to repeal: to annul, to end officially

1952: The McCarran-Walter Act repealed the Chinese Exclusion Act of 1882 and loosened restriction on Asians. Special legislation admitted displaces persons from World War II (1948), refugees from Hungary (1958), refugees from Cuba (1959–1964), and in 1979 the "boat people" from Vietnam.

1965: The US Immigration Act abolished the quota system. Instead it allowed up to 290,000 immigrants annually, who had special qualifications or skills.

1986: The Immigration Reform and Control Act was passed to deal with illegal immigration from Mexico. It prohibited the hiring of illegal aliens and offered amnesty to all who had illegally immigrated before 1982.

1990: The Immigration Act of 1990 established a yearly limit of 700,000 immigrants for each of the following three years, and a limit of 675,000 per year thereafter. The Act established a special annual quota of 140,000 for immigrants with job skills needed in the United States.

1996: The Illegal Immigration Reform and Immigrant Responsibility Act of 1996 made it easier to deport aliens attempting to enter the USA without proper documents, and established an income test for those trying to bring family members from abroad to the USA.

2001: The USA PATRIOT Act was a reaction to the terrorists' attacks of September 11, 2001. It gave the government wide powers to arrest suspected terrorists

without charge and to deny them their normal legal rights.
2005: The Real ID (identity document) Act of 2005 strengthened the laws on asylum and deportation of aliens for terrorist activity and established national standards for drivers' licences and non-drivers' identification cards.
2006: The Comprehensive Immigration Reform Act (CIRA) improved border security by building a fence along the U.S.-Mexican border and granted citizenship to long-time illegal immigrants. From 2013 onwards Obama's new non-deportation policy has made it easier for illegal immigrants with U.S. relatives to apply for a visa without returning to their home countries.

Social Divisions and Groupings

The question whether social classes are meaningful to Americans has for a long time been the subject of scholarly debate. On the one hand it has been argued that the New World offered **a break from European traditions**, that the United States has always been an open and relatively egalitarian society and that, therefore, class terms should be rejected as foreign. Others have countered that the USA is the country with the **biggest social differences** of any industrial nation and that since the 19th century ethnic affiliation has become increasingly important.

The term "class" is not accepted by all Americans to describe social groupings, but can be useful.

Socio-economic Models

American sociologists have adapted the basic class model of three main socio-economic groups to contemporary American society. The American social critic Vance Packard (1914–1996) distinguishes **two distinct classes** (in: *The Status Seekers*,1959, pp. 4, 10, 38) which can be split into several sub-classes:

The Diploma Élite	%	The Supporting Classes	%
I The Real Upper Class	5	III The Limited Success Class	25
II The Semi-Upper Class	15	IV The Working Class	40
		V The Real Lower Class	15

These are "horizontal" divisions in American society. Alongside them Packard places the "vertical" dimension of race.
The diploma élite comprises both the principle of selection by family and of selection by merit, but the selection by family is the real upper class and the selection by merit (meritocracy) is generally the semi-upper class.
Other sociologists have offered variations on the class structure, based on social, economic and ethnic factors. The most current model is a **five-point scale** which will be used for the following description of social strata in America:

upper – upper middle – middle – working – lower

The most current socio-economic model has 5 divisions.

Class Stratification

Social groupings

The **upper class** consists of industrialists, financiers, politicians and military leaders, often from historically important families.

The **upper middle class** is made up of doctors, lawyers and executives at the top of their professions.

The **middle class** is the largest and most influential. Teachers, social workers, shopkeepers and skilled craftsmen are among the members of this grouping.

The **working class** includes those who do have regular jobs but at a low level of pay.

The **lower class** is composed of the unemployed, casual workers, the poor including migrant labour.

WASPs: short form for White Anglo-Saxon Protestants. The term refers to the early settlers of West and Northern European descent.

janitor (AE): doorkeeper, caretaker of a building

The top of American society is formed by a power élite consisting of multimillionaires, business investors and financiers on the one hand, and high-prestige politicians and military leaders on the other. This combination of political and financial power, linked with a "good" family name, constitutes the **upper class** in America. For a long time families whose names could be traced back to the early settlers, the so-called WASPs, have had important positions in American society. Today their influence has not altogether disappeared.

Next to the upper class comes an **upper middle class** consisting of professionals (doctors and lawyers), business executives, managers, and technologists. The **middle class** is quantitatively and qualitatively the most powerful force. It comprises schoolteachers, social workers, small businessmen and shopkeepers, white-collar workers (clerks, supervisors in offices and stores) and blue-collar workers (foremen in factories, skilled craftsmen, and technical aides).

Forty years after the 1960s struggles, about a third of the Blacks have managed to rise into the middle class. They have profited from economic growth, expanding industries and from Government pressure on white industrialists to achieve equal opportunity on the labour market. They have improved their economic situation, obtained skilled jobs and moved into well-to-do suburbs.

The **working class** consists of regularly employed, semi-skilled workers, such as assembly-line factory workers, deliverymen, truck drivers, miners, janitors, and shop assistants.

The **lower class** comprises the unemployed, casual labourers (e.g. migrant farm workers), the poor who live in miserable conditions in shabby "downtown" areas. Most of them are Blacks or Hispanics.

Occupation of Employed Persons by Sex, Jan 2015, 16 years and over (in thousands)

	Total	Men	Women
All occupational groups	146,552	75,364	66,894
Management, professional, and related occupations	57,367	27,465	29,537
(Management, business, and financial operations occupations)	(23,447)	(13,271)	(10,098)
(Professional and related occupations)	(33,920)	(14,194)	(19,497)
Service occupations	25,342	10,134	19,440
Sales and office occupations	33,114	12,207	13,497
Natural resources, construction and maintenance occupations	13,007	12,190	0,571
Production, transportation, and material moving occupations	17,722	13,368	3,885

Source: U.S. Dept. of Labor

Characteristics of Social Class

- Americans are not only geographically but also socially "on the move". **Social mobility** is more frequent than in European countries and class lines are less fixed and less stable.
- In the United States there is **no hereditary royalty and nobility**, therefore family and tradition have been of less importance than in Britain.
- In spite of obvious social and economic inequalities there is still a strong belief that each man is fundamentally equal to every other. "Equality" does not mean economic equality but **equality of opportunity**: everyone is free to achieve wealth by his own efforts.
- This idea of equality of opportunity, however, has hampered the development of a working-class party, a strong trade union movement, and an efficient welfare system.
- The American worker believes in the structure of American society. He identifies with striving for success, and he works hard to participate in the American Dream. Therefore, there is no idealistic gulf between the workers and the middle classes, as there is in Britain.

Social groupings are much less fixed than in many other countries. There is no hereditary nobility at the top, but a belief in the idea of equality of opportunity to rise through the classes.

to hamper: to hinder

On the whole, class bonds are less marked in the United States than in Britain. They are, however, strengthened by **race bonds**. Social class and ethnic affiliation are closely interrelated with each other, forming a hierarchy of prestige. As to ethnic origin, Western Europeans are at the top of the class system and ethnic minorities at the bottom.

For the ethnic minorities this means that their subordinate racial status reinforces their lower class membership and that they are caught in a vicious circle of social class and race.

In practice, social grouping depends largely on ethnic origins, which make upward movement difficult though not impossible.

Commentary on the Results

The noble egalitarian principles of US society have only partly come true. Social status and race are still important factors.

In retrospect we can say that American society has only partly been able to live up to and to realize its high egalitarian principles, and that for millions of Americans, especially for members of ethnic minorities, the **American Dream is a sheer illusion**. Class and social status are determined to a great extent by **ethnic affiliation**. US society is a predominantly white society with Indians, Hispanics and Blacks at the bottom of the social scale. Legislation since the 60s has done a lot to ease upward mobility for the underprivileged, but has not been capable of compensating completely for centuries-old injustice. Due to the vastly growing number of ethnic minorities, the future picture of America will be a **minority of the white European American**. It has been prognosticated that in the year 2056 the average 60-year-old American will not trace his or her descent to Europe.

Due to this, there have been **basic social and cultural changes**:

The growth in the population of Hispanics and Asians leads to predictions that white Europeans will be in the minority in 50 years time.

The Blacks still have the most social problems. They find it hard to escape slum living, unemployment and poverty.

- As the Hispanic groups are so numerous, and the Asians are a fast-growing group, the needs of the Blacks are receiving less priority.
- Whilst the Hispanic and Asian ethnic groups have more **cultural problems**, the Blacks, even today, have more basic **social problems**. The Asians are often economically successful and achieve good educational qualifications. The Hispanics have an extraordinary work ethic. Most of them have blue-collar jobs which they seldom lose or leave. However, many Blacks do not manage to overcome their underprivileged social position.
- An important change is that **Spanish** has developed into **a second lingua franca**. Street signs or political information are often bilingual and there are numerous Spanish television and radio stations and Spanish newspapers.

In some states in the South like California, New Mexico and Texas minority groups now form the majority of the population.

In 1999, California, the most heavily populated state in the USA, became the first **"majority minority" state**, i.e. the non-Hispanic white population fell below 50% of the total. This development was seen as a milestone in the growth of ethnic diversity. As recently as 1970, about 80% of California's population were white, yet in 2000 non-Hispanic Whites accounted only for about 47% of the state's residents. Hispanics made up 33%, Asians 11%, and Blacks 7%. By 2005 Hawaii, New Mexico and Texas joined California as states in which minority groups, taken together, account for a majority of the population.

The 2010 census confirmed this trend. Between 2000 and 2010 the population increased by 9.7% to 308,745,538 residents. Never before had the nation been so diverse:

- Ethnic minorities now make up more than one third of the population (37%), up from one 25.1 % in 2000 and one fifth in 1990.
- Nationally about 9 million Americans, i.e. 2.9 %, described themselves as multiracial, that is stemming from more than one race.
- In five states the population was "majority-minority": Hawaii (77.3 %), District of Columbia (65.2 %), California (59.9 %), New Mexico (59.5 %) and Texas (54.7 %).
- With more than 50 million (16 %) people the Hispanics today constitute by far the largest ethnic minority group (one in 6 people of the United States) followed by the Black population with about 39 million (12.6 %). This demographic shift has had a major impact on politics and culture at the start of the new millennium.
- Overall, the Sun Belt continued to gain. The South with a rate of 14.3 % and the West with 13.8 % continued their population expansion, whereas the Northeast (3.2 %) and the Midwest (3.9 %) showed the slowest growth. This means America is divided between increasingly young, multi-ethnic gateway states like California, Florida, or Texas and regions such as the Northwest or the Midwest that are mostly white, or white and black in the South.
- As in the 2010 census population gains varied widely by states, the South (e.g. Texas, Arizona, Florida) and the Mountain West (e.g. Nevada, Utah) added 11 seats in Congress. On the other hand states in the Northeast (e.g. New York) and Midwest (e.g. Michigan, Ohio) lost a total of 11 congressional seats.
- One of the most pressing challenges to face these immigration regions will be to prevent the states and their cities from dividing into ghettos of different racial and ethnic groups, and to encourage the development of a new integrated social and cultural identity.

Census 2010 showed that more than a quarter of the population are non-white with Hispanics being the dominant ethnic group.

The South and the West of the US are growing strongly compared with the traditional rich regions of the Midwest and the Northeast. Both growth and decline bring their problems to the new century.

A major challenge of US society: integrating the different ethnic groups

Social Structure of the United States

Social Structure of the United States: A Nation of Immigrants
Its basic values and beliefs are the ideal of the American Dream, the "melting-pot theory", and the frontier spirit.

The American Dream
- Americans have common motives for immigration: religious persecution, political oppression, and economic problems.
- They are strongly committed to egalitarian ideals: dream of a new classless society where one is free to develop one's abilities (cf Declaration of Independence: "inalienable rights" of "life, liberty, and the pursuit of happiness").

The "Melting-pot Theory"
- describes the creation of one nation under God;
- implies immigrants would give up their national identity, culture, language.
- This ideal however only worked to a limited extent among white settlers.
- A biological fusion of races and mixing of religion has not taken place.
- New metaphors for the US population are the salad bowl or the pizza.

The Frontier
The frontier (border region between wilderness and civilization) has made a strong impact on American society:
- "Going west" has become synonymous with a new beginning, with leading a free life and with independence from any restrictions.
- The frontier way of life means self-reliance and "can-do" spirit.

The Population Structure: Europeans
- Colonists (1607 – 1776) and "old" immigrants (1800 – 1880) mainly of Germanic (Northern, Western and Central European) descent and Anglicans or Protestants;
- "new" immigrants (1880 – 1960s) mainly from Southern and Eastern Europe (Catholics).

The Population Structure: Minorities

Indians (Native Americans)
- Today about 2,9 million. Some 800,000 live on reservations.
- Their original way of life was opposed to that of the Whites (nomads, no exploitation of resources, no private property).
- They were expelled from their territories by the Whites and put in reservations;
- were almost exterminated by warfare, European diseases, or suicide.
- The phase of military action between Indians and Whites (1860 – 1890) ended with the massacre at Wounded Knee (1890).
- After that the attempt of the US Government to assimilate Indians into mainstream America failed.
- In the 1960s they organized protest actions and formed a Red Power Movement.
- After many years of resistance they were granted self-determination on the reservations and the preservation of their own culture.

Blacks (Afro-Americans)
- Their history as slaves in America started as early as 1619.
- After the end of the Civil War (1865) slavery was abolished and Blacks were given citizenship in 1868, but discrimination in the South went on.
- In 1896, the Supreme Court pronounced its "separate, but equal" doctrine.
- The rejection of this doctrine 1954 marked the beginning of the Civil Rights Movement.
- It ended with the victory of the black population: segregation and discrimination were officially abolished and equal status in all social matters was announced.
- Today about 2/3 of the Blacks are middle class, a third lives in the slums of the big cities.

Hispanics (Spanish-speaking Americans)
- have mainly come for economic reasons, often illegally across the Mexican border;
- have now overtaken the Blacks and form the biggest immigration group;
- are often unwilling to assimilate, continue to speak Spanish and live in enclaves.
- The establishment of bilingual classes poses a problem for the unity of the nation.

Asians
- are the most rapidly growing minority group;
- integrate well into the American way of life and are among the best students of the nation.

Immigration Policy
- Immigration was up to 1880 unrestricted.
- 1882: Chinese labourers were excluded.
- 1924: The so-called "quota system" was introduced, favouring Western European countries.
- 1965: The "quota system" was abolished; instead a fixed annual number of 290,000 immigrants with special skills was admitted.
- The Immigration Act of 1990 established a limit of about 700,000 immigrants a year.
- The Illegal Immigration Reform of 1996 made it easier for US authorities to deport illegal immigrants.

Social Class in the USA
On the whole "class" is in the USA much less marked than e.g. in Britain because
- social mobility is more frequent and class lines are less stable;
- there are no hereditary titles;
- the ideal of a classless society is deeply rooted in US society.

On the other hand there are factors that promote the idea of "class":
- the USA is the country with the biggest social differences of any industrial nation;
- people with a "good" family name (i.e. WASPs) enjoy a high prestige;
- social class and ethnic or racial group are closely interrelated with each other: Western Europeans are at the top of the class system and minorities are at the bottom.

Florence Nightingale

- in the 19th century practically no social legislation
- social security and health based upon private initiative (e.g. family, church)
- up to 1945 only sporadic welfare programmes such as old age pensions and unemployment insurance
- after World War II creation of the modern welfare state by the Labour government

- National Health Service (NHS): largely free of charge, availabe to all residents, British and foreign
- comprehensive security "from cradle to grave"
- need of social services
- the Welfare State: a controversial issue
- today's crisis in Britain's health service and the growing importance of a private medical insurance (private patients)

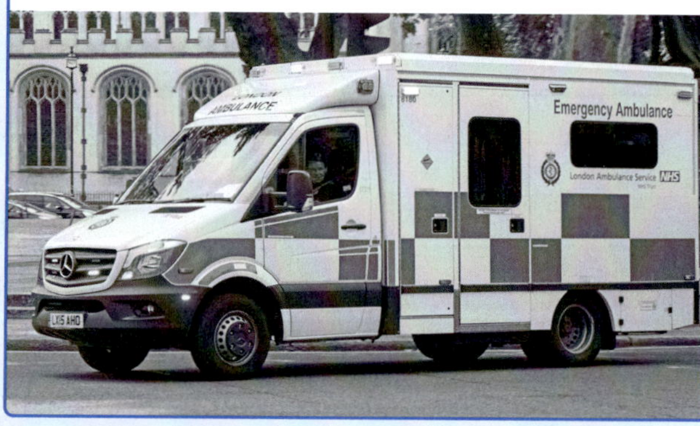

Social Welfare in Britain

National demonstration in central London, to defend the NHS against government cuts, closures and privatisation.

3 Social Welfare in Britain and the United States

Homeless man in San Francisco

- gaps in the public welfare system
- up to the 2010s 44% millions of Ameri-cans (18%) without health protection

- tradition of Protestant work ethic
- importance placed on the free individual and self-responsibility prevented the development of a comprehensive welfare state as in Britain: the ideal of self-help and self-reliance
- Social Security Act introduced by Franklin D. Roosevelt in 1935 during the Great Depression
- today Americans have to pay more than 10% out of their own pockets to receive necessary treatment
- private insurance is of utmost significance for Americans

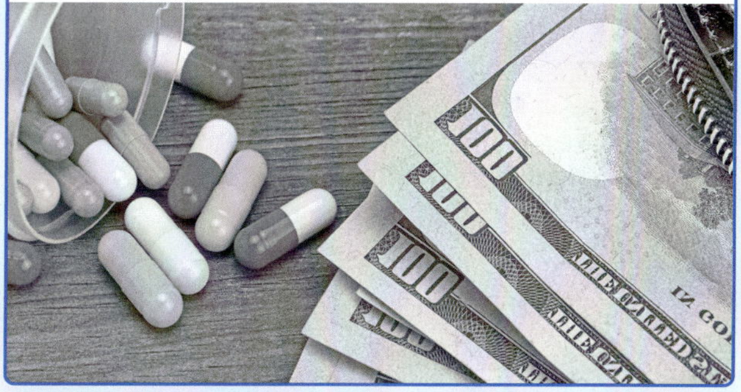

Social Welfare in the United States

- introduction of "Obamacare" (healthcare reform) in 2015
- Donald Trump wants to repeal the Affordable Care Act by President Obama because of the immense costs
- importance of private charity organizations

IN BRIEF

3 Social Welfare in Britain and the United States

- The British welfare state was created after World War II.
- The National Health Service (NHS) and the social security system provide the bare necessities of life for all citizens.
- There are both pros and cons in such a "cradle to grave" service. The USA relies on self-help by the individual in place of a state welfare system.
- Roosevelt's "New Deal" policy sought to relieve the worst effects of the Great Depression of the 1930s.
- As of 2016 there is still no compulsory legal health insurance in the USA.

3.1 Social Welfare in Britain

The Creation of the British Welfare State

Social security was seen as a largely private responsibility in Britain before the 20th century.

to alleviate: to make pain or suffering less or easier to bear

Up to the turn of the 20th century **social security** was generally considered a problem to be **solved individually**. Large parts of the population thought economic and social insecurity inevitable. Social legislation alleviating the workers' hardships caused by disease, old age, or unemployment remained sporadic. Social services were thought to belong to the private sector (families, neighbours, charitable or religious organizations). Germany was the first country, under Bismarck (1815–1898), to introduce comprehensive social legislation for workers, covering sickness and old age (1880s).

At the turn of the 20th century the idea of **public responsibility** also gained ground in Britain and the liberal government of Lloyd George introduced **laws modelled on German legislation**:

- the Old Age Pensions Act (1908) fixed pensions for persons over 70;
- the National Insurance Act (1911) provided for health and unemployment on a contributary basis.

A **comprehensive social security system** "from cradle to grave" was developed after WW II.

to conceive: to think of

During World War II a climate for **large-scale social legislation** developed. The war experience involved many people from different classes of society united for a single effort. This, in turn, created a greater sense of community and contributed to a more heightened social conscience of the well-to-do. The result was a **social revolution, the Welfare State**, conceived and created by the war-time Government of Winston Churchill (British Prime Minister from 1940 to 1945) and the Labour Government of Clement Attlee (British Prime Minister from 1945 to 1951).

It was based on the **Beveridge Report** (1942) which recommended a programme of **comprehensive security "from cradle to grave"**. The Welfare State became the ideal of the post-war Labour Government (1945–1951). Its fundamental goals were:

- social justice;
- social security as a right rather than a privilege;
- the redistribution of the national income;
- the creation of an egalitarian society;
- a higher living standard for the working classes.

Social welfare was established through the following acts:

- Family Allowances Act (1945);
- National Health Service Act (1946);
- Town Planning Act (1947);
- National Assistance Act (1948).

  These acts covered family and children's allowances, health-care, unemployment, additional grants for the needy, and the building of "council houses" (→ pp. 54, 98 ff).

The British Welfare System

The **Welfare State** is based on the idea that the state should ensure that everybody has the basic necessities of life and that the government has primary responsibility for the individual and for the social welfare of its citizens. The British welfare system today comprises

- social security;
- the National Health Service (NHS);
- social services.

The basic idea of the welfare state was to make the government responsible for the well-being of all its citizens.

The system includes social security, the National Health Service (NHS) and social services.

The system of **social security** consists of financial support for the unemployed, sick and disabled persons, retired persons and families.
The costs for these four areas of social welfare are paid by contributions of employers and employees to the **National Insurance** as well as by general taxation. Young people leaving school must join one of the government training schemes if they have not found full employment. If they refuse to join one of these schemes without good reason, their unemployment benefit is withheld.
The number of people receiving such financial support had grown so fast that the new coalition government of David Cameron decided in 2011 to introduce reforms in order to cut costs:

- raising the state pension age to 66 years, for both women and men;
- stricter rules on unemployment and disability payments;
- efforts to get disabled people back into work.

The National Health Service

The National Health Service aims to provide medical care free or almost free to all residents at the time of need.

The **National Health Service** follows the principle that

- medical care and advice should be completely or largely free of charge;
- it is available to all residents, British and foreign.

It is one of the largest employers in the world with a workforce of nearly 1 million people. Over 79% (2000) of the costs of the health service is paid through general taxation, 13% through the NHS element of the National Insurance contribution, 8% through charges on prescribed drugs and dental treatment, and the rest through other receipts. Under the NHS each person is free to choose a general practitioner in the area where he/she lives and to register on a list. Once registered he/she must normally go to this doctor. All general practitioners (GPs) work exclusively for the NHS. Only senior hospital doctors (consultants) may treat patients under the NHS and privately.

consultant: *Chefarzt*

Visits to a NHS doctor and hospital treatment are free, but adults below pensionable age have to contribute to the costs of prescribed medicines, spectacles, and dental treatment. About five million (10%) Britons have a **private medical insurance**. These private patients are free to seek medical treatment and doctors of their choice.

The NHS was seen as a model for health care systems all over the world, but suffered a crisis in the 1980s when demand grew faster than the money to pay for it.

For a long time the NHS was admired as a model among Western democracies for its efficiency and egalitarianism. It was one of the most expensive health care systems in the world. Costs and demand for health care rose sharply, however, so that symptoms of a **crisis in Britain's health service** were noticeable in the 80s. The UK devoted 5.4% (1987) of its Gross Domestic Product (GDP) to health care, much less than most of the Western democracies. This resulted in:

- a notorious waiting list for medical treatment;
- shortages of hospital staff;
- insufficient medical equipment and run-down hospital buildings;
- underpaid hospital staff.

The Labour government increased spending on health care in the 2000s, and produced a new NHS Plan.

To improve the situation the **Labour Government** increased its spending on the health service steadily during its 13 years in power, so that public funding rose from 7.6% (2002/03) to 9.2% (2007/08) of the GDP.

The **National Health Service Plan**, issued by the Government in 2000, intended to modernize the NHS to meet the **changing needs** of the people of the 21st century. It aimed in particular at

- making all parts of the health and social care system work better together;
- improving clinical performance and health service productivity;
- providing new modern hospitals with smaller wards;
- increasing the NHS staff (consultants, doctors, nurses, therapists).

Much progress was made in raising standards of health care, but at a higher cost than taxes could pay for. The Cameron government pledged to maintain existing NHS expenditure, but future rising costs and demands would have to be met from increasing efficiency.

Most of the **social services** are directed towards elderly or disabled people, young families with social problems, children deprived of a normal home life, and young **offenders**. They are performed by professional social workers, charities, "self-help" groups, or religious organizations, and include such programmes or organizations as "Meals on Wheels", the Red Cross, the Samaritans, the Salvation Army, or the National Society for the Prevention of Cruelty to Children.

The social services are directed towards those in need.

They are provided by a mixture of professional workers, charities and other "self-help" groups.

offender: someone who has committed a crime *(Straffälliger)*

Reforms between 1991 and 1993 gave the social services a new financial and managerial framework aimed at supplying a quality service for those who need it. Government grant aid to voluntary organizations dealing with health and social services is an important factor. The money is given to national organizations helping children, the elderly, ethnic minorities, HIV/AIDS sufferers and against alcohol or drug abuse. The British public also generously donate to such organizations.

grant aid: financial support

The tension that has always existed, between being generous to those in need (electorally popular) and running a fair, efficient and cost-effective budget (essential for long-term prosperity) was greatly increased by the 2008 world financial crisis. In the second decade of the 21st century, the debate continues, with growing concern about the effect of an aging population.

Pros and Cons of the Welfare State

Pros

- It helps the poorest part of the population to survive.
- It meets in particular the needs of the coloured minority which constitutes the majority of unemployed people and of large families.
- It is a means of promoting social justice and of avoiding violence and discontent.
- It is an important means of social reform and of an egalitarian view of society's responsibilities.

The welfare state remains a controversial issue. In its favour, it does a lot of good work to help those in need, and is a means of social reform. Against this, its very size makes it inefficient, slow to respond to changing needs, and discourages private responsibility.

Cons

- The enormous costs swallow up a considerable part of general taxation badly needed for economic investment. These costs will continue to increase because
  - a longer life expectancy will push up the costs of health care and pensions;
  - a declining birth rate will put a greater tax burden on the working population (change of age structure);
  - mounting numbers of jobless workers increase the costs of unemployment benefit.
- The Welfare State discourages people's private initiative and responsibility for themselves.
- It tends to encourage abuse of the social services.
- It encourages people's growing demands for public welfare.

3.2 Social Welfare in the USA

The American Point of View

Whereas Britain has made comprehensive health coverage a right for every citizen, the United States has remained the only industrialized society in the Western world that does not provide basic medical insurance for all its citizens. From the beginnings of the nation's history, Americans developed the **ideal of self-help and self-reliance** which is personified in the pioneer and frontiersman. Health and well-being were regarded as a private matter, and dependence on others, especially the Government, was rejected. According to Calvinist thought (→ pp. 146, 149 f), material success was a visible sign of God's grace. America was viewed as the land of unlimited possibilities. All the immigrants had to do to reach a better life was to work hard. Those who were jobless or poor were thought to deserve this lower standard of living. It was believed that they could not be helped because they would not help themselves.

The **ideal of self-help** and **self-reliance** is founded in US history. Many early settlers believed in the Calvinist ethic, linking material success to God's grace and blaming the poor and jobless for their own failures.

Even though changes have been made to improve social conditions during the 20th century, it cannot be said that the USA has developed a genuine welfare state.

genuine: real, true

The **Great Depression of the 1930s**, a period of unprecedented economic decline, called for a radical change of the traditional viewpoint. Franklin D. Roosevelt's **"New Deal"** (→ p. 32) policy introduced the **Social Security Act** (1935). It established a social insurance to protect the elderly. Social insurance membership and contributions were made compulsory.

The **Great Depression** in the 1930s led to changes in this viewpoint. President Roosevelt's **"New Deal"** brought in a federal Social Security Act.

Today, **social security**, the largest of all federal programmes, is financed by a tax (7.65 % for employers and employees and 15.3 % for the self-employed) which is deducted from the wages of all working people. Social security and Medicare hospital insurance benefits are paid without regard to financial need to retired persons, surviving dependants, and disabled workers. So practically everyone who works fairly regularly is covered by social security.

to deduct: *einbehalten*

dependant: *Angehörige(r)*

Unemployment Insurance is provided for by the individual states and is largely financed from employers' taxes. Generally the unemployed person receives half of his/her salary as unemployment benefit. However, each state determines its own maximum limit. Unemployment benefit is paid for 26 weeks in most states. Exceptions are Massachusetts and Washington where it is paid for 30 weeks. For example in Massachusetts the maximum weekly unemployment benefit is between two and three times higher than it is in Alabama.

Unemployment Insurance is run by each state, with varying provisions.

Since 1935, more than 70 public **welfare programmes** outside the social security have been established. A few of the most important ones are:

Since 1935 many major welfare programmes have been introduced to help those who cannot look after themselves.

assistance: *Unterstützung, Sozialhilfe*

recipient: *Empfänger*

- The Temporary Assistance for Needy Families (TANF) programme of 1996 provides assistance and work opportunities to needy families. It changed the nation's welfare system into one requiring work in exchange for time-limited assistance. Welfare recipients must participate e.g. in work experience, community service or vocational training.
- Medicaid is a health-care programme for the poor.
- The Supplement Security Income (SSI) guarantees a minimum income for the elderly (over 65), the blind, and the handicapped. It was set up in 1974 and currently supports over 6 million people.

nutrition: *Ernährung*

- The Food Stamp Programme is a nutrition programme (it distributes food products to low-income or poor families).
- School Meal Programmes provide free meals to schoolchildren.

to grant: *gewähren*

- Public Housing Programmes grant apartments to people on low incomes.

Gaps in the public welfare system

mandatory: *obligatorisch*

As of 2017 the United States is in the process of introducing **mandatory legal health insurance** to be complete after 2018. However, the USA has developed a very costly mixed system of private and government responsibility for health (altogether 17.1% of the GDP in 2014).

- The vast majority of Americans rely on employment-based private health insurance, paid for by employers and employees, or by employers alone. However, not all employees enjoy an insurance cover, as many small and middle-sized companies do not offer their employees any private insurance schemes at all.

Health care remains the responsibility of individuals through insurance, but the elderly and the very poor are supported by **Medicare** and **Medicaid**.

- About 46 million Americans (16%) do not have any health protection. Most of them are workers who, with their families, live close to the poverty line and cannot afford to purchase private insurance.
- The elderly and the very poor are covered by government-financed programmes like **Medicare and Medicaid.**

Even when there is an insurance cover, Americans often have to **pay out of their own pockets** to receive necessary treatment, about 12% of all medical costs. Hospital services are as a rule usually covered (with about 3.4% self-contributions), whilst medicine is hardly covered (with about 55% self-contributions). Furthermore, there are **no uniform regulations on salary payments during sickness**. Neither Medicare nor Medicaid offer complete cover of costs. Therefore, the elderly who receive Medicare assistance often take out additional private insurance, or have to fall back on Medicaid assistance, if they are eligible. Through Medicaid, the poor do have better access to the care system, but in comparison to other health systems, the American Welfare Programme offers relatively poor medical health care.

to take out insurance: *eine Versicherung abschließen*

eligible: *berechtigt*

Contemporary Issues

Like in all Western countries the debate over welfare is an important political topic in the USA, especially in election times. The **Republicans** hold that government deficit spending and unemployment are, among others, caused by too costly welfare programmes. They believe that lower taxes and a less costly government will induce people to buy more goods and thus increase business production. This again will create new jobs and thus help the poor more than welfare programmes do.

to induce: *(dazu) bewegen*

Their opponents, the **Democrats**, maintain that it is a major responsibility of government to provide a sufficient welfare programme for the poor, to avoid the creation of a permanent underclass. When the Democrats under President **Clinton** came into office in 1993, one of their main promises was to guarantee lifelong health protection for all Americans including the uninsured. This law, however, was never passed by Congress. Similarly President **Obama** (→ pp. 36 ff, 69, 89, 107 ff), in his electoral campaign in 2008, proposed sweeping changes in the health care system. The Affordable Care Act was finally passed in 2010. It aims to include a further 32 million Americans by 2018, with private health insurance for the general population and Medicaid for the needy. The passage of the health care bill was particularly important for Obama because he had made it one of the main goals for his presidency. Republicans strongly opposed "Obamacare", but in 2012 the Supreme Court ruled that Obama's landmark healthcare reform was constitutional, though at the same time allowing states to stay with the old system. When the Republican Donald Trump won the 2016 election, one of his major pledges was to undo the Affordable Care Act ("Obamacare") and replace it by a new American Healthcare Act (AHCA). This bill was intended to cut healthcare costs severely, but in early 2017 the Republican majority in Congress were unable to reach a consensus about the plan, thus forcing President Trump to withdraw the new healthcare bill before a vote in Congress.

Public welfare is an election issue for political parties in the USA as it is in all Western countries. The Republicans stick to the traditional self-help policy, while the Democrats propose more public social and health provision. When it comes into effect, President Obama's new health care reform will provide Americans with better health security.

The importance placed on the ideal of the free individual prevented the development of a comprehensive welfare state. But this lack of governmental responsibility paved the way for a broad spectrum of **private charities** and voluntary organizations.The best-known business-funded organizations are the Carnegie, the Ford and the **Rockefeller Foundations** (→ pp. 103, 150) which promote scientific and educational programmes.

Private charities and voluntary organizations, mostly financed by big business, help to fill the gaps left by government programmes.

Social Welfare in Britain

Creation of the British Welfare State

- The beginnings of the modern welfare state date mainly back to the Beveridge Report (1942), which recommended a programme of comprehensive security "from cradle to grave".
- The post-war Labour Government (1945–1951) put these ideas into practice: it introduced family and children's allowances, health-care, unemployment, additional grants for the needy, and the building of "council housing".

The British Welfare System

comprises social security, the National Health Service (NHS), and social services.

- It is based on the idea that the state should ensure that everybody has the basic necessities of life.
- The Government has primary responsibility for the individual and for the social welfare of its citizens.

Social Security

consists e.g. of unemployment benefits, retirement pensions, and family allowances.

The National Health Service

is paid by general taxation and contributions of employers and employees. It is based upon the principle that

- medical care and advice should be completely or largely free of charge;
- it is available to all residents.

Social Services

are directed towards e.g. elderly or disabled persons and young families with social problems.

Social Welfare in the USA

Principles

- The tradition of the Protestant work ethic prevented the introduction of welfare legislation.
- The idea of self-help and self-reliance is deeply rooted in the American character.
- Health was considered a private matter, therefore the USA has not developed a genuine welfare system.

Social Security

- developed late during the Great Depression (1930s) as part of the "New Deal".
- The Security Act (1935) established a social insurance to protect the elderly.
- Today this government programme provides a pension for all regular workers, which is financed by a tax for employers and employees.
- An unemployment insurance of six months is provided for by the individual states and financed from employers' taxes.

Welfare Programmes

- Many other welfare programmes (e.g. The Food Stamp Programme, School Meal Programmes, Public Housing Programme) have been established to help poverty-stricken families, the elderly and handicapped.
- There is a broad spectrum of private charities and voluntary organizations with e.g. scientific or educational programmes.

Health Care

- As of 2017 the USA is introducing mandatory legal health insurance.
- Most Americans have a private health insurance paid for by employers and employees.
- Some 44 million Americans (18%) do not have any health protection; most of them are workers who live close to the poverty line and cannot afford to purchase private insurance.
- The elderly and the very poor are covered by government-financed programmes like Medicare (support for the elderly) and Medicaid (support for the poor).

- rise of the British economy: the Industrial Revolution
- Great Britain as first industrial nation of the world
- development of mechanization
- focus on basic industries (coal, textile, iron and steel)

Factory in Birmingham, 1851

- the labour movement
- economic decline in the 20th century
- deteriorating industrial relations in the 1960s and 70s resulting in numerous strikes
- decline in heavy industry and discovery of North Sea oil
- the "British disease"
- "Thatcherism"
- the North-South divide

Factory in steel industry

The British Economy

- rise of the service industries
- London as an international finan-cial centre
- an unsolved problem: unemployment particularly of young people in inner city areas
- guarantee of a national minimum wage

Finance District in London

4 The British and American Economies

- large supply of natural resources
- principle of free trade
- the importance of big business
- weak labour unions
- structural changes in American industries
- post-industrial era in the 1980s/90s
- the problem of the national debt

Cargoship in the San Francisco Bay Area

The American Economy

- Laissez-faire economy or government intervention
- restriction of a laissez-faire economy during the Great Depression (1930s) by protectionist measures
- decline of the basic industries in the Manufacturing Belt in the North and East (coal, steel)
- rise of new industries in the South and West (oil, aerospace, computer)
- highest consumption of mineral resources and energy
- problems of environmental pollution

Office building in Silicon Valley, California

4 The British and American Economies

- Britain became the world's leading economic power in the 19th century.
- Through most of the 20th century Britain's economy declined.
- Traditional heavy industries, such as mining, steel, shipbuilding and textiles gave way to service industries such as banking.
- Today Britain is suffering a severe recession as part of the worldwide economic crisis.
- The economic strength of the USA still makes it the world's superpower.
- The US economy is based on free trade, with occasional periods of protectionism.
- Big business is dominant, with relatively weak labour unions.
- Post-industrial America sees far fewer workers in manufacturing and agriculture, but service industries have sharply increased.
- The economic crisis began in 2008 in the USA and soon spread all over the world.

IN BRIEF

4.1 The British Economy

Rise to Economic Supremacy

The **Industrial Revolution** began in Britain, using machines to replace manual labour in manufacturing.

In the 19th century Britain became the leading economic and trading power in the world. This rise was caused by an interplay of several factors:

- the **Industrial Revolution**: Britain was the first country in the world to introduce mechanization of manufacturing and to replace the domestic handicraft system by the factory system. After 1750 rural Britain was transformed into an industrial country. This economic revolution was made possible by a series of epoch-making inventions.
  The textile industries (woollen industry in Yorkshire, cotton industry in Lancashire), coal-mining and the iron and steel industries, particularly those of the Midlands (the "Black Country"), played a crucial part in the growth of the British economy.

Inventions

1764	"spinning jenny"
1769	steam engine
1785	machine loom
1814	steam locomotive

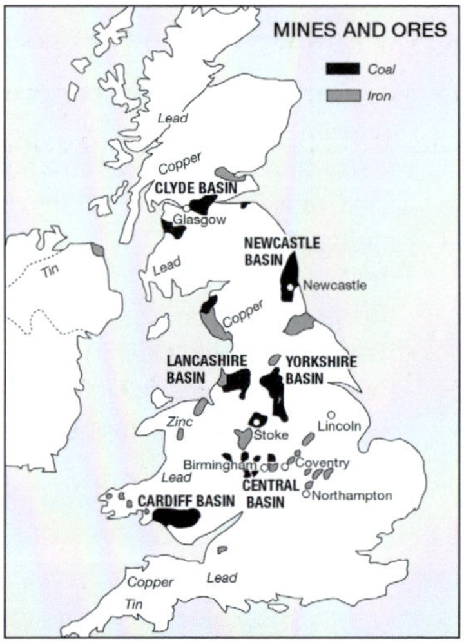

- abundant natural resources like coal, iron ore and cheap supplies of raw materials from the colonies (cotton, wool);
- secure markets in the colonial Empire for British manufactured goods;
- Britain's important merchant fleet;
- the rapid extension of a transportation network of waterways and railways;
- the spirit of enterprise of British entrepreneurs who were ready to invest capital in technological innovation;
- the emergence of a strong banking and credit system.

Plentiful natural resources such as coal and iron, plus cheap imports of raw materials from the Empire using a large merchant fleet encouraged the rapid growth of the economy.

Government legislation favouring **free trade** resulted in rapid economic expansion, and Britain took the lead in manufacturing, banking and investment of capital. The **Great Exhibition of London** (1851) demonstrated the industrial and commercial superiority of British capitalism to the world.

Up to the turn of the 20th century, British industry kept its leading position, although other European nations (notably Germany and France) and the United States had become powerful industrial nations and began to close the gap. In 1939, Britain still held second rank behind the USA in terms of per capita GDP.

In the early 20th century other countries began to catch up.

per capita: *pro Kopf*

GDP: Gross Domestic Product

Economic Decline

In the decades after 1945, especially in the 60s and 70s, Britain lost its position as one of the leading industrial nations in the world. In 1986 it only ranked 19th behind Italy. Industrial decline and economic stagnation characterized this period:

- a rate of **inflation** rising up to 16% in 1974 and 23% in 1975; comparative figures for the Federal Republic of Germany: 1974: 7%, 1975: 6%
- the **devaluation** of British currency (1960: £1 = 12 DM, 1980: £1 = 4 DM);
- the worst **strike record** among Western industrial nations; In 1979 almost 30 million days were lost by strikes, the worst strike record of the nation.
- **stagnation** in the **car industry**.

These factors added up to the "**British disease**", a period of economic decline.

The **"British disease"**, as this process of staggering economic decline was called on the Continent, resulted from a combination of economic, political and social factors. Some of the causes can be traced back to the 19th and the beginning of the 20th century, others developed after World War II.

WW II left Britain victorious but exhausted.

Politico-economic Reasons

- Loss of British capital during the two world wars.
- Loss of colonial markets after the disruption of the Empire. Many newly independent countries developed their own manufacturing industries (e.g. textile industry in India).

Loss of the Empire reduced both raw materials and markets.

- Antagonistic economic principles of the alternating post-war Labour and Tory Governments contributed to instability and lack of continuity in the economy.

Political disagreement on measures such as nationalization led to instability and lack of investment.

- Lack of innovation and modernization, mismanagement and low productivity, especially in the traditional industries (coal, iron, steel, textiles), made the British economy uncompetitive. At first, the nationalization of mining, shipbuilding, steel, and textiles by the post-war Labour Government sheltered these industries from competitive market forces. However, after the loss of its colonial markets, Britain had to expose its industries to the more dynamic and modernized industries of her European rivals, and the long-term structural obsolescence and equipment deficiency became apparent.

to expose sth: *etwas (z. B. einem Risiko) aussetzen*

obsolescence: *veralteter Zustand*

equipment deficiency: lack of e.g. machines

- Flight of British capital to foreign countries underlined the lack of confidence in the British economy.
- Weak balance of payments because of low exports of British-made goods and increasing dependence on foreign-manufactured imports.
- Inadequate infrastructure: insufficient traffic system of motorways and electrified railways.
- Bad industrial relations between the powerful Trade Unions and management leading to numerous official and unofficial (or so-called "wildcat") strikes.

Neglect of infrastructure (roads, railways etc), bad industrial relations and numerous strikes brought Britain to its low point in the late 1970s.

During the 60s and 70s, industrial relations deteriorated, and strikes in mining, shipbuilding, the car industry, and printing began to increasingly paralyze the country. In the winter of 1978/79, the amount of strikes brought the British economy to a near standstill and swept the Tories to power, as they promised drastic union reform.

to deteriorate: to become more difficult

to paralyze sb.: to make sb. unable to act or function properly *(jdn. lähmen)*

Socio-economic Reasons

The structure of British society has also played a major part in the country's economic downturn.

The country's **rigid class system** (→ pp. 46 ff) has also played a key role in the decline.

- Upper class people are generally prejudiced against manufacturing careers.
- A shift in attitude of the upper middle class, in the 19th century the class of entrepreneurs and captains of industry, can be observed. Today, they tend to follow the upper class and turn to politics, law, banking, or the Civil Service rather than to industry.
- The "them-and-us" class antagonism of the British working class inevitably leads to industrial conflicts instead of industrial cooperation.
- Moreover, **class distinctions** make it difficult for the talented and ambitious of the lower classes to move up the social scale.

- The **dual school system** of state and private education increases the gap between employers and employees.
- The **lack of prestige of managerial jobs** has led to a crisis of industrial management. British managers are often inadequately prepared for the commercial and technological conditions of the modern world (e.g. inadequate knowledge of foreign languages) and are frequently unfamiliar with the particular problems of the countries where they have or seek markets.

Structural Changes in the British Economy

Over the years, the traditional industries (steel, textiles, coal) in South Wales, Merseyside, the Midlands, North-East England, and Scotland have lost their important role, causing unemployment and poverty. Instead, the rise of new, **fast-expanding industries** can be observed in areas that have a supply of skilled workers, a well-developed transportation system and that are in the neighbourhood of international trading centres. Examples are aerospace, electrical and electronic engineering, computer manufacturing, manufacture of consumer goods, the chemical, pharmaceutical and the plastic industries.

The decline in heavy industry in the Midlands and North gave way to growth in new technology in Scotland and the South-East.

- Light and high-tech industries are centred in Scotland, Cambridgeshire, and the Southeast, mainly in the London conurbation. This industrial concentration decisively increased the gap between North and South.
- The discovery and exploitation of North Sea oil and gas in the 70s gave rise to a new off-shore petro-chemical industry in North-East Scotland and the Orkney and Shetland Islands. It has also had a significant effect on the economy, easing the balance of payments. Britain has become self-sufficient in terms of oil and is today the world's fifth largest oil-producing country.
- Like all other countries in the Western World, Britain has experienced another change in the economic structure: from manufacturing to service industries (rise of the "white-collar" worker). In 2010, 81 % of the labour force was employed in the service industry compared to about 18 % in manufacturing. The service industry contributed 77.1 % of the GDP.
- London has maintained and – in recent years – even strengthened its important position as an international financial centre.

conurbation: large urban area

The exploitation of North Sea oil and gas had a major effect on the economy of the country.

"Thatcherism"

"Thatcherism" reversed the 30-year decline in Britain's prosperity. The emphasis was on self-reliance, small government, and a complete renewal of society in a climate of productivity and efficiency.

Membership of unions for manual workers fell, and there were fewer strikes, in protest against cuts in jobs and pay.

In the 80s, **Margaret Thatcher** (1979 – 1990) introduced and carried through a tough monetary reform programme of the British economy. But **"Thatcherism"** was more than a mere economic concept. The term describes a social, political and economic philosophy aimed at a renewal of society, in which the qualities of **self-reliance, private initiative**, and **economic commitment** were essential. The reform policy was intended to create an economic climate of competition, production, and efficiency. Government influence on the national economy was withdrawn more and more to release the creative capacity and the responsibility of the individual.

Tough labour laws were introduced, leading to a fall in union membership; there are now less than half as many union members as there were in 1979. Those leaving the unions were mainly male manual workers in declining manufacturing industries, while "white collar" membership actually grew. This in turn led to a long-term reduction in strikes; in the dark days of the 1970s the average was 12.9 million days lost per year, while it was about a quarter of a million by 2015, mainly in public administration and education in protest against job reductions and pay cuts.

One of the aims of the Conservative Government was to encourage the extension of share-ownership and to create a "share-owning democracy". The campaign for **privatization** of nationalized industries can be understood as a counter-movement to the nationalization of the Labour Government in the 1940s. The Thatcherite ideology was to withdraw from state-run industries and to turn people who work in the newly privatized companies into shareholders, thus raising their interest in profitability. At the end of 1998, 22 million British people (about 45 %) were shareholders.

Privatization aimed to create a "share-owning democracy". Social housing was sold at a home ownership.

Another element of privatization was the sale of social housing ('council houses', owned by the local authority) to tenants at a discount. By 1998, 68% of the British people were home owners – though mostly with a big mortgage debt.

The sale of public property continued under John Major. Unemployment rose to 3 million in the 1990s.

"Thatcherism" met with a lot of criticism; people felt that the emphasis on competition and individual responsibility was destroying values considered to be typically English. After the fall of Margaret Thatcher in 1992, however, her successor John Major continued many of her policies. Electricity, gas and water were privatised, as were British Airways and British Railways. Inevitably the cumulative effect of these changes led to job losses. Indeed, government policy of maintaining only productive jobs and of abolishing overmanning and subsidizing of uncompetitive industrial plant led to many closures of factories and other job providers, destroying 25% of manufacturing jobs. In the early 90s unemployment peaked at nearly three million.

Tony Blair (1997 – 2007)

The approach of the Blair Government was to accept the Thatcher/Major reforms, and to "fine-tune" them to make them more effective. It did not re-nationalize any industries; its aim was to regulate the private firms to protect customers from exploitation. At the same time, it introduced to British industry many of the EU Social Chapter reforms, such as those governing working hours and consultation of the workforce, which the Major Government opted out of. Up to 2007, the economic situation in Britain was characterized by **continuing economic growth**, higher than that of its European rivals. This growth had been achieved e.g. by strengthening competition in domestic markets and by providing incentives for enterprise and risk-taking, as well as by the exploitation of North Sea oil. However, Britain was not immune to the economic problems that arose world-wide in 2008. The UK economy deteriorated dramatically and entered a recession due to the world economic crisis. Gross Domestic Product (GDP) declined sharply to a record low of -5.9% in June 2009. Recovery began in 2009, but not enough to keep **PM Gordon Brown** (→ pp. 15, 20, 30, 174) and Labour in power after the election in 2010.

Blair did not renationalize any industry, but he did introduce EU social reforms.

to fine-tune: *eine Feinabstimmung vornehmen*

The new century brought an economic boom, followed by world-wide recession in 2008.

incentive: *Anreiz*

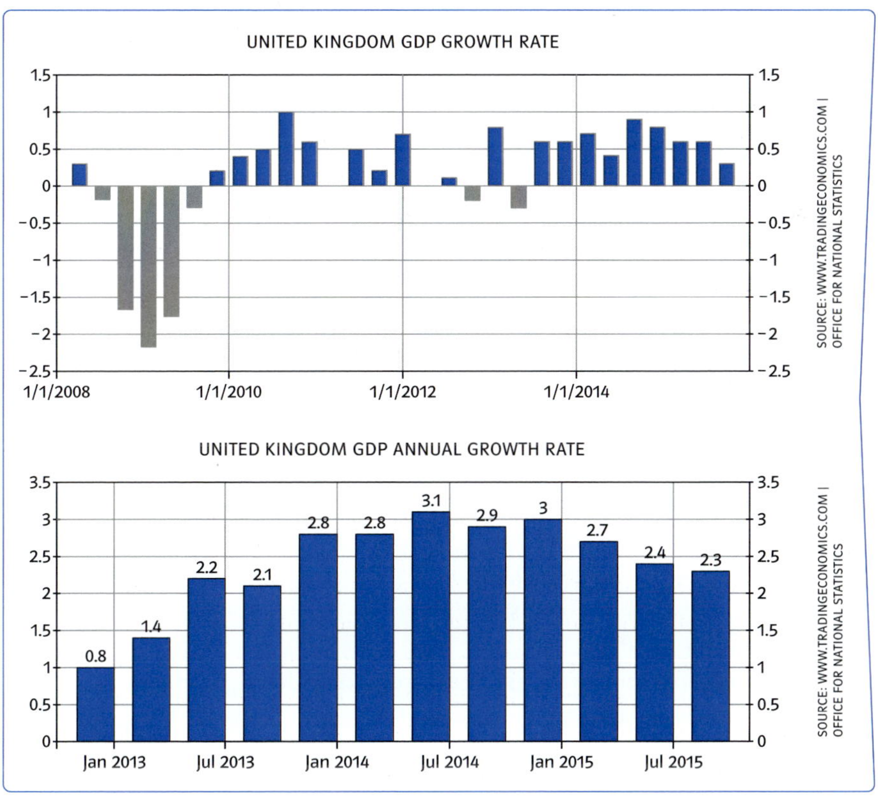

Annual growth in gross domestic product in real terms (United Kingdom)

Gross Domestic Product per Head 2015 (EU 28 = 100%)

Luxembourg	271
Ireland	145
Netherlands	129
Germany	125
Sweden	123
United Kingdom	110
France	106
Italy	95
Spain	92
Portugal	71
Greece	73
Romania	57
Bulgaria	46

Source: Eurostat

The coalition government (2010-2015)

There was a long, slow struggle to recover from recession, with low rates of inflation and interest, while the national debt grew.

The new coalition government took early steps to solve the problem of the national debt, and the country faced a long period of economic hardship. This involved very low interest rates (Bank rate at 0.5% for six years), low inflation rates and incomes which for most people were still below those of 2010 as the next election in 2015 approached – and still the country's national debt was growing.

Median weekly pay for all employee jobs in the UK, Apr 2015 by country / region	£ per week
United Kingdom	**527,7**
London	659,9
South East	552,1
Scotland	527,0
East	517,5
West Midlands	493,1
South West	492,8
North West	488,8
North East	488,7
Yorkshire/Humberside	486,4
Northern Ireland	484,9
East Midlands	479,1
Wales	473,4

Annual Survey of Hours and Earnings

Demand for housing was strong, thanks to low interest rates, high immigration, people living longer and cheap mortgages.

In spite of these economic problems, demand for housing continued to be strong, for several reasons. The population of the UK was growing due to immigration (half a million in 4 years, mostly from eastern Europe), people were living longer, families were more fragmented (divorce, single parents), people saw mortgages as an investment at a time of low interest rates, while paying rent was "throwing money away". Most houses are built for the private sector for sale to owner-occupiers. Housing associations are now the main provider of "social housing" and replace the old council housing scheme.

Unsolved Problems

Unemployment figures have improved, but the economy remains much better in the South-East than in the North.

During the Coalition period, the UK economy has been on the road to recovery and at the end of 2015 the jobless rate stood at 5.1%. Unemployment rates across the UK, however, varied widely depending on region, kind of industry and age of the workforce. They ranged from 3.5 % in the East to 8.0 in the North East. Unemployment of young people (18–24 years) was up to three times the overall rate, often caused by lack of skills and experience. It was at 14% in 2016. Many inner city districts and former industrial areas have the lowest employment rates. Due to the economic recession Black unemployment (16–24) rose to more than 30% in 2016.

Young people and ethnic minorities suffer most, in spite of government efforts which have had some success.

A comparison between North and South regarding unemployment in general and of youngsters in particular, income, GDP, and quality of life reveals that Britain is geographically, politically, socially and economically a divided country: a burst of entrepreneurial activity and new prosperity in the South on the one hand, and gloom and industrial decay in the North on the other, have resulted in widening inequality **in the North-South divide**, one of Britain's greatest problems, in spite of Government encouragement of inward investment in the North. In recent years some of the most serious **regional inequalities** have been gradually reduced as migration of labour from North to South became less attractive. For example the Japanese companies Toyota and Nissan built factories in the North of England to manufacture their cars.

entrepreneurial: *unternehmerisch*

Unemployment in the UK, Dec - Febr 2016 by country / region (%)	Rate of Unemployment (%)	Unemployment in the UK, Dec - Febr 2016 by country / region (%)	Rate of Unemployment (%)
North East	8.0	North West	5.0
Yorkshire / Humberside	6.3	East Midlands	4.5
London	6.3	South West	3.8
Northern Ireland	6.3	South East	3.8
Scotland	6.2	East	3.5
West Midlands	5.5	United Kingdom	5.1
Wales	5.0		

Source: Labour Market Statistics

Another basic problem was the **shortage of vocational training** and of technical colleges. However, today Britain is acknowledged as an innovative world leader in open and flexible learning (open university and open college). Employers spend over £20,000 million a year on employee training and development. The Government also funds various training, enterprise and vocational educational programmes. Its labour market policies include:

- the promotion of job creation;
- improved training of unemployed people in order to move them from welfare into jobs (Welfare-to-Work Programme, 1999; under this programme young unemployed are required to accept training, with the promise of jobs at the end, but with the loss of benefits if they decline);
- new measures to ensure that the UK workforce has the necessary skills to meet the challenges of a rapidly changing world economy;
- the provision of better learning opportunities by bringing further education and training closer together;
- the availability of career development loans to help people pay for vocational or further education;
- the guarantee of a national minimum wage (£6.95 an hour in 2016 for those aged 21 or over).

The government seeks to improve vocational education and training by using threats and promises:
if you take a training course, you are promised a job; if you decline to do so, you lose benefits.

The national minimum wage rises.

4.2 The American Economy

Leading Industrial Nation of the World

America has reached and retained its position as the world's leading industrial economy by maintaining free market principles.

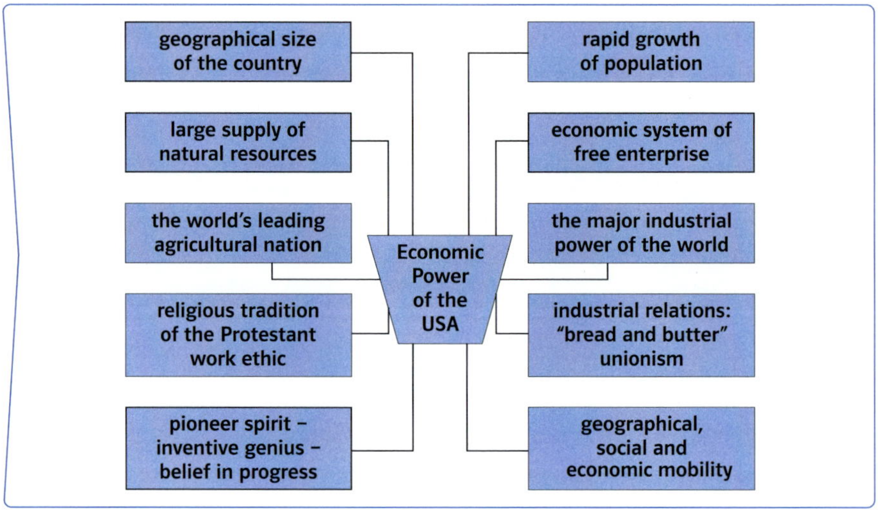

The USA is the leading industrial nation of the world. With about 4.5% of the world population it manufactures 19% (2014) of the total industrial production of the world. Its Gross National Product (GNP) is higher than that of the EU and, along with China, it is the world leader in the export of industrial goods.
During the 19th century, the north-eastern region developed into the **Manufacturing Belt**, the biggest industrial area of the world. The interaction between abundant resources, cheap immigrant labour supply, and the inventive genius of its people made the Northeast the "work shop" of the nation (iron, steel, automobiles, electrical industries), and the USA the industrial giant of the world. Since 1945, the USA has had the greatest productive capacity of the world's nations. During the second half of the 80s, America had the strongest economy due to its agricultural and industrial production.
However, this leading position has now been seriously challenged by its main competitors China, Japan and Germany. Although the export of finished products has expanded on the world market, America's exports in this field have fallen.

Major Themes

From the very beginning of the nation Americans favoured a **laissez-faire economy** based on the principles of free market, competition, and private property. This system seemed best suited for the young democracy that had made civil liberties its fundamental principles. Government control was considered to hamper economic progress. Thus, ideal conditions were created for the numerous success stories and the rise of the business tycoon. Famous tycoons were Andrew Carnegie (1835–1919), John D. Rockefeller (1839–1937) and Henry Ford (1863–1947).

to hamper: to hinder

This period of almost unrestricted capitalism ended when monopolist tendencies of business began to threaten competition, and Government, thereupon, introduced Anti-Trust-Laws (1890 and 1914). It was the **Great Depression** (→ pp. 32, 37, 87, 181) that eventually demanded massive government interference in this free economy. New laws for stricter control of manufacturing and prices brought about a fundamental change in American capitalism. Whilst the Reagan Administration restressed the importance of a free market, it again lost its importance under the Clinton Administration.

Government only intervenes when things go badly wrong, such as in the **Great Depression** in the 1930s. It tries to control any trend towards monopolies or protectionism.

In 2008, at the end of G.W. Bush's second term, the **global financial crisis** forced the US government to take decisive measures in order to save the banking sector and the automobile industry. Facing an economic crisis of historic proportions, the Federal Reserve had to put a multi-billion dollar package into the US economy in an effort to stabilize the financial system. As certain banks and insurers had become so big that the government could not allow them to go bankrupt, the Fed was forced to provide costly bail-outs or to nationalize them.

The **financial crisis from 2008** onwards has again forced the government to step in as banks fail and unemployment rises.

bail-out: *Rettungsplan*

The **role of government** is also an important issue in trade policy. In times of economic depression, manufacturers demand protectionist measures (high tariffs) against foreign competition, and in times of an economic boom, a policy of free trade is pursued.

For example, the demand for **protectionism** was high in times when the American steel industry was put under pressure from increasing foreign imports, or when rapidly developing countries such as Taiwan, Korea, and China swamped the market with cheaper products. In the same way, in 2005, the USA imposed import restrictions on cheap Chinese textile products to protect American manufacturers.

to swamp: *überschwemmen*

The importance of big business

Big business has normally been seen as a good thing in the USA, but it can be a danger for small-scale enterprise and becomes a dis-advantage when companies are too big to fail.

Today, American business is subject to many laws and regulations. Nevertheless, the **trend towards big business** has proved to be very strong. About 80 % of the US economy is carried by a few hundred companies. Since the 1960s, many corporations have developed into even larger conglomerates by putting very different firms under the same management.
Today, the USA has some of the biggest corporations in the world. It is feared, however, that big business eliminates too many small businesses and has too much influence on politics through lobbying. Supporters of big business point out that the high living standard for the majority of the American population and the expansion of output, scientific know-how, and international competitiveness of the American economy have been brought about by business concentration.

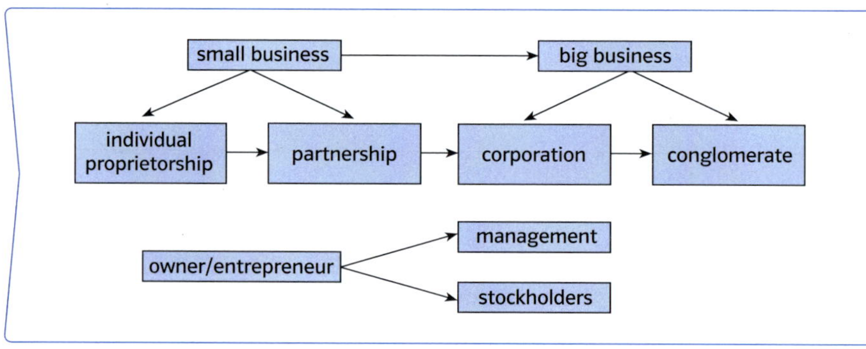

The current trend, however, tends to emphasize the **importance of small businesses**. There are many more small business owners in the House of Representatives than in the early 90s. They are striving to pass legislation and to reduce environmental and other regulations, so that the small businesses will have a better chance of being more profitable.

Labour unions in the USA have never been political. They work for better wages, health care and pensions.

Industrial relations between management and labour unions have never been as hostile as in Britain. The Hartley Act (1947) forbids "closed shops" and allows the President to postpone a strike for 80 days ("cooling-off" period). Due to the absence of a strong left-wing party and of a rigid class structure, **American unionism** has never been revolutionary in its objectives. Its main concern has always been a greater share of wealth and benefits like insurances, pensions, and health care plans. Therefore, American unionism is also sometimes called **"bread-and-butter" unionism**. In the 70s and 80s its bargaining power decreased, as heavy industries, the stronghold of unionism, declined, and the number of "blue-collar" workers decreased.

Structural Economic Changes and Problems

Development of the USA into a Service Society Contribution by sector in GDP (%)				
	1960	1980	2000	2015
Agriculture	4.0	2.4	1.6	1.6
Goodsproducing industries	33,9	30.0	24.9	20.8
Serviceproviding industries	62.1	67.6	73.5	77.6

In the past century the economic importance of manufacturing and agriculture drastically declined, but that of service industries sharply increased.

The United States economy underwent a fundamental change in the 80s and 90s, a process that has its roots in the three previous decades.
The country has moved into a "post-industrial era". This "post-industrial" economy is characterized by a drastic decline in the proportion of American workers employed in agriculture and manufacturing. Simultaneously, the service-providing businesses (banking, telecommunications, wholesale and retail trade, hotels and restaurants, transportation, administration) have sharply increased and dominate the economy. Nine out of ten newly created jobs today are in the service sector, with only one in manufacturing.

wholesale and retail trade: *Groß- und Einzelhandel*

American agriculture, which leads world production and export of wheat, corn, soya beans, cotton, tobacco, and vegetable oil, has experienced fundamental structural changes since the 1880s, when it was still the most important sector of the US economy:

- Large-scale mechanization with the help of modern farm machinery, electricity, and oil has led to a large increase of productivity and efficiency in farming, but also to an exodus of farm workers to the cities. The results of this development have been urban unemployment and social problems.
- The traditional system of agricultural belts (monoculture) has been replaced by crop rotation and mixed farming in order to promote soil conservation and to achieve highest intensity of agriculture.
- The original self-sufficient, small family farms (homesteads) have been increasingly replaced by high-technology "mega-farms" or "agri-business", which include e.g. food processing industries or manufacturing of farm equipment. Giant conglomerates like Coca-Cola, Goodyear and Boeing have expanded into agri-business.

Agriculture in the USA employs far less labour than in the early 1900s, due to mechanization, increased crop productivity and the move from "farms" to "agri-business".

The downside of these changes has included soil erosion, damage from excessive use of chemicals and over-production leading to low prices.

The main result of these changes was the large **increase of productivity per worker**: in 1950 one farm worker nourished 10 persons, in 2005 85 persons.

In spite of its outstanding position in the world today, American agriculture is beset by many problems:

- soil erosion as a consequence of continuous monoculture;
- environmental damage by extensive use of artificial fertilizers and toxic chemicals;
- overproduction (crop surpluses), especially of wheat and corn, which causes a low-price policy and consequently economic difficulties. Small and even middle-sized family farms cannot compete with "agri-business" and often have to be closed.

Government programmes try to cope with the situation in the agricultural sector by granting subsidies to farmers who agree to remove part of their land from production (acreage limitation) and by providing payments to make up for low prices (price-supports).

As the largest consumer of mineral resources and energy the USA has to cope with environmental problems.

The USA has the highest consumption of **mineral resources** and energy of all nations. In 2016 the world oil market produced 91.3 million barrels per day. The USA, with 4.5% of the world's population, daily consumes 19.6 million barrels i.e. 21.0% of the world's total. It is confronted with the problems of **environmental pollution and exhaustion of various mineral resources**. The USA has developed into a country dependent on imports, of mineral oil (55% of its consumption is imported) in particular, but the new technology of recovering gas by "fracking" has made the USA self-sufficient in gas and reduced the national debt. The present US government has set the goal of reducing the country's oil dependence, e.g. by the use of renewable and other alternative energy.

Since the Sixties, remarkable **structural changes in American industries** have been taking place:

In recent decades the **Manufacturing Belt** has lost some of its former importance. Instead, new industries (oil, aerospace, computer) in the South and the West are playing a key role in the American economy.

- While still concentrating half of the industrial work force on 18% of the land area of the USA, the **Manufacturing Belt** has lost part of its dominant position due to the world-wide overproduction of steel, EU and, in particular, Japanese competition in the car industry, lack of investment in modernization of plants, and a tendency towards industrial decentralization.
- As the "old industries" declined, there was a growth in new areas such as services, communication and information.
- Rise of industries in the "sunbelt" because of financial advantages (lower taxes, wages, costs for building sites), closeness to mineral resources (oil), and supply of skilled workers;

- the petrochemical industries (plastics, synthetics) centred around Houston (Texas);
- aerospace and computer industries in California; microelectronics are mainly centred around Stanford University.

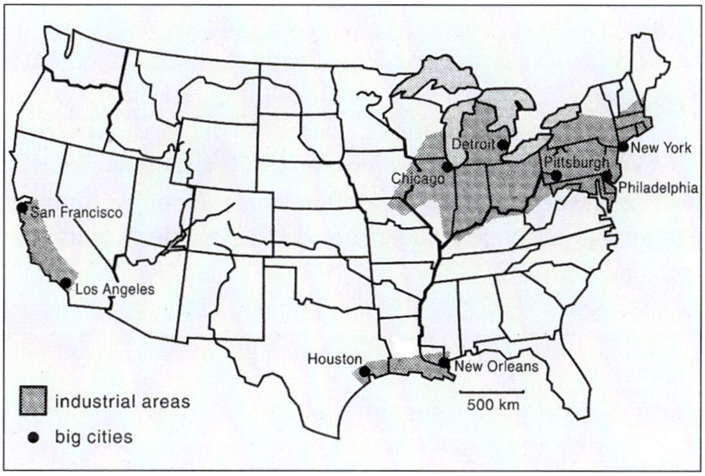

Under Reagan and George H. Bush the **national debt** escalated from $1 trillion to $4 trillion, and exceeded $5 trillion under the Clinton Administration. With G.W. Bush's presidency and his war on terrorism the national debt increased from $5.7 trillion in 2001 to more than $8.7 trillion in 2007. Due to measures to cope with the economic crisis, defence spending and reduced income from the recession, the national debt rose between 2008 and 2010 to over $10 trillion and hit the debt ceiling of about $14.3 trillion in 2011. This was more than 100% of GDP. After a heated debate between Obama's Democrats and Republicans, Congress decided to raise the debt limit to $16.4 trillion in order to guarantee the creditworthiness of the United States and to avoid an economic and a political disaster. In Sep 2012, however, national debt rose above $16 trillion for the first time in American history.

dept ceiling: Schuldenobergrenze

As Obama and the Republicans failed to agree a new budget and to raise the nation's debt limit, the debt-ceiling debate led in 2013 to a 16-day-long shutdown of the U.S. federal government, the third longest in American history. This meant that the American government had to shut its non-essential services and hundreds of thousands of federal employees were put on unpaid leave. After this very unpopular phase of confrontation the two opposing parties re-started talks seeking a continuing resolution. In

Total Public Debt

Year	Public Debt (in millions)
1980	907,700
1985	1,823,100
1990	3,233,300
2000	5,674,100
2007	8,780,980
2010	12,311,000
2012	16,066,000
2016	19,936,000

the end they agreed to suspend the debt ceiling and compromised on a budget deal up to the end of Obama's presidency in 2016. The government's most recent borrowing limit is at $20 trillion. It remains to be seen whether the Trump administration will find a way to avoid a government shutdown and to get the debt ceiling raised.

The USA in the 2010s

The boom years of the 1990s and into the new century led many to believe that prosperity would never end. Even the terrorist attacks of 9/11 caused only a short-term economic decline. However, the boom did collapse in 2008, when the country was hit by the **global economic crisis**.

The United States experienced its longest economic expansion during the 1990s, and entered the 21st century with an economy that accounted for more than 25 % of the world's output. Unemployment was down to 3.9 % in 2000, and real wages had grown for five consecutive years, the best performance since the 1960s. Critics of the American "job miracle" maintain that the increase in jobs was not due to the economic boom but to the availability of poorly paid jobs ("McJobs") and multiple job holding.

At the end of the year 2000 there were, however, signs of a global recession. The Administration of George W. Bush had to deal with an economic slowdown accompanied by low growth and a substantial rise in business failures. This **economic downturn** accelerated after the terrorist attacks of Sept 11, 2001. The American economy, however, showed strength and recovered comparatively fast from this shock, driven by substantial gains in labour productivity and by consumer spending, despite damage caused by hurricanes. This boom came to an end in 2008 when the credit crisis hit the country and the world. The bursting of the housing bubble led to falling property prices, billions of losses by banks, a high jobless rate and the longest economic recession (2008–2009) of the USA since the Great Depression. The government responded to the financial crisis by various fiscal measures such as stimulus programmes as well as tax cuts, but by 2012 the economic recovery of the country proved to be rather weak and joblessness high (more than 8 %). Since then the economy has shown stronger signs of an improvement and the jobless rate decreased to about 4.5 % at the beginning of 2017.

Long-term problems of the US economy include a sharp increase in energy prices, considerable trade and budget deficits, rapidly rising medical and pension costs as people live longer and lack of income growth for poorer families.

After many years as a creditor nation, the USA has been in debt since the 1970s. In the last 30 years the **trade deficit** has grown, caused by a strong dollar, a flood of cheap imports from East Asian countries, and sales difficulties for American-made products. The Clinton / Gore Administration managed to transform this deficit into a surplus by 2000. The war in Iraq, however, shifted resources to the military and resulted in new record trade and budget deficits.

The world's leading trading nations, 2015 est. (in thousand millions)					
Exports			**Imports**		
China	$	2,275	USA	$	2,308
USA	$	1,505	China	$	1,682
Germany	$	1,329	Germany	$	1,050

Source: statistica.com

In the 1990s the American economy was more closely linked with the global economy than it had ever been. Clinton, like his predecessors, continued to work for the **elimination of trade barriers**. In 1994 a North American Free Trade Agreement (NAFTA) further increased economic ties between the United States and its nearest trading partners, Canada and Mexico. The General Agreement on Tariffs and Trade (GATT) treaty, signed in 1994, lowered trade barriers and created the World Trade Organization (WTO) which seeks to enforce trade agreements and to resolve disputes. In 1999 Clinton signed a trade agreement with China to reduce barriers between the countries, making it easier to export US products. The government under George W. Bush favoured a free-trade zone throughout the Americas, from Canada to Argentina, but no agreement had been reached by the end of his presidency.

In 2013 the USA and the EU started talks about establishing a free trade agreement, the so-called Transatlantic Trade and Investment Partnership (TTIP). Its aim is to decrease trade barriers, to boost the economy and to reduce unemployment in both economic areas. Critics claim that such an agreement would lower the EU's health and safety standards and weaken its environmental policy. Moreover they maintain that it would mainly serve the interests of corporations and favour the world of finance.

The British Economy

Rise to Economic Supremacy
In the 19th century Britain became the leading economic and trading power in the world because of
- the Industrial Revolution (mechanization of manufacturing, the factory system);
- epoch-making inventions (steam engine, "spinning jenny");
- abundant natural resources (coal, iron ore) and cheap raw materials from the colonies (cotton, wool);
- secure colonial markets;
- a government policy of free trade.

Economic Decline after 1945
Britain lost her position as one of the leading industrial nations of the world due to
- the "British disease" (industrial stagnation, rising inflation, devaluation of the British currency; a strike record; lack of innovation and modernization; nationalization of major industries);
- consequences of World War II (loss of British capital, of colonial markets);
- socio-economic reasons (lack of prestige of managerial jobs, class antagonism of employers and workers).

Structural Changes
- decline of the basic industries causing unemployment mainly in the North, Scotland, and Wales;
- rise of light and high-tech industries and of the chemical, pharmaceutical and plastic industries in e.g. the Southeast and Cambridgeshire;
- discovery of North Sea oil and gas in Scotland;
- change from manufacturing to service industries ("white-collar" workers) in e.g. transport, communication, banking, business service, health, and education.

Thatcherism (1980s–1990s)
Prime Minister M. Thatcher carried through a tough reform programme to cure the country from the "British disease" by
- diminishing the power of the Trade Unions;
- privatizing nationalized industries;
- selling council houses to tenants thus encouraging home ownership;
- cutting public spending.

The Situation Today
- regional (inner city districts, former industrial areas) and youth unemployment;
- the North-South divide: economic and social inequalities of the "two Britains" are gradually being reduced;
- investment in training and further education;
- guarantee of a national minimum wage;
- low rate of inflation; moderate economic growth; low unemployment.

The American Economy

The Economic Power of the USA

is based on the geographical size of the country, a large supply of natural resources, the Protestant work ethic, a belief in progress and pioneer spirit, a system of free enterprise, rapid growth of population, cheap immigrant labour supply.

Major Themes

- Laissez-faire economy or government intervention: the USA was originally a laissez-faire economy based on the principles of free market, competition, and private property; however, this capitalist system was restricted during the Great Depression (1930s) by new laws favouring a stricter control of manufacturing and prices (Anti-Trust Laws, Labour Unions, welfare programmes).
- Protectionism or trade: in times of an economic boom a policy of free trade is pursued; however, in times of an economic depression, protectionist measures are introduced.
- Big business or small business: there is a strong trend towards big business with the result that the USA has some of the biggest corporations of the world; presently, Government tries to counteract this development and to pass legislation in favour of small business.
- Industrial relations: American unionism is called "bread-and-butter" unionism, as its main aims have always been a greater share of wealth and social benefits.

Structural Changes

The USA has moved into the "post-industrial "era:

- drastic decline of workers employed in agriculture and manufacturing;
- increase of service-providing businesses;
- decline of the "old industries" in the Manufacturing Belt in the Northeast;
- rise of new industries in the sunbelt.

Agriculture

- leader in world production of e.g. wheat, corn, cotton, tobacco;
- traditional system of agricultural belts (monoculture) has been replaced by crop rotation and mixed farming;
- small farms are subsidized or go bankrupt because of high-technology "mega-farms" or "agri-business";
- large-scale mechanization has led to overproduction.

- the UK's dual school system of state and private education
- comprehensive schools with mixed-ability classes vs grammar schools (more academic curriculum)
- Public Schools: their high academic standards and social importance
- the "old-boy network" and "the old school tie"

English pupils

The British Educational System

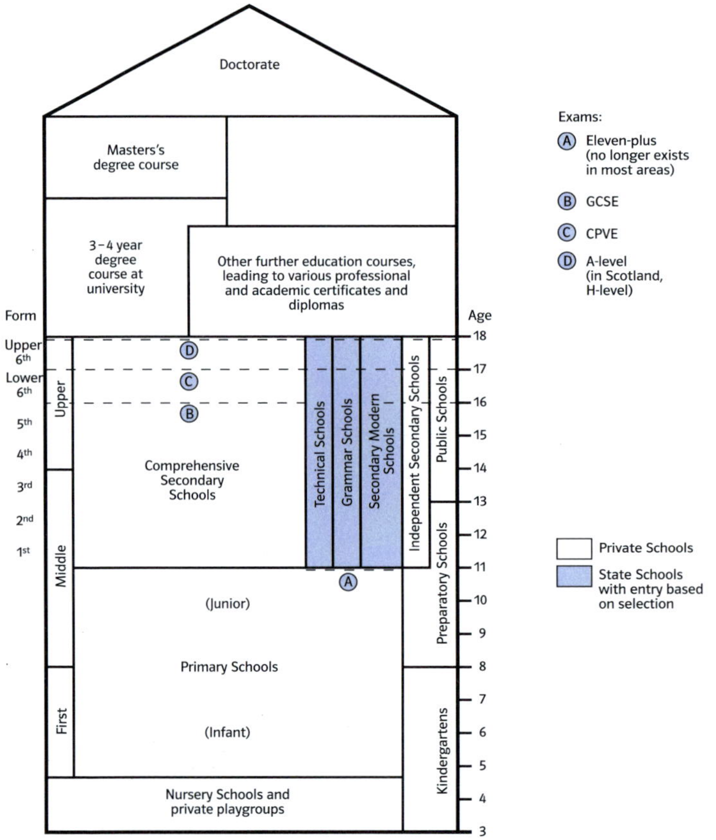

5 Education in Britain and the United States

- school as a unifying factor in the US for shaping a nation of immigrants
- provision of free public education for every child
- a comprehensive high school system for all children
- schools offer a wide range of courses (vocational and academic programmes)
- racial issues in education

High school Soccer team

The United States Educational Structure

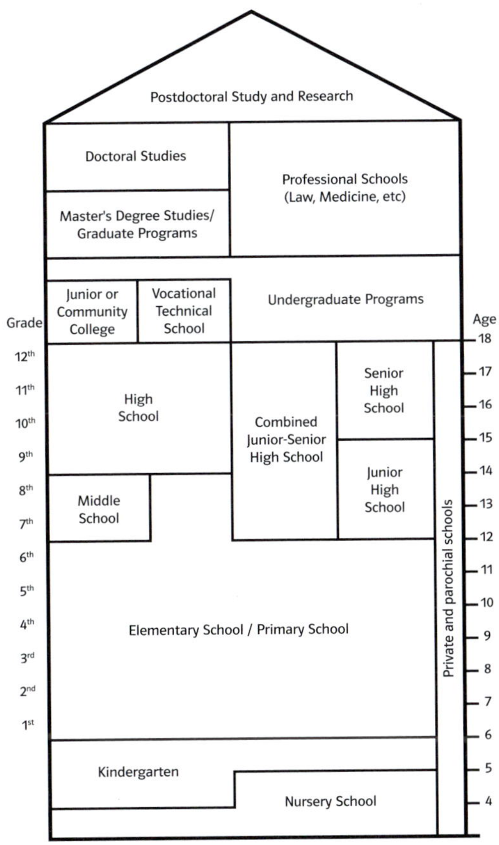

College graduation, USA

5 Education in Britain and the United States

IN BRIEF

- British education provides a dual school system consisting of state schools and private schools.
- Comprehensive schools are large state secondary schools for children of all abilities.
- Public schools are fee-charging private institutions which have gained a reputation for their high academic standards.
- According to the National Curriculum nationwide examinations take place at the age of 16 and 18.
- Education in the USA has always emphasized the integration of different immigrant groups into society.
- The American high school is comprehensive, i.e. a school for all children offering a great variety of courses.
- In the USA state governments and local communities are responsible for their education system.
- Apart from the free public school system there are also prestigious private colleges and universities with high fees.
- Ethnic minorities often do not achieve a similar educational attainment to whites.

5.1 Education in Britain

According to the Butler Act (1944) British state education is free and compulsory from 5–16 years.

Present-day state education is based on the **Butler Act of 1944**:

- State education is free (including equipment and books) and compulsory from the age of 5 to the age of 16 (since 1973).
- Responsibility for providing school education is devolved to the governments of England, Scotland, Wales and Northern Ireland, and administered by (today) 211 Local Education Authorities (LEAs). This means that there are many variations in detail within the general concept of universal education.

About 9.6 million pupils attend almost 30,000 schools. The average class size is 26 in primary and 21 in secondary schools.

State Education

About 94% of British schoolchildren attend publicly financed state schools, 6% private schools. Almost all three- and four-year-olds in Britain attend nursery school. 9/10 of all pupils attend comprehensive schools (→ pp. 46, 49, 115, 119 ff), whilst 1⁄10 attend the still-existing grammar and secondary modern schools, which involve a selection process at the age of eleven.

Compulsory schooling (5–16) is divided up into **primary** (5–11) and **secondary education** (11–16/18). Primary education consists of a two-year Infant School (5–7) and a four-year Junior School (7–11). All state primary schools are co-educational. Secondary education comprises the years 11 to 16, but may also lead up to the age of 18 if the Sixth Form is included. Basically there is only one type of secondary state school (publicly financed) left: about 95% of all British children attending state schools go to **comprehensive schools**. This school type was initiated by the Labour Government in 1966. Comprehensive schools are attended by children of all abilities and provide all types of secondary education. Ideally they are non-selective and are attended by all children in a district; classes are mixed-ability. In practice pupils are put into different classes according to ability (e.g. top set and bottom set). Opposition to comprehensive education remains, however, and LEAs are no longer required to abolish selective schools. About 5% of schoolchildren attending state schools are selected at the age of eleven, according to their total school performance, and move on into three types of selective secondary schools:

- **Grammar schools**: their curriculum is strictly academic, i.e. they prepare children for a university education or for entry into a profession. Some of them are single-sex schools.
- **Secondary modern schools**: they provide general education on a somewhat lower level, including vocational courses.
- **Technical schools**: they put greater emphasis on practical and technical preparatory work and stress the more career-oriented subjects.

British education provides **two separate school systems**: 94% of schoolchildren attend state schools and 6% private schools.

State-run schools are divided up into **primary** and **secondary schools.**

The main type of secondary school is the comprehensive school, a school for children of all abilities.

About 5% of schoolchildren go to selective grammar, secondary modern or technical schools.

Examinations and the National Curriculum

Because of the complexity of the British school system and due to recent educational developments a variety of school exams which a child may have to take in his school career can be distinguished.

The **National Curriculum**, which was introduced in 1989 in England and Wales, laid down guidelines for a unified educational system from primary school onwards. Core subjects are English, mathematics, science with religious education, history, geography, technology, music, art, and physical education. At secondary school a foreign language is included. Attainment targets were laid down stating the knowledge, skills and understanding which are expected at each level. Tests take place in English, maths and science at ages 7, 11 and 14 to assess the level of attainment.

The **National Curriculum** of 1989 provides guidelines for a unified educational system (e.g. core subjects, level of attainment).

attainment target: *Bildungsstandard*

to assess: *beurteilen*

School exams at the age of 16: GCSE and GNVQ

At the age of 16 (after 5 years of secondary education)

- GCSEs (General Certificates of Secondary Education) are taken by most children. It is a subject-based examination although only English, maths and science are compulsory.
- The GNVQ (General National Vocational Qualification) has also been introduced, which is a more practical vocational alternative to GCSEs. It is run by 5 regional examination groups, but their syllabuses must be validated by the Schools' Council. For most subjects, coursework assessment marked by the pupils' own teachers is an important feature. Grading is from A to G; grade C is generally considered to be a pass. Emphasis is placed on practical work and problem solving rather than on mere factual recall.

syllabus: programme of school lessons *(Lehrplan)*

to validate: *bestätigen*

Pupils who leave school at the age of 16 may continue their education at e.g. a Technical College, a College of Art or an Evening Institute.

The two-year Sixth Form is intended for students preparing for the "A" level examination at the age of 18.

At the age of 18 (at the end of the Sixth Form)

The Sixth Form is made up of the Lower and Upper Sixth (years 12 and 13) and is largely geared towards preparation for A-levels at the end of two years. In some areas, the Sixth Form is part of a comprehensive or grammar school, in others it is a separate college.

- **A-level (Advanced level):** Normally a pupil takes 3 A-level subjects; no subject is compulsory, but it is common to take maths plus two sciences or English plus two languages. The grading system is A to E; B or C is usually required by universities. A-levels take two years of concentrated study with a mock exam in the middle of the final year.
- **AS-level (Advanced Supplementary level):** This exam, introduced in 1989, provides an opportunity for Sixth-Formers to study a wider range of subjects. It is intended to be of the same academic level as A-level, but includes only 50 % of the content of A-level. It takes half the study time of A-level and counts as half an A-level for university entrance qualifications.
- **S-level (Scholarship level):** This is an additional paper taken in the same subject as A-level, intended for the most able pupils. Questions are very broad, seeking evidence of mature thought rather than mere knowledge of facts. It is taken mainly by Sixth-Formers aiming at Oxford or Cambridge, as an alternative to the Colleges' own Entrance Exams.

mock exam: simulated exam so that pupils can practise and prepare for the real exam

Higher Education

Sixth-Formers who successfully complete their A-level courses may go to a university at the age of 18. Students wishing to become teachers may alternatively attend a College of Education.
First degree courses usually last 3 or 4 years. The most common titles for the first degree are Bachelor of Arts (BA) or Bachelor of Science (BSc). Postgraduates who are interested in research may, after 1–2 years' study, obtain a Master's degree or, after further years of specialized research, a Doctor's degree (PhD).

Students at a university may obtain a Bachelor's degree or a Master's degree.

Universities

There are over 300 institutions which offer degree courses in Great Britain. Oxford and Cambridge retain their pre-eminence in terms of academic excellence, social standing, and international prestige. "Oxbridge" requirements are the same as those of other universities in principle; in practice they usually require the highest grades. "Oxbridge" is open to all those who have the necessary grades, but the public schools tend to have the academic standards that continue to produce "Oxbridge" students.
The main group in terms of student numbers are the so-called "Redbrick" universities, mainly in the major cities (London, Manchester, Bristol, Birmingham etc), often founded a century ago by major industrialists. Since the 1950s many new universities have been established, often on a parkland "campus" in or close to historic medium-sized cities like Norwich, Lancaster, Canterbury, and York. In the late 60s they tended to be very left-wing, but are now firmly established in the mainstream of higher education. In recent years polytechnics, where courses tend to be more oriented toward the needs of industry and commerce, have all merged with universities in the same town or have become universities in their own right.
The Open University is a non-residential university which provides study by means of correspondence courses, radio and television programmes. It is "open" to anybody and leads to the BA (Open) and higher degrees.

There are about 300 universities and colleges in Britain, among them **Oxford** and **Cambridge**. These ancient universities require the highest grades for entrance.

Private Education

Private education was neither abolished by the Butler Act of 1944 nor by later Labour Governments.
About 6% of British children attend independent schools. These schools must be registered and are subject to official inspection. They charge fees averaging £26,000 per year for senior boarding pupils, but usually offer scholarships and free places for pupils from less well-off families.

About 6% of British schoolchildren attend private schools. They are fee-charging and subject to inspection.

Preparatory Schools (Prep Schools)

The private school system is divided up into prep schools (7–13 years) and public schools (13–18) years.

These schools are for children aged 7 to 13, although many of them maintain pre-preparatory departments for younger children. They provide education that "prepares" the future public school pupil for the Common Entrance Examination, which is the same for all public schools.

Public Schools (→ pp. 47, 50, 117 ff, 151 f)

Many of Britain's public schools are long-established and have gained a reputation for their academic excellence as well as their development of the pupils' personal and social qualities.

The largest and most important of the independent schools are the public schools (13–18 years). The word "public" derives from the fact that originally pupils from all over the country could enter the school and not just from the immediate neighbourhood. Most of them are boys' schools, but today some of them also accept girls as Sixth-Formers. Public schools are long-established and have made a notable contribution to English education, which aims at developing the personal and social qualities of the pupils as well as their intellectual faculties. Some of the most famous are Westminster (1382), Winchester (1382), Eton (1440), Rugby (1557), and Harrow (1571).

Public school ideals and values:

- formation of character through practice of sport ("fair play" ideal);
- emphasis on social behaviour ("Manners makyth Man" is the motto of the Public School of Winchester, summing up the ideal of public school education);
- training for leadership positions;
- discipline is regarded as an important feature, but pupils are also encouraged to take responsibility.

Special Features of British School Life

British schools show a variety of typical features, e.g. they are all-day schools, younger pupils wear school uniforms, extra-curricular activities play an important part in school life.

- Compulsory schooling covers the age-groups from 5 to 16. A-level (16–18) is voluntary.
- It is a **dual system** consisting of state and private schools.
- English schools are **all-day schools** (lessons from 9–12 and 2–4 from Monday to Friday) with school meals provided at lunch time.
- The schoolyear is divided up into three terms (autumn, spring, summer).
- The schoolday begins at 9 o'clock with a 15-minute **assembly** with pupils and staff present. It usually consists of a religious part (prayer, hymn) followed by the Head Teacher's announcements for the day. State schools

must provide religious education. The syllabuses must reflect Christianity whilst taking account of other main religions practised in Britain. However, parents have the right to withdraw their children from religious education classes and collective worship.

- **School uniforms** are worn by many primary and younger comprehensive school children (up to year 11) and public school pupils. They are supposed to remove social differences, preventing competition in dress, and to promote equality among pupils.
- The **prefect system** was introduced to give specially selected senior boys and girls responsible tasks to assist the staff. Thus prefects help the teacher to organize trips, run school facilities or supervise younger children in the teacher's absence. The prefect system has been abandoned in many comprehensive schools.
- **Extra-curricular activities** (e.g. drama, school magazine, photography, music) play an important part in English school life. The most traditionally English of these activities is the **debating society** in which pupils learn to develop their oral skills and to speak according to democratic rules. The meetings imitate the debates held in Westminster Parliament. Today "drama" has taken over from "debating" in many comprehensive schools.

extra-curricular: activities outside the classroom studies

- The English concept of the school as a **community** combines formal learning with the acquisition of social values such as cooperation, loyalty, team spirit, readiness to help. This educational principle is exemplified with the help of e.g. the prefect system, out-of-class activities, and community schemes. These aims were developed originally by the private schools and later adopted by state schools, too.

Educational Problems in Britain

A dual school system does not promote equal opportunities.

The basic problem of British education lies in the fact that there is no common, but a dual system of education, which sustains inequality. In the 1970s, the antagonism between supporters of grammar schools and of comprehensive schools split the country. After the almost complete abolition of the tripartite system in favour of an egalitarian system, the more profound dualism between publicly maintained state schools and fee-paying private schools continues to exist in the new millennium.

Pros and cons of comprehensive schools

truancy: practice of children staying away from school without permission

Comprehensive Schools	
For	Against
• provide a social mixture • provide greater equality • give more chances to more children • forge young people capable of dealing with all social levels in their later lives	• lower academic standards • bad reputation because of truancy and vandalism • reduction in spending by authorities on state schools • too big, but current demographic trends are making schools smaller, i.e. the decline of the proportion of young people

For many British parents a public school education for their children is of great importance.

The root of the educational problem in England is the social importance of private schools, constituting only 6% of all schools. More and more middle-class parents doubt the efficiency of comprehensive schools and try at all costs to enrol their children at one of the public schools. Private education is generally deemed superior.

The Social Ladder

Public Schools	
For	Against
• high academic standards • house system (groups of 50 under the care of a house-master) • carefully selected teachers many of whom studied at "Oxbridge" • a high staffing ratio (i.e. small classes) • high proportion of successful pupils	• favour an educational élite • are only available to the few whose families (predominantly upper and middle class) can afford it • are old-fashioned in clinging to traditions • favour social isolation from other classes which could be a handicap for the pupils' later careers • promote arrogance and snobbishness in public school pupils

Pros and cons of public schools

staffing ratio: *Lehrer-Schüler-Relation*

Traditionally, the ruling classes were recruited from former public school pupils. Although the conditions have changed and more emphasis is placed on merit today, public school pupils still have a big advantage over pupils from comprehensive schools. Educational privilege, social prestige, and the "old-boy network" (→ p. 49) may help the public school leavers to achieve high positions in all fields of life. The "old school tie", especially that of a public school, guarantees professional success. Therefore, the existence of a separate system of education for the wealthy is an important factor in preserving and perpetuating class distinction in Britain. The educational ideal of equal opportunities for all is not provided by the present educational system.

Because of their superior education and their connections, **public school students** have big **advantages** over students from comprehensive schools in their later lives.

New problems for the British education system arose through the existence of ethnic groups concentrated in special areas. However, today most ethnic minority children were born in Britain and have the same interests and aspirations as any other child in Britain. Young Asians have adapted well to the British school system. They are very ambitious and often achieve good results, whereas West Indian children frequently leave school without any qualification. The addition of countries in Eastern Europe to the European Union has led to a large increase in immigration, especially from Poland. This is causing problems with overcrowded schools and the need to teach English to the new arrivals.

Ethnic minority pupils and new immigrant children from Eastern Europe have posed a new challenge to the British educational system.

The Way Ahead

The guidelines of the National Curriculum have helped to give the educational system in Britain a unity, although many people think it is too narrow and prevents teachers from being innovative and imaginative. Today, state schools enjoy a younger staff who are highly motivated to help their pupils achieve their full potential. More and more schools are becoming academies. This means with parental support they are pulling out of local authority control. Many areas of management (finance, staffing, equipment) are now in the hands of the individual schools rather than local authorities. Every school now has to be inspected every four years by a team of independent inspectors. Parents are sent a summary of the inspection report, which is published.

New trends in British education: the introduction of academies and a more global orientation of university studies.

In the last decade Britain has encouraged links between educational institutions in Britain and other countries. The European Union Scheme ERASMUS gives grants for students to study in other countries. The Union's LINGUA programme seeks to improve and widen competence in foreign languages. It gives grants towards study abroad for language students, joint educational projects, and exchanges for young people in professional, vocational and technical education. The British educational trend is at present towards a more global awareness.

5.2 Education in the USA

From America's very beginnings schooling was considered vital for the shaping of a distinctive American nation. In this role it played a major part in Americanizing immigrants by providing them with the basic skills necessary to become responsible American citizens. The American school was turned into a melting pot to fuse children from different national and ethnic backgrounds together. Therefore, in spite of the diversity and the size of the country, the role of the American school remained similar throughout the land. The provision of free public education for every American citizen became one of the fundamental aims of US society.

In the USA schools have always played a major part in the process of integrating different groups of immigrant children. The principle of **free education** for all is fundamental to American society.

Structure of the Educational System

About 90 % of American schools are free and public. In the last few years there has also been a growing number of Protestant parochial schools. Most of them are co-educational. The rest are fee-charging private schools, mostly Roman Catholic parochial schools. Private schools are mostly single-sex schools. The organization and curricula of private schools are similar to those of the public schools. American education comprises three levels: elementary, secondary and higher education. Schooling is compulsory from the ages of 5 or 6 to 16.

parochial school: *Konfessionsschule*

About 90 % of American schools are free and public.

Nursery Schools (age 2–3) and **Kindergartens** (age 4–5) are not compulsory. Kindergartens are sometimes part of the public school system. Whilst the Kindergartens are free, the parents have to pay to send their children to nursery schools. In this educational sector there exist 1,8 million private schools compared with 1,2 million public schools.

There are several structural patterns in use, depending on the location.

6–3–3 plan		
Elementary School:	grades	1 - 6
Junior High School:	grades	7 - 9
Senior High School:	grades	10 - 12
8–4 plan		
Elementary School:	grades	1 - 8
High School:	grades	9 - 12
6–6 plan		
Elementary School:	grades	1 - 6
High School:	grades	7 - 12

Different plans of public education have been introduced.

All plans lead to high school graduation at about 17 or 18 years of age.

Elementary Education

Elementary Schools are for children from the ages of 6 to 12 or 14. They are usually public and co-educational. Historically, educational efforts focused on elementary schools because of their integrational effect on the young children of immigrant parents. Lessons begin between 8.00 am and 8.30 am and end at about 3.00 pm. There is no school on Saturdays. The lessons are centred on reading, writing, and arithmetic.

Secondary Education

Secondary schools comprise either 4 years (age 14–17) or 6 years (age 12–17). The six-year high school is divided up into a junior (age 12–14) and a senior high school.

The **American high school** is a comprehensive school with greater freedom to choose courses.

The **American high school** offers educational facilities for all children aged 12/14–17. It shows best the egalitarian tendency of American education in making children of all social classes attend the same type of school as long as possible. It is a **comprehensive school** which mirrors the American ideals of equal opportunities and equality of social status and serves, just like the elementary schools, as an integratory force in the making of the nation.

High schools offer a mixture of academic subjects and practical skills (commercial classes and vocational training).

The basic problem of US high school education is whether it should provide vocational or general education. Therefore, all larger high schools offer a number of different programmes, which can be taken with the different courses.

- The **academic curriculum** prepares children for college; the basics for high school graduation requirements are English, mathematics, science, social studies, computer science, and a foreign language if students go to college.
- **Commercial classes** include typing, shorthand, bookkeeping.
- **Vocational programmes** offer courses in auto mechanics, printing, agriculture, homemaking, cosmetology, marketing/sales skills.

The four objectives of high schools are:

- general education for all future citizens;
- equipment with practical skills for the marketplace (career education);
- preparation for college and a professional career;
- community service programmes through extra-curricular activities.

High School Dropout Rate by Race, 2014 (%)	
All races	6.5
White	5.2
Black	7.3
Hispanic	10.6
Asian	1.1

Child Trends Data Bank

The high school reflects the pragmatic character of American education in its mixture of classical subjects and necessary practical skills.

Higher Education

Three out of four pupils graduate from high school, and more than half of the high school graduates continue their education. The post-secondary education system in America is complex, as many different types of programmes are offered by the more than 3,000 colleges and universities. It consists of four basic types of institutions:

1. the two-year Junior or Community College;
2. the two-year Technical College;
3. the four-year undergraduate institution – the College of Liberal Arts (18–22) – leading to the Bachelor's Degree (BA or BSc);
4. the university, which normally comprises a college for undergraduate students seeking a Bachelor's Degree and one or more graduate schools or professional schools for those seeking Master's or doctoral degrees.

More than half of high school graduates continue their education at college or university with the aim of obtaining a Bachelor's or a Master's degree.

Higher education is very expensive in the USA, especially at the prestigious private institutions.

A school in any of these categories might be public or private according to its source of funding. Although higher education can be expensive in America, a student can seek funds through scholarships, financial aid (needs based) or guaranteed government student loans. The average tuition fees lie between $4,000 and $12,000 depending on whether it is a public or a private college. At the old and respected universities like Harvard or Yale, the tuition fees are $20,000.

scholarship: If you get a scholarship to a university, your studies are paid by the university or by some other organization.

loan: a sum of money that you borrow

tuition fee: money used to pay for teaching

Acceptance to most colleges depends on a number of possible factors: high school records, recommendations from high school teachers, scores on the Scholastic Aptitude Test (SAT) (which tests maths and verbal skills) and sometimes interviews at the college or university. Acceptance to many institutions is quite competitive, as there is a hierarchy of universities according to prestige, academic standards, and facilities.

Many institutions of higher learning were established by churches, e.g. Harvard 1636, Yale 1701, Princeton 1746 by Protestant denominations. Some of the private universities like Harvard, Yale, Princeton, Northwestern University, Washington University, or Stanford are among the oldest and most highly regarded institutions in the country. They are felt to be élitist because of their high academic standard and their prestige.

Private institutions set high standards.

Control and Financing of Education

Education is the responsibility of local authorities and state governments.

Historically, education has been considered a state and local responsibility, rather than a federal matter. Local communities are given broad authority to run schools. They decide on the school budget, employ teachers and school personnel, provide schoolbuildings and transportation for pupils. State governments have their own departments of education which determine school policy (e.g. curricula, graduation requirements) and enact educational laws.
There is no national public examination system. In public elementary and secondary schooling, local districts determine and maintain standards. But students who apply for college and professional schools (higher education) take the nationally recognized Scholastic Aptitude Test (SAT). They are tested by the College Entrance Examination Board or the Educational Testing Service.
The US Department of Education has little authority and no direct control over education. There are federal standards for all states, but beyond this state governments have control. Only in the last 30 years has federal intervention become more frequent, e.g. in granting federal aid when educational costs became too high for state and local communities.

Educational Attainment by Race and Hispanic Origin, 2015

High school completion or higher (%)		Bachelor's degree or higher (%)	
White	93.3	White	36.2
Black	87.0	Black	22.9
Asian	89.1	Asian	54.4
Hispanic	66.7	Hispanic	15.5

Digest of Education Statistics

Current Issues concerning American Education

Educational issues concern e.g. the ideal of **equal opportunity for all** with regard to inner city schools and educational attainment by race, **bilingual education** as regards the Hispanics and questions about student achievement in general.

American education is beset by many problems. The most important concern:

- **Equal opportunities for all**: Efforts are still necessary to ensure that every child has access to a uniformly high quality of education. Differences still exist among and within states. In the past they concerned urban and rural areas; nowadays they are between inner city schools and other urban and suburban areas. Pupils in inner cities, mostly those from low-income and minority group families, have generally low results compared to suburban, middle-class schoolchildren. But the problem of social integration with the help of job facilities after school is even greater than that of equal education. The improvement of the situation for minorities is a major social and educational problem for the coming decades.

- **Racial issues** still have a great impact on schools. Although racial segregation of schools was declared illegal, many schools still reflect basically white or black neighbourhoods. Schools, however, are doing better in the desegregation of society than other sectors of life (e.g. housing, jobs).
- **Bilingual education** and mother-tongue teaching are controversial subjects as regards the growing numbers of Spanish-speaking immigrants mainly in the South and Southwest.
- **Student achievement and curricula reforms**: Again and again educationalists have been alarmed at the decline in pupil achievement. Especially since the **Sputnik shock** in 1957, when the American public became aware of the necessity of technological competition in the space race with the Soviet Union, demands for the development of nation-wide examinations and for higher levels of performance have been made. After a decade of freedom of choice for pupils, the 1970s saw a return to the basics, the three "Rs" (reading, writing, arithmetic) and science. Since that time, course requirements have been tightened to raise the standards of performance in each subject. Still, many Americans are not satisfied with the standards and curricula. In particular they complain about the wide range of electives and merely practical skills pupils can take as subjects to obtain credits, and demand higher intellectual student ability and more academic curricula.
- **School prayer**: During the conservative Reagan era (1984), an amendment to the Constitution to introduce school prayer was rejected. It is, however, currently under discussion whether to reintroduce school prayer.
- **Inner-city problems**: There is a growing dissatisfaction with the public schools in many areas, especially in the inner cities where social problems, such as rising availability of drugs and increasing violence, are prevalent. Increasing difficulty in raising money through taxation to support public education intensifies the problem. As a result there is an increase in the number of parochial and private schools, as well as a growth in "home-schooling", where the parents educate and test their children themselves, rather than sending them to school.

This survey of some major educational issues in American education shows that schools reflect the state of society, and that social problems in society at large have their impact on school life and educational institutions.

to tighten: to make stricter and more efficient *(verschärfen)*

elective (AE): *Wahlfach*

Education in Britain

State Education

- Present-day state education is based on the Butler Act of 1944. It is free (including equipment and books) and compulsory (from the age of 5 to the age of 16).
- 94% of British schoolchildren attend state schools, 9/10 comprehensive schools, and 1/10 grammar schools and secondary modern schools.
- Schooling is divided up into primary (5–11) and secondary (11–16/18) education.

School Types
Comprehensive Schools (11–16/18 years) are attended by children of all abilities and their classes are mixed-ability.

A small percentage of schoolchildren are selected at the age of 11 and move into two types of selective secondary schools:

Grammar Schools (11–16/18 years) have a more academic curriculum and prepare children for a university education.

Secondary Modern Schools (11–16 years) provide general education on a lower level and include vocational courses.

Main Examinations

- GCSE (General Certificate of Education) at the age of 16: an exam with English, maths, and science being compulsory;
- A-level (Advanced Level) at the age of 18 after years 12 and 13 is required for university entrance and taken in three or more A-level subjects.

Higher Education

- Sixth-Formers who successfully complete their A-level exams may go to university at the age of 18.
- University degree (BA or BSc) courses usually last 3–4 years.
- After 1–2 years of research postgraduates may obtain a Master's degree (MA).

Private education

About 6% of British schoolchildren attend independent fee-charging schools.

School Types
Prep Schools (7–13 years) prepare the future public school pupil for the Common Entrance Examination.

Public Schools (13–18 years)

- form the character through practice of sport ("fair play");
- emphasize social behaviour;
- encourage pupils to take responsibility;
- stress the importance of discipline;
- have high academic standards (small classes, carefully selected teachers).

Public school leavers have a big advantage over children from comprehensive schools. Educational privilege, social prestige, and the "old-boy network" normally guarantee professional success.

Education in the USA

General Concept

The provision of free public education for all became a fundamental aim of US society:

- Schooling was considered vital for the shaping of the American nation.
- School was turned into a melting pot to fuse children from different backgrounds together and to Americanize them.

Structure of the Educational System

- About 90% of American schools are free and public; the rest are fee-charging private schools.
- Education is normally organized according to the "6-3-3" plan.
- High school graduation is at the age of 17 or 18 years.

Elementary School (6 – 12 years)

- is usually co-educational.
- The traditional programme focuses on skills in reading, writing and arithmetic.

The High School (12 – 17 years)

- is a comprehensive school which mirrors the American ideal of equal opportunities.
- Its four objectives are: general education for all citizens, equipment with practical skills, preparation for college, and community service programmes.
- It combines general and vocational programmes: the academic curriculum prepares students for college (e.g. English, science, social studies, foreign language); commercial classes include e.g. typing and bookkeeping, and vocational programmes offer courses e.g. in auto mechanics, homemaking, or marketing.

Higher Education

- Post-secondary education consists of four basic types: the two-year Junior College; the two-year Technical College; the College of Liberal Arts (18 – 22) leading to the Bachelor's degrees; the university leading to a Bachelor's or Master's degree.
- Higher education is very expensive, as public and private colleges and universities demand high tuition fees, especially those of high academic standard.
- College admission depends on: high school records, recommendations from high school teachers, scores on the Scholastic Aptitude Test (SAT), personal interviews.

- Because of its influence in public affairs the British press is often called the "Fourth Estate".
- most important national quality papers: the *Times, Guardian, Daily Telegraph, Independent, Financial Times*.
- most important populars: *Sun, Daily Mirror, Daily Star*
- national papers generally have a conservative leaning
- tendency of press concentration (e. g. Rupert Murdoch)
- the *British Broadcasting Corporation* (*BBC*) renowned for its high standard of reporting
- *ITV* channels are commercial companies financed by commercial advertising.

BBC Broadcasting House London

Mass Media in Britain

- important role of the press in forming public opinion
- British press unrestricted by censorship
- highest newspaper circulation in the world
- typical aspects of the "yellow" press
- Increasingly important role of the Internet for the provision of information

6 The Mass Media in Britain and the United States

- freedom of the press guaranteed in the Bill of Rights
- tradition of investigative journalism (e.g. Watergate affair)
- Newpapers do not have a political leaning (e.g. Democratic or Republican).
- The presidential press conference is of great importance.
- widely known newpapers: *USA Today, The New York Times, The Wall Street Journal*
- tendency of press concentration like in Britain
- absence of a nationwide press due to the size of the country

Politician giving an interview

Mass Media in the United States

Telecommunications satellite dish and communications tower

- nationwide television: a unifying factor of American society
- commercial television entirely financed by advertising
- non-commercial public television *PBS* financed by the Federal Government
- US commercial TV programmes widely criticized for their focus on popular entertainment and sensational presentation of serious news

IN BRIEF

6 The Mass Media in Britain and the United States

- In Britain the press has an important role in forming public opinion.
- There are basically two kinds of national newspapers: "quality" and "popular" papers.
- Television is provided by two authorities: the British Broadcasting Corporation (BBC) and the Independent Broadcasting Authority (IBA).
- In the USA freedom of the press has a long tradition: it is guaranteed in the Bill of Rights.
- Due to the size of the USA no nationwide press comparable to the British press has developed.
- Most of the US radio and TV networks and stations are commercial. Advertising and popular entertainment are typical features.

6.1 The Mass Media in Britain

The British Press

General Features

British people buy more newspapers per person than any other nation in the world. Therefore the press has a strong influence on the readers' opinions.

In Britain more national and regional newspapers are sold per head than in any other Western country, a fact which emphasizes the important role of the press in forming public and political opinion. It is quite common for English people to read a national daily and a local evening or weekly paper, and a Sunday paper. Reasons for the high circulation of newspapers are:

- Complete information can only be obtained by reading both a national and a regional paper.
- Newspaper reading is part of the traditional British Sunday.
- **National dailies** have a circulation of about 15 million, **national Sundays** of about 16 million copies. The national press caters for a much larger reading public than in many other countries. The regional or local press is comparatively less significant, except in Scotland and Wales, which still have a strong national identity expressed through papers like *The Scotsman*.
- The British press is unrestricted by censorship or state control. It is considered to be an instrument for controlling and criticizing government and decision-makers. It has considerable influence in public affairs and is therefore sometimes called the "Fourth Estate".

to cater for: to take account of and provide with what is necessary

estate: *Stand*

- The **Press Council** (1953) was set up to safeguard the freedom of the press and to maintain the highest professional standards.
- Unlike most other European countries the British press receives no subsidies and relatively few tax and postal concessions.

The National Press

National newspapers (dailies and Sundays) are distributed throughout the country, but are mainly produced in London (in the Docklands area in Wapping) and Manchester. They are traditionally classified as either **"quality"** papers or **"popular"** papers.

Most important are the national newspapers that can be divided into "quality" and "popular" papers.

The British press owes its international importance to seven papers with the highest standards. Characteristics of the **"qualities"** or "broadsheets":

Quality papers provide the educated reader with reliable and full coverage of news.

- reading public: the educated, the élite;
- format: mostly broadsheet;
- content: reliable and full coverage of news, often with additional background information; also a wide range of feature articles (e.g. on legal or financial affairs); articles are mostly written by experts on the subject and signed;
- style: formal, matter-of-fact, highbrow, sometimes literary;
- Saturday and Sunday newspapers include colour supplements with articles on travel, food, wine, and leisure topics.

coverage: recording of events

feature: a special article in a newspaper or magazine

highbrow: intellectual, academic, difficult to understand

Populars are mass-circulation tabloids, which are cheaper in price and of lower standard. Typical aspects of the "popular" or "yellow" press:

Popular papers are written for the less demanding reader and focus on sensational news and "human interest stories".

- reading public: the lower middle classes and working-class people, commuters on their daily way to work;
- format: the handy tabloid;
- layout: words in bold face type, sensational headlines, illustration with (colour) photos to attract the reader's attention;
- content: sensational treatment of news with emphasis on "human interest" stories and scandals; some of them are down-market in their use of sex to boost sales; political reporting is superficial; articles are sometimes more openly tendentious;
- style: more emotional, colloquial, informal, use of everyday English.

tabloid: newspaper with small pages

down-market: popular and cheap and not very good in quality

to boost: to increase, to raise *(ankurbeln)*

It is important to note that the striking difference between "quality" papers and the sensational press reflects the gap between Britain's social classes.

As the name describes, the **mid-market papers** cover the intermediate market and are also tabloid (small-sheet).

Survey of national dailies and Sundays

National Newspapers		
Title and foundation date	**Controlled by**	**Circulation 2016/2017**
Dailies:		
Populars		
Daily Mirror (1903)	Trinity Mirror	724,888
Daily Star (1978)	Express Newspapers	443,452
Sun (1964)	News International	1,666,715
Mid-market		
Daily Mail (1896)	Associated Newspapers	1,511,357
Daily Express (1900)	Express Newspapers	392,526
Qualities		
Financial Times (1888)	Financial Times	188,924
Daily Telegraph (1885)	Telegraph Group	472,258
Guardian (1821)	Guardian Newspapers	156,756
Independent (1986)	Independent Print	55,193
Times (1785)	News International	451,261
i (2010)	Independent Print	266,768
Sundays:		
Populars		
Sun on Sunday 2012	News International	1,375,539
Sunday Mirror (1963)	Trinity Mirror	629,277
People (1881)	Trinity Mirror	240,846
Daily Star Sunday (2002)	Express Newspapers	256,801
News of the World (1843)		closed in July 2011
Mid-market		
Mail on Sunday (1982)	Associated Newspapers	1,257,984
Sunday Express (1918)	Express Newspapers	335,772
Qualities		
Sunday Telegraph (1961)	Telegraph Group	359,400
Independent on Sunday (1990)	Independent Newspapers	91,644
Observer (1791)	Guardian Newspapers	185,752
Sunday Times (1822)	News International	792,324

Audit Bureau of Circulations

Current Issues concerning the British Press

- The great majority of the national papers (70% of the circulation figures) express a conservative affiliation. This fact has frequently given rise to some criticism of the British press.
- The monopolistic tendencies of the British press are another area of criticism. 90% of the total circulation of the national press are controlled by only five "Press Lords" or newspaper groups. The Australian **Rupert Murdoch** (News International) already owns one third of Britain's national press (*The Times*, *The Sunday Times*, *The Sun*). In July 2011, however, a scandal caused by journalists hacking into private voicemails led to the closure of the oldest and biggest Sunday newspaper, the *News of the World*.

There are e.g. concerns regarding the mostly conservative political leaning of the national newspapers and the problem of press concentration in Britain.

affiliation: leaning

- Most British newspapers are situated in the Docklands of East London. Here they take advantage of modern computerized printing systems which were introduced to keep pace with soaring costs and competition from cable television.
- To encourage sales and distribution, overseas editions of the Financial Times are printed in Frankfurt, Northern France, New Jersey, and Tokyo, whilst the *Guardian* prints an international edition in Frankfurt.
- Numerous weekly, fortnightly and monthly ethnic minority publications are published by members of ethnic minorities (e.g. *Asian Times*, *Asian Trader*, *Caribbean Times*).
- The **Press Complaints Commission** was established in 1991 by the newspaper and periodical industry due to growing criticism of press standards, especially with regard to unjustified invasion of privacy and inaccurate and biased reporting (e.g. the Royal Family "scandals"). The Government is considering possible legislative steps to deal with intrusion into personal privacy.

biased: not objective, unfairly influenced in favour of or against sb. or sth.

- Until 1986 *The Times* always presented an unbiased and balanced view of the political scene. Since the acquisition by Rupert Murdoch the reporting has reflected the owner's political views, and the paper, almost a national institution, has lost its dominant position in forming and reflecting opinion at the highest levels.

The Times, formerly known for its unbiased stance, now mirrors its new owner's political views. Some observers feel that it has gone downmarket.

- Some *Times* readers have switched to papers like the *Independent* (founded in 1986), a quality paper which is not committed to any political stance.

stance: standpoint

- *The i*, a new compact quality paper (2010), is designed to complement the *Independent*, its sister edition, for 20 p.
- The circulation of British newspapers has diminished by 20% over the last five years, far above the European average. Reasons are the bad economic performance of the country, decreasing advertising revenues and the growing competition of the internet, including online editions of the newspapers themselves.

British Radio and Television

Radio programmes are produced by the BBC and a great number of independent commercial radio stations.

Sound broadcasting is available on analogue and digital channels, both on air and on line, from the British Broadcasting Corporation (BBC) and from many independent commercial stations. BBC radio provides ten national services plus 48 local radio stations and the World Service. Every aspect of life is covered, including news, current affairs, sport, entertainment and all kinds of music.

Television is provided by the BBC and the IBA. BBC runs four national TV networks BBC 1, 2, 3 and 4; the commercial IBA controls ITV 1, 2, 3 and 4, as well as Channel 4 and Five.

Television Audience Share Figures, UK, Apr 2017

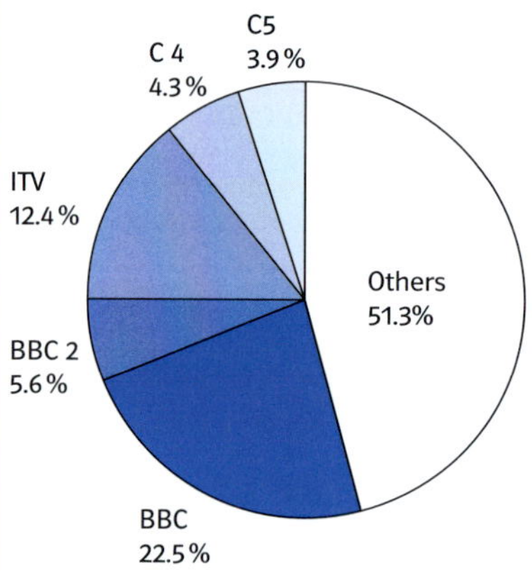

BARB/Broadcasters' Audience Research Board Ltd 2015

All **television** in the UK uses digital technology; terrestrial programmes are provided by two authorities, the **British Broadcasting Corporation (BBC)** and the **Independent Broadcasting Authority (IBA)**. Satellite channels (BSkyB and many other commercial stations), cable (Virgin Media) and online services are increasing their share of the market. The BBC (founded in 1922) is directed by a Board of Governors appointed by the Government. It is primarily financed by licence fees and sales of television programmes, recordings and publications. BBCTV (founded in 1936) broadcasts four channels.

BBC 1 presents programmes of more general interest such as light entertainment, sports, news, current affairs, and children's programmes. **BBC 2** transmits more specialized programmes like documentaries, travel, serious plays, and international films. The BBC does not broadcast any commercial advertisements or sponsored programmes. It is renowned worldwide for its high standard of reporting and documentary presentation. It has become a model of TV journalism, as all other TV reporting and presentation has often been judged by the BBC standard. **BBC 3** and **BBC 4** carry programmes of minority interest, and also many repeats of popular series from the main channels.

The **IBA** (1972) is appointed by the Home Secretary. It was set up to coordinate independent television and radio stations. Its function is not to produce programmes, but to appoint companies to produce programmes, to supervise programme arrangement, and to control advertising.

The IBA controls the four ITV (Independent Television) channels, while **Channel 4** and **Channel 5** are commercial companies. Finance for these television channels is provided solely by commercial advertising, but advertisers are not allowed to influence programmes. Advertisements ('Ads') interrupt programmes every 15 minutes or so.
ITV 1 offers a great variety of subject matter: news, information, current affairs, and light entertainment. It broadcasts such popular productions as the **soap operas** "Emmerdale Farm" or "Coronation Street". **ITV 2, 3** and **4** present items of minority interest, repeats of popular programmes and films.
Channel 4 (1982) has used its independence to provide a wide range of programmes, in any aspect of life which it thinks will attract viewers.
Five (1997) is aimed at the younger viewer, and seeks to widen the range of programmes available. Finance is provided by advertising.
Advances in digital technology have led to the introduction of High Definition (HD) broadcasting and to the appearance of very many new commercial TV and radio channels.

Current Issues concerning British Television

- In 2010 around 4.2 million homes in the UK were receiving multichannel television, internet, email and telephone services by cable.
- Direct broadcasting by satellite (DBS) has been available in Britain since 1989. Satellite channels include British Sky Broadcasting, Eurosport, MTV (pop videos), and CNN (news).
- In 1994 the BBC announced a new organizational structure named BBC Worldwide. Its main service is BBC World which broadcasts radio programmes worldwide using English and 42 other languages. It features mainly news and language programmes.
- The role of the Internet has become increasingly important for the provision and distribution of information and entertainment. Most newspapers and broadcasters have set up their websites where they offer a wide range of information and advertising services, for example *The Times*, *The Guardian*, *The Daily Telegraph*, *The Independent*, BBC, ITV.

Technology continues to change the media. New developments in Britain's media landscape concern the spread of cable and satellite TV and the growing importance of the Internet.

6.2 The Mass Media in the USA

The American Press

Typical features of the **American press:** Freedom of the press is guaranteed in the Bill of Rights. There are practically no nationwide national papers, newspapers do not have a political leaning and investigative journalism plays an important role.

In the history of the press, America has always been a forerunner. As early as the beginning of the 18th century the Americans regularly issued newspapers, and in 1830 mass press was born in the form of *The Sun*.

- **Freedom of the press** has a long tradition in the States as it is guaranteed in the First Amendment to the Constitution: "Congress shall make no law [...] abridging the freedom of speech, or of the press [...]."
- Of great political importance is the presidential press conference, an instrument for the President to answer journalists' questions and to expound his political stance on current affairs. Newspapermen thus play a significant part in the democratic political process of the country.
- There are no papers with a clear Democratic or Republican **leaning**. American newspapers tend to be impartial and unbiased in their news reporting. Objective information and personal comment are clearly separated.
- There is a long tradition of **investigative journalism** with reporters acting as "private eyes" to detect political corruption or to dig out secret military documents which are of public interest. Newspaper investigation proved e.g. that President Nixon was involved in the Watergate affair (→ pp. 28, 185).
- Due to the size and the federal character of the USA, it is virtually impossible to have a nationwide press comparable to the British press. However, three big newspapers have succeeded: *The Wall Street Journal*, *The New York Times* and *USA Today*.
- There are about 2,400 different daily and Sunday papers with a circulation figure of 115 million copies, the highest number for any country in the world.
- Press organs of international excellence are furthermore *The Christian Science Monitor* and the two weekly news magazines *Time* and *Newsweek*.
- The *Wall Street Journal* and *The Herald Tribune*, with their different editions in Europe and Asia, have started a new era, that of the world paper.
- Most American dailies are "quality" papers and reflect responsible journalism. Sensational press products like *New York Daily News* are more of an exception.
- US newspapers are mainly funded by advertising. Many of them, especially Sunday editions, consist of a bulk of several hundred pages, 60% of which are filled by advertisements.

Largest Daily US Newspapers (May 2016)

Newspaper	Total Circulation
USA Today	2,301,917
The Wall Street Journal	2,101,611
The New York Times	1,337,376
The Orange County Reg.	467,309
The Los Angeles Times	424,721
San Jose Mercury News	384,962
New York Post	356,768
Daily News	321,296
Newsday	299,538
The Washington Post	298,759

Cision

Current Issues concerning the American Press

- There is a growing tendency of press concentration like in Britain (e.g. the Hearst Newspapers).
- A rising distrust is to be noticed with regard to investigative reporting which is often felt to violate the right to privacy and fair treatment (plain muck-raking) and to thereby defame the American nation.
- Ordinary American papers are written for the middle-of-the-road white American. Minority groups maintain that their interests are not adequately covered and that there is not enough serious criticism of the drawbacks of American society.

Controversial issues are the growing press concentration, the violation of the individual's right to privacy and the lack of coverage of minority interests in newspapers.

muck-raking: the act of finding and spreading scandal relating to public figures e.g. the Clinton/Lewinsky affair

drawback: disadvantage

American Radio and Television

From the very first broadcasting in 1920, radio became the most important medium until it was replaced by television. There are about 12,500 radio stations in the United States. Over 10,500 are commercial, the rest are non-commercial. **Commercial radio stations** offer specialized programming promising high ratings, such as light music, "top-40", Country music, "oldies", hard rock. Others present news, interviews, and phone-in broadcasts. **Non-commercial radio stations** are either educational or religious. They are run by universities, boards of education, or churches, and concentrate on cultural programmes, features, news, current affairs, and entertainment.

American radio and television are licenced by the **Federal Communications Commission** (FCC), an independent federal authority, but the networks and their programmes are not subject to control by any governmental body. Moreover, sound broadcasting and television are free of charge for the American audience. American TV viewers receive about 2,000 stations, 1,660 commercial and more than 330 non-commercial. Besides the three major networks NBC (National Broadcasting Company), CBS (Columbia Broadcasting System), and ABC (American Broadcasting Company), **commercial television** has an increasing number of networks. Among them are CNN, C-Span (live coverage of Congress), Fox Television, ESPN (sports), CBC (Canadian Broadcasting Corporation), and TNT (Turner Network Television). These companies provide programmes for the individual television stations. Commercial TV is entirely financed by **advertising** revenues. American advertising agencies and sponsors even influence the choice of programmes suitable for advertising. Therefore, sponsors avoid controversial issues and special interest topics, preferring programmes that appeal to the masses. Even serious news about war, hijacking or national catastrophes is frequently interrupted by sales messages which present an ideal world without problems.

The great majority of US radio and television stations are **commercial**. They are free of charge and entirely financed by advertising. Programmes are chosen that promise high ratings and appeal to the masses.

The non-commercial public television (PBS) is funded by the Federal Government. It provides cultural and educational programmes.

Non-commercial public television was developed in 1967 to counter-balance the profit-oriented private television companies and to promote quality programmes. The Public Broadcasting Service (PBS) with approximately 300 TV-stations is nowadays the biggest TV-network. It is financed by the Federal Government and by donations from viewers and corporations.

The **non-commercial Pay TV** is financed by an additional charge and therefore has no commercials. It meets the need of cultural and educational programmes, such as concerts, operas, plays, documentaries, and children's programmes (e.g. "Sesame Street"). As the cost of the pay TV is quite high, critics note a social division of TV viewers: those wealthy enough to pay for non-commercial TV and those who cannot afford it and have to be satisfied with commercial TV.

to proliferate: to spread

Altogether, there seems to be a trend towards channels that either broadcast only one theme (sports, news, music, films), or aim at a certain proportion of the viewers (e.g. the Spanish-speaking population). Radio and television "Talk Shows", where the public can call in with their opinions and where there are interviews with ordinary people who are in the midst of a crisis, have proliferated throughout the country.

Current Issues concerning American Television

Television has become a major factor in shaping the American family and the nation as a whole. But it is also widely criticized because of its focus on popular entertainment, its shallowness and its sensational presentation of serious news.

to glean: *erfahren*

- Nationwide television has become a unifying factor of American society like no other medium, providing the American people with the same culture and common experiences.
- Television is said to have weakened traditional family life. In 2006 84 % of all US homes were cabled, 98 % had at least one TV set. In 2004 the average daily viewing time per home was 4 hours 30 minutes. Most Americans gleaned their news from the TV.
- Television plays a very important role during election campaigns. Over 50 % of the election finance budget is spent on television spots. This is a welcome source of income for the privately owned TV companies.
- US commercial TV programmes are generally criticized for their shallowness, their presentation of a dream world combined with a bombardment of advertising, programmes which, however, are sold worldwide with great success. Commercial television continues to supply audiences to advertisers instead of providing programmes for the audience.
- Another criticism of commercial TV in particular is that the news programmes are putting increasing value on the entertainment element. They are often presented as talk shows where the main points are sensational stories rather than more serious news; for example the sensational reporting oft he Gulf War (1991) (→ pp. 148, 186 f) was heavily criticized.

The Mass Media in Britain and the United States

General Features of the British Press

It plays an important role in forming public and political opinion, as there are more national and regional newspapers sold in Britain than in any other Western country.

National Newspapers (Dailies and Sundays)

- are mainly produced in London and Manchester;
- are traditionally classified as either quality papers or popular papers.

Quality papers (e.g. *Times, Independent, Guardian*) are papers with the highest standards:

- reading public: the educated, the élite;
- content: reliable and full coverage of news, often with background information; wide range of feature articles; articles mostly written by experts.

Popular papers (e.g. *Daily Mirror, Sun*) are mass-circulation tabloids, of lower standard:

- reading public: lower middle classes and working class;
- content: sensational treatment of news, emphasis on "human interest" stories and scandals, political reporting is superficial, articles are sometimes tendentious.

British Radio and Television

The British Broadcasting Corporation (BBC)

- provides five radio services (Radio 1 to 5), local radio stations, and four TV programmes (BBC 1, 2, 3 and 4);
- is renowned for its high standard of reporting and documentary presentation;
- is financed by licence fees, sales of programmes, recordings, and publications.

The Independent Broadcasting Authority (IBA) controls many local radio stations and TV programmes which are financed only by commercial advertising. The TV programme companies sell time to advertisers, but there is no sponsoring of programmes like in the USA.

General Features of the American Press

- Freedom of the press is guaranteed in the First Amendment to the Constitution;
- American newspapers tend to be unbiased;
- because of the size of the country it is impossible to have a nationwide press.

American Radio and Television

- **Non-commercial radio stations** are either educational or religious; they are run by universities or churches and concentrate on quality programmes.
- **Commercial television** is entirely financed by advertising revenues; American advertising agencies even influence the choice of programmes suitable for advertising (e.g. game shows, sitcoms, soap operas).

The majority of the British people are Christians.

St. Paul's Cathedral

Religion in Britain

1. **Christian** 37,770,000 | 63.0 %
2. **No religion** 17,320,000 | 28.9 %
3. **Muslim** 2,560,000 | 4.3 %
4. **Hindu** 800,000 | 1.3 %
5. **Sikh** 370,000 | 0.6 %
6. **Jewish** 280,000 | 0.5 %
7. **Buddhist** 250,000 | 0.4 %

Other religion 570,000 | 1.0 %

Source: ONS Labour Force Survey, 2011 (Jul – Sep 2011)

7 Religion in Britain and the United States

In the United States there is a big variety of different churches.

Afro-American Christians in a gospel choir

Religion in the United States

1 **Roman Catholic Church** 68,200,000

2 **Southern Baptist Convention** 16,200,000

3 **United Methodist Church** 7,800,000

4 **Muslims** (estimated) 5,800,000 – 6,600,000

5 **The Church of Jesus Christ of Latter-day Saints** 6,200,000

6 **Jewish** (estimated) 5,200,000 – 6,100,000

7 **Church of God in Christ** 5,500,000 members

8 **National Baptist Convention, U.S.A., Inc.** 5,000,000

9 **Evangelical Lu-theran Church in America** 4,500,000

10 **National Baptist Convention of America, Inc.** 3,500,000

11 **Assemblies of God** 2,900,000

12 **Presbyterian Church (USA)** 2,800,000

13 **African Methodist Episcopal Church** 2,500,000

US Religious Bodies with Membership over 2,500,000
Source: *2012 Yearbook of American and Canadian Churches/ThomRainer.com 2014*

IN BRIEF

7 Religion in Britain and the United States

- The Church of England (Anglican Church) is the official church of the UK.
- The Church of Scotland ("Kirk") is an established Presbyterian Church.
- Free Churches (Dissenters / Nonconformists) are Protestant churches that did not conform with the English Reformation.
- British Puritanism has had a strong influence on British society.
- The Puritan heritage has had a great impact on the religious, social and political development of the USA.
- Religious life in the USA is characterized by a great diversity.
- Contemporary religious America is divided between liberal Protestantism and conservative fundamentalism.
- The Electronic Church in the USA combines religious fundamentalism with the techniques of the entertainment industry.

7.1 Religion in Britain

Britain is a religiously diverse country.

At first sight, Britain appears to be a country of great religious unity, which is overwhelmingly Protestant. But at a closer look one is astonished to find a great variety of denominations:

„established church": state church

- the Anglican Church as the "established" Church of England;
- the Presbyterian "established" Church of Scotland;
- a dominant Methodist Church in Wales;
- a Protestant majority and a substantial Roman Catholic minority in Northern Ireland.

The Church of England

The Church of England, the official church of the UK, was created in the 16th century, when Henry VIII separated from Rome. It is made up of two branches: Anglo-Catholics and Evangelicals.

Foundation	
1534	Act of Supremacy: Henry VIII separated from Rome and the British Sovereign became the "Head of the Church of England"
1559	Book of Common Prayer (order of worship)
1562	39 Articles (Anglican doctrine)

The Church of England or Anglican Church is the official church of the United Kingdom. It dates from the English Reformation of the 16th century. There are **two branches**:

- Anglo-Catholics (High Church) put emphasis on church ritual and believe in the authority of the clergy.
- Evangelicals (Low Church) attach greater importance to preaching and the interpretation of the Bible and stress simplicity of worship.

Its secular head is the Sovereign, and its religious head the Archbishop of Canterbury. England is divided up into two provinces (Canterbury and York), dioceses, and parishes, administered by bishops, priests, and deacons.

The Anglican Church occupies a middle position between the Roman Catholic and the Protestant Churches.

The **General Synod** is the central governing body of the Church of England. It meets to discuss spiritual, educational, social and administrative questions. The Anglican Church has a middle position between

Catholicism		Protestantism
· The Nicene Creed · The Historic Episcopate · liturgy · monasteries · no ordination of women (up to 1992)	and	· no supremacy of the Pope · the sacraments are only: Baptism and Holy Communion · marriage is no sacrament · service in English

creed: *Glaubensbekenntnis*

Holy Communion: *Abendmahl*

The Anglican Church is not supported by the State, e.g. through a church tax, but finances itself from land property and private donations.

There is a close relationship between Church and State in the UK.

Apart from financial matters, the relationship of **Church and State** is one of mutual obligation and control. The monarch holds the title "Defender of Faith" (F. D.). He/She is not only the "Head of the Church", but also appoints important church dignitaries on the advice of the Prime Minister. Moreover, Parliament must approve of Church legislation, e.g. revision of the liturgy. The established status of the Church of England is also illustrated by the fact that the Lords Spiritual (the two archbishops and 24 bishops) are members of the House of Lords and can thus take an active part in British policies.

dignitary: *Würdenträger*

The Church of Scotland ("Kirk")

The Church of Scotland is Scotland's official national church. It is Protestant (Presbyterian) and has complete freedom in all spiritual matters.

Foundation and Development	
1559	John Knox, the Scottish reformer, founded the Calvinist Presbyterian Church.
1707	In the Treaty of Union its status as the national Church of Scotland was acknowledged.
1921	The Church of Scotland Act confirmed the complete freedom of the church in all spiritual questions.

episcopal: *bischöflich*

elder: official in some churches

The Church of Scotland is an established **Presbyterian church** that originated in the Protestant Reformation. It rejects the episcopal form of church government and replaces it with a more democratic government by elders. All of them, including the ministers, enjoy equal status. Church government is performed by local, regional and national committees. Each year, the **General Assembly** elects the **Moderator** as head of the "Kirk". Presbyterian dogma and the form of divine service resemble those of Continental Protestant churches.

The Free Churches (Dissenters / Nonconformists)

The Free Churches are non-established Protestant Churches. They derive from the Puritans who disagreed with the English Reformation.

The Free Churches are Protestant churches that did not conform with the English Reformation and the establishment of the Anglican Church as Church of England in the 16th and 17th centuries. These "Nonconformist" churches derive from the Puritans who opposed the middle position of Anglicanism and separated from the Established Church on points of ritual and doctrine:

- For most dissenting groups the Bible is the sole authority. The individual is directly responsible to God.
- Church hierarchy is abolished and replaced by a democratic church organization emphasizing equal status of ministers and laymen, of men and women.
- Simple worship services are held in plain chapels.
- Much stress is laid on practical Christianity.

British Puritanism

The historical significance of Puritanism exceeds the scope of ecclesiastical struggles. The Dissenters have had a strong impact on British culture and society. Puritanism has promoted:

- the ideal of the self-controlled, independent personality that does not show his feelings or lose his temper;
- to a certain extent an anti-authoritarian outlook on life, as Nonconformists have tended to be critical of state authority ever since their persecution in the 17th century;
- an inclination towards individualism, as e.g. Congregationalists and Baptists practise a loose and individualistic form of church organization;
- the observance of the "British Sunday" as a day of churchgoing, prayer, and rest. However, since 1994 shops are allowed to open every Sunday for a maximum of 6 hours;
- excessive prudishness and righteousness in the Victorian Age, qualities that developed from the ideal of a virtuous life and the condemnation of personal pleasure and idleness;
- social reform and legislation in 19th century Britain. By placing stress on practical Christianity the Free Churches committed themselves to improve the situation of the new industrial proletariat in the cities (e.g. end of child labour, better working conditions, prison reform, schools for the poor). Apart from relief work they campaigned against slavery in Britain and the colonies. Slavery was abolished in 1833;
- value of hard work, leading to material prosperity.

The Puritan heritage of the Free Churches has had a profound influence on British social and cultural life.

Roman Catholics

After the Reformation the Catholic minority were denied many civil rights. The so-called Penal Laws, for example, removed their right to vote and excluded them from public office and from university education. In the late 18th and early 19th centuries a process of Catholic emancipation started in Great Britain and Ireland. This finally resulted in the Catholic Relief Act of 1829, which marked the end of all major restrictions. Since the mid-19th century there has been a revival of Catholicism (**Oxford Movement**), but the monarch is still not allowed to be a Catholic. The only part of the United Kingdom where religion is still a cause of hostility and unrest is Northern Ireland (→ pp. 192 ff).

For a long time Catholics were disadvantaged in Britain. Since the 19th century, however, they have regained all major civil rights.

Non-Christian Religious Communities

Overseas immigration after WW II has strongly increased non-Christian beliefs in Britain.

Since the 1950s Britain has not only developed into a multiracial nation, but also one with many religions. Immigration from Asian and Black African countries has resulted in a variety of non-Christian beliefs. Over the last decade adult membership of Trinitarian churches has fallen by 16%, whereas the number of Muslims and Sikhs has more than doubled. Britain's Muslim minority has been involved in major issues such as the Salman Rushdie affair, arguments about Islamic schools, the Gulf War (1991), and international terrorism (2001). In 2000 there were over 1,000 mosques in the UK.

Current Religious Issues in Britain

Current religious issues concern e.g. the rapidly declining church membership and attendance, the close relationship of Church and State in Britain and the political and charitable commitment of religious organizations.

- **Decline in membership and church attendance** in all traditional religious communities, especially in the Anglican Church, reflecting a generally declining influence of Church on society.
- Concern about a sufficient **supply of young clergymen** in the Anglican Church.
- The **ordination of women** had been discussed since 1975. In 1992 the General Synod agreed to admit women to the ministry and in 2015 the first female bishop of the Anglican Church was consecrated.
- The **relationship of Church and State** is another pressing question for Anglicanism. Some members favour a complete separation of Church and State, as Parliament (which includes also non-Anglican MPs) decides about Church legislation.
- The British Catholics are split over the Pope's view of birth control and celibacy.
- Church influence on **Northern Irish politics** and school education is definitely the most urgent problem to be solved.
- Significant growth of **youth sects** since the 1970s poses a great problem for the traditional Churches.
- The **Church and the bomb**: the Campaign for Nuclear Disarmament (CND) is supported by a substantial number of church members and ministers, especially from the Free Churches, which have passed anti-arms resolutions.
- There is a growing tendency towards cooperation among the churches. The council of "Churches together" coordinates the work of its 32 member churches in such areas as church life, missionary work, and inter-faith contacts. In 1999 the Church of England and the Methodist Church began formal discussions on a move towards unity.
- The churches are increasingly playing an active, often controversial role in British life. Many comment directly on social problems e.g. homelessness, poverty, drugs, and AIDS. Many are active in social issues e.g. helping drug addicts and the homeless.

celibacy: the state of being unmarried, esp. as the result of a religious promise *(Zölibat, Ehelosigkeit)*

7.2 Religion in the USA

The Early Settlers

The break between Catholicism and Protestantism and the lack of internal unity of the Reformation provided America with the most influential group of religious immigrants to shape the nation up to the present. Suffering from intolerance and persecution, religious dissenters of all shades emigrated to the New World **in search of religious and political freedom.**

In the 17th century different religious groups of dissenters emigrated from Britain to the New World in search of religious and political freedom.

From 1620 onwards Separatist Pilgrims (→ pp. 59, 66, 149, 159), Puritans (→ pp. 59, 146 f, 159), Roman Catholics, and Quakers settled the eastern coast of North America. Puritanism was to become the dominant spiritual force during the colonial period. The new immigrant society brought forth some of **the basic principles of modern America:**

- Rise of **self-government and democratic principles** derived from the Puritan congregations and "covenants".
- 1620: Mayflower Compact; 1639: "Fundamental Orders" of Connecticut (the first written constitution in North America).
- Establishment of **religious freedom** and tolerance by Baptists (Rhode Island), Catholics (Maryland), and Quakers (Pennsylvania).
- **Separation of Church and State** to safeguard true religious freedom was practised by the Baptists of Rhode Island.
- **Social and humanitarian commitment** developed early: German Mennonites and English Quakers from Pennsylvania drafted "The First Vote against Slavery" in 1688, a document that initiated the abolitionist movement (→ p. 66).

They established basic values of modern America such as the democratic principle of self-government (Mayflower Compact) or the idea of religious freedom.

to draft: *entwerfen, verfassen*

The Puritan Heritage

Of particular importance for the development of the United States was **Calvinism** with its **values of prayer and prosperity, work and wealth.**

- Founded by a pious people, America has developed into a country where religion is a much more important factor than in other countries.
- Even today, America is a predominantly **Protestant country** as a large percentage of the upper and middle classes are Protestant. Although the middle class in America today is diverse, WASPs (→ pp. 33, 74) have always had great influence in American society.
- The concept of America as a country that has received God's special blessing shows how **religion and patriotism** are interlinked in what many regard to be a "national religion". This has its origin in the notion of America as the "promised land" where God had led his "chosen people" (the Puritan settlers).

The impact of the early Puritan settlers can still be felt today: America has become a largely Protestant country with WASPs playing an important part. The concept of a "national religion" and the Calvinistic work ethic have shaped the nation.

- Some scholars believe that the economic ideal of **material success** in US society derives from Calvinism. According to Calvinistic doctrine, material wealth is interpreted as proof of God's favour and as a sign of being elected by God. Others believe that this success is not related to religious doctrine, but to the basic political and economic principles of America, such as free enterprise and the freedom of the individual. It is important to state that the Protestant work ethic influenced members of practically all the many religious groups in America.
- The **Protestant work ethic**: material success is achieved through the virtues of hard work, thrift and self-discipline. These virtues, which encourage the individual to save and to invest money instead of spending it on personal pleasures, are considered to have influenced the development of industrial growth and business life in America.
- Material gain was not considered as an aim in itself, but was to be given away to help others and, as a sign of gratitude, was also to be used to support **charities and public endowments**. This idea was taken up by 19th century Protestantism, for example the Rockefeller Foundation (→ pp. 89, 103).

Development of Religious Life

Historical overview of religious life in America

1740s	The **First Great Awakening**, an evangelical "revival" movement, influenced by German Pietism and British Methodism and directed against 18th century **deism** and rationalism.
1791	The **First Amendment to the Constitution** guaranteed free practice of religion and complete separation of Church and State.
1800	The **Second Great Awakening**, a nationwide movement, renewed religious activity. Characteristic of it were great open-air religious services (camp-meetings) held in a highly emotional atmosphere and resulting in numerous conversions.
1830	Foundation of the **Latter-Day Saints (Mormons)**, the biggest religious group of American origin. Exodus to Utah and founding of Salt Lake City in 1847.
1880s	The arrival of growing numbers of non-Protestant groups, in particular Catholics and Jews, resulted in a **triple melting pot** determined by religious affiliation.
1920–33	**Prohibition Laws**: struggle for temperance by leading Protestant Churches resulted in nationwide prohibition.
1950	Foundation of the **National Council of the Churches of Christ** in the USA promoted **ecumenism** among Protestant denominations.
1960s	Strong commitment of the **Black Churches** to the **Civil Rights Movement**.

temperance: total avoidance of alcoholic drinks *(Alkoholabstinenz)*

1960 – 2000s	Increase of **other world religions**: adherents of Islam, Buddhism and Hinduism reflect recent immigration from Asian countries or conversion of Blacks to Islam. **Tensions within the denominations** about the stance of the Church on political issues (e.g. Communism, Vietnam War, US policy in Central America), about abortion, school prayer, environmental protection, human sexuality, race relations, and the ordination of women.

The United States is a country of unparalleled religious diversity. Now-adays there are more than 250 religious bodies. Though smaller in numbers, other denominational groups have acquired importance in the US such as the **Disciples of Christ**, the **Seventh-Day Adventists**, **Jehovah's Witnesses**, and **Christian Science** (which publishes *The Christian Science Monitor*, a newspaper of international importance), the **Quakers** and the **Amish People**. Apart from the latter two, all these religious groups were founded in America.

The USA is a country of unprecedented religious diversity, but only few religious groups are of American origin.

General Characteristics of Religious Communities

Church Adherence in the USA (2016)

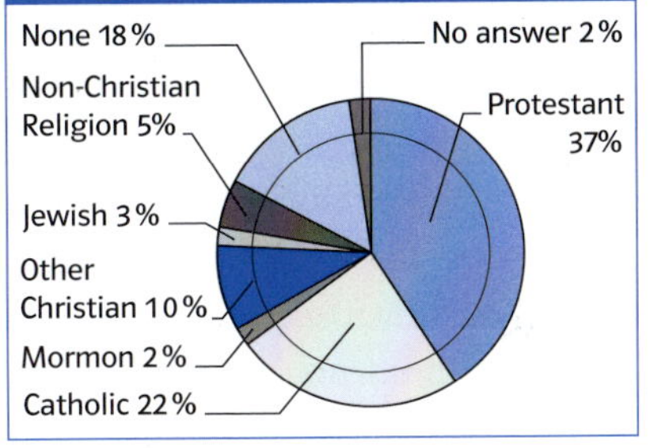

Gallup

- Religious communities are independent and are supported by voluntary contributions from their members.
- Members of a congregation are normally from the same social class. Churches reflect black and white neighbourhoods. Black Churches normally form an organic whole of black members, but integration has been achieved in a significant number of congregations.
- The church is not only a place of worship but often the centre of social activities. The reasons for this particular aspect are historical: the traditional high mobility of the American population and the absence of a historic town or village centre, where community life could take place, have made the church a meeting place to cultivate friendship with neighbours and other church members. Also ethnic and language considerations led many immigrants to group themselves into congregations where not only the faith is practised and cultivated but also "old country" traditions are enjoyed.
- The separation of Church and State prevents the giving of formal religious instruction in public schools. Therefore, Sunday Schools play an important part in the religious education of children.

Due to the strict separation of Church and State, religious communities are financially supported by their members. Other characteristics are that they are the centre of social activities and that they stress practical Christianity.

- Application of Christian religion to practical situations, stress on practical tasks to help the neighbour, serve the community, the society or even the nation.
- Continuously growing religious diversity, but growth of non-religious people in the 2000s and 2010s (more than 15%).
- Decrease in membership of main-line liberal religious bodies and increase in membership of conservative denominations or extreme religious fringe groups.
- Growing importance of sects. Today, more and more sects are not only of spiritual importance, but also show a strong interest in the economic and political situation of America, such as the Scientology Church.
- There seems to be a trend towards the opening of church-related schools, especially for primary, secondary and senior high children.

fringe group: *Randgruppe*

"Return to Religion"

Present-day religious America is marked by the retreat of main-line liberal Protestantism and the growth of religious fundamentalism.

Fundamentalism is a conservative religious and political movement. It is characterized by a belief in the strict interpretation of the Bible and the importance attached to traditional moral values.

Contemporary America presents us with two conflicting religious currents, dividing the country morally and culturally. **Main-line liberal Protestantism**, particularly active in the 1960s (Civil Rights Movement, Vietnam War protests, Feminist Movement), focuses, in general, on social and racial justice, peaceful coexistence, the ecumenical movement, and strict separation of Church and State in educational affairs (no religious instruction and prescribed prayer in public schools). Since the 1970s, the strength of this liberal trend in religion has been declining. It was superseded by a resurgence of **fundamentalism**. This "religious revival" is characterized by:

- a literal interpretation of the Bible;
- the resurgence of the religious Right;
- strong anti-communism;
- a struggle against the "permissive society", against abortion, premarital sex, the Feminist Movement, pornography and against the acceptance of homosexuality as a permissible lifestyle;
- support of school prayer and religious instruction as a subject in schools, strong opposition against Darwin's evolution theory and the attempt to replace it by teaching creationism in the school curricula;
- emphasis on personal experience of religious conversion, on self-examination and inner religious conflict.

to supersede: to replace

resurgence: *Wiederaufleben*

permissive society: *tabufreie Gesellschaft*

premarital: before marriage

The Electronic Church

The Electronic Church is a particular phenomenon of contemporary religious life in America. The 70s and 80s saw the development of many religious programmes quite independent of any church body. Many of these programmes which are evangelical or fundamentalist in tone, have used radio and TV very effectively not only to present "the message", but also to entertain. The techniques of the entertainment industry with music, staging, lighting etc have been used to capture the interest of viewers. Very often these televangelists make strong appeals for financial support through donations and the sale of books.

Electronic Church: church on television

televangelist: preacher on TV

The Electronic Church plays an important part in contemporary religious life. It uses radio and television to spread its fundamentalist message and to entertain the audience.

In 2000 the American religious scene shows two strong trends: extremely high religious affiliation rates and an ever more pluralistic religious composition. Liberal progressive churches are declining while conservative churches, for example Assemblies of God and Pentecostal Church of God, are growing. This tendency towards conservatism mirrors the rise of traditional values in America as a whole.

The Sept 11, 2001 (→ pp. 108, 184) attacks on New York and Washington led to a new wave of religious patriotism, a "national religion" documented by flags and flag-waving during the funerals and memorial services of the more than 3,000 victims. The result of the 2004 Presidential Election showed a similar picture: Bush's doctrine of the three Fs – Family, Faith, and Flag – proved to be very successful among frequent churchgoers, especially among fundamentalist Christian groups. Bush won 79% of their 26,5 million votes. The Evangelicals' concern for "moral values" on issues such as abortion, same-sex marriage, and stem-cell research was one of the key issues of the election and assisted G. W. Bush to his victory.

Contemporary America shows a rise of traditional values: a new religious patriotism developed after 9/11. Similarly G.W. Bush's re-election in 2004 reflected Fundamentalist concern for "moral values".

Religion in Britain

The Anglican Church

- is the "established" (official) Church of England which dates from the English Reformation (16th century).
- Its secular head is the Sovereign, its religious head the Archbishop of Canterbury.
- It combines Catholic and Protestant elements.
- It is not supported by the State (e.g. through a church tax), but finances itself from land property and private donations.
- The Lords Spiritual (the two archbishops and 24 bishops) are members of the House of Lords.

Other Christian denominations

- The Church of Scotland ("Kirk") is an established Presbyterian Church; it rejects the episcopal form of government and replaces it with a more democratic government by elders.
- The Free Churches (Dissenters/Nonconformists) are Protestant churches that did not conform with the English Reformation; they derive from the Puritans who separated from the Church of England.
- Roman Catholics were first discriminated against by anti-Catholic laws; since the 19th century, however, Catholicism has been on the increase in Britain.

Westminster Abbey, London

Religion in the USA

The Early Settlers and their Heritage

- Suffering from intolerance and persecution religious British dissenters (Separatist Pilgrims, Puritans) fled to the New World in search of religious and political freedom.
- Puritanism became the dominant spiritual force and brought fourth some of the basic principles of modern America: rise of self-government and of democratic principles (Constitution), establishment of religious freedom (Bill of Rights), separation of Church and State.
- Calvinism with its values of prayer and prosperity, work and wealth has shaped America.
- America was considered to be the "promised land" where God had led his "chosen people" (close link of patriotism and religion; concept of a "national religion").

Characteristics of American Churches

- Protestants, Catholics and Jews are the major religious communities.
- There is an unparalleled religious diversity in the country.
- Religious communities are independent from the State and are supported by voluntary contributions from their members.
- As formal religious instruction is not given in public schools, Sunday schools play an important part in the religious education of children. The church is often also a place of social activities, a centre of community life.
- Decrease in membership of main-line liberal bodies; increase in membership of conservative groups or extreme religious fringe groups and growing influence of sects.

Fundamentalism

Since the 1970s a "return to religion" can be observed.

- It is based on a literal interpretation of the Bible, strong anti-communism, a struggle against the "permissive society" and against Darwin's evolution theory.
- It supports family life, school prayer, religious instruction as a subject in schools, and teaching of creationism in the school curricula.
- It is characterized by evangelical or fundamentalist programmes on TV (Electronic Church) with emphasis on entertainment and strong appeal for financial support (business).

Making of the Empire (1497 – 1583)

- exploration and discovery
- establishment of trading posts
- emigration and settlement

1607: Jamestown (Virginia) first permanent settlement

"First British Empire" (1607 – 1783)

- West Indies
- Canada
- Bengal (India)
- North America

1783: loss of the 13 American colonies

1497 – 1583 | **1607 – 1783**

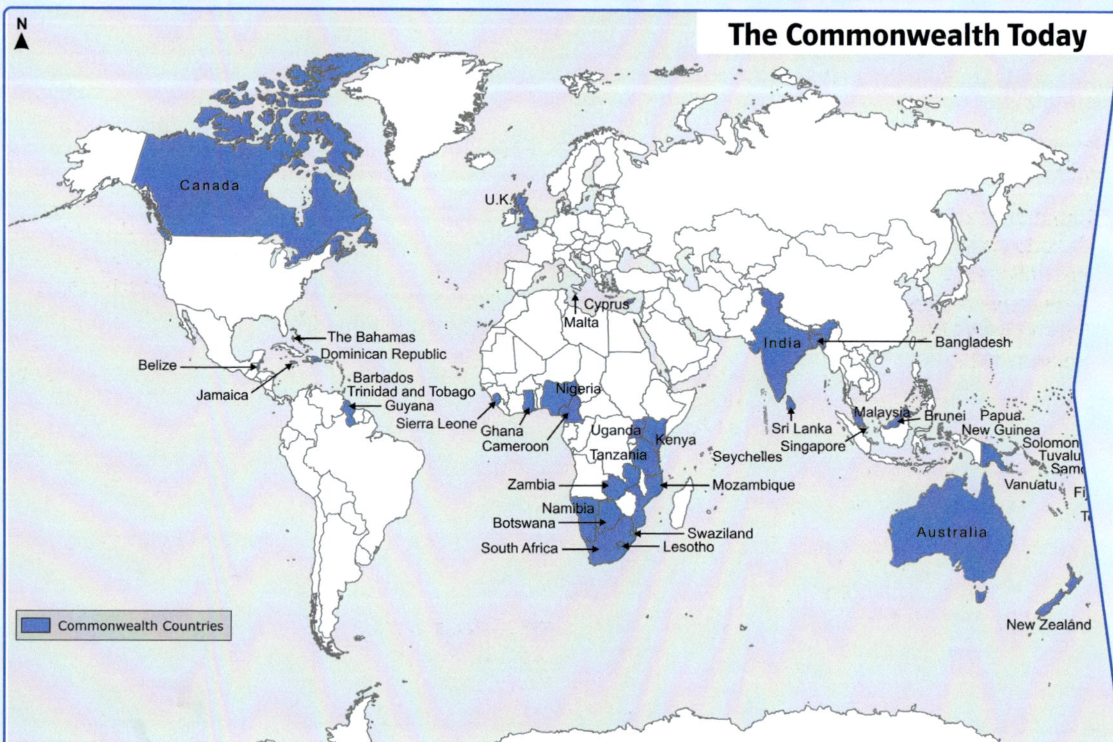

8 British Empire and the Commonwealth

1783 – 1918/45

"Second British Empire" (1783 – 1918/45)

- Cape Colony (1795) / Union of South Africa (1902)
- Australia (1813)
- British Indian Empire (1858 – 1945)

1876: Queen Victoria was crowned Empress of India.

From Empire to Commonwealth

Development in the "white" colonies

"Dominion status" for
- Canada **(1867)**
- Australia **(1900)**
- New Zealand **(1900)**
- South Africa **(1910)**
- Ireland **(1922)**

1931: Statute of Westminster replaces "Empire" by **"British Commonwealth of Nations"**

1945 – 1997

Decolonization and decline of the British Empire (1945 – 1997)

development in African and Asian countries: process of decolonization after WW II

First colonies to become independent:
- in Asia: India **(1947)**
- in Africa: Ghana **(1957)**

end of empire:
handover of Hong Kong to China **(1997)**

1950s: "New Commonwealth" members: recently decolonized, non-white countries

1951: official name **"Commonwealth of Nations"**

today

Legacy

15 British Overseas Territories (e.g. Gibraltar, Falklands)

The Commonwealth of Nations today

a voluntary association of 52 independent sovereign states, most of which are former British colonies

8 British Empire and the Commonwealth

IN BRIEF

- The British Empire was the largest empire in history.
- The First British Empire ended with the American War of Independence. It was replaced by the Victorian Empire.
- In the 19th century Britain pursued a policy of imperialism.
- The development from Empire to Commonwealth first started in the "white" colonies at the end of the 19th century.
- Development of independent status took place in three major stages: crown colony – self-governing colony – dominion.
- The Commonwealth of Nations today is a voluntary association of 52 independent countries.

The Making of the British Empire (→ p. 169)

The British colonial Empire was the largest empire in human history.

peak: the highest point of a development

The **British Empire** was the largest colonial empire in history. At the peak of colonization, at the beginning of the 20th century, it comprised nearly one fifth of the land surface and one quarter of the world's population. It has shaped the world of today, insofar as North America and Australia have become white English-speaking continents, and large parts of Africa and Asia mirror a strong British impact in their culture and institutions.

With the discovery of America a struggle for supremacy among European powers developed.

Baltic: Baltic Sea *(Ostsee)*

With the **discovery of the American continent**, the cultural and economic leadership of the Mediterranean countries and the northern states centred around the Baltic came to an end. The future lay in the hands of those countries whose sea routes faced the New World. In the 16th century, therefore, a struggle began between Spain, Portugal, Holland, France, and England for commercial and naval supremacy. England was the last to join the colonial powers, but about a century later it outdid its rivals and became the most important colonizing country. The reason for this was that, in contrast to Britain, its main European rivals, Spain and France, were always divided between a policy of colonial extension and a policy of European conquest.

Britain's colonial interests were basically economic.

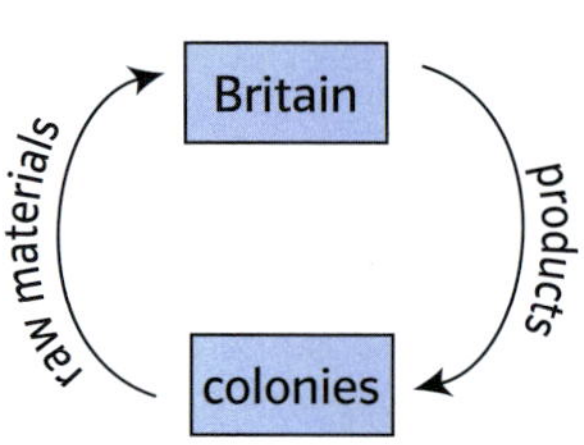

British colonialism from the 16th to the 19th century basically pursued **economic interests**. England's main aim was self-sufficiency, i.e. economic independence. Colonies were sought that would provide the country with precious metals, raw materials, and convenient markets, where Britain could sell her manufactured products.

The shaping of the British Empire proceeded in **three major stages**. England's large sea-going community provided the Crown with **explorers**, adventurers, and pirates that paved the way for the Empire.

The foundation of the Empire proceeded in three stages:

- exploration and discovery
- establishment of trading posts
- emigration and settlement.

	Explorers
1497	John Cabot discovered Newfoundland (1497); Francis Drake sailed around the world (1577–1581).
1607	Sir Walter Raleigh founded Virginia, England's first permanent colony.
1770	Captain James Cook discovered Australia and New Zealand.
1618	John Hawkins engaged in slave-trade on the Gold Coast in West Africa.

Trade was the most influential motivation of colonization. It meant profits for the merchants and the enrichment of the Crown's treasures. To this end the Crown chartered trading companies which had the privilege of settling in overseas countries with land grants. Trade was soon followed by taxation and administration. The most important trading companies were:

- East India Company (1600);
- London (Virginia) Company (1606).

In the early phases of colonialism there was, with the exception of North America, no massive emigration of English colonists. Britain dominated the sea and established her trading posts along the coast, e.g. in India, without controlling the interior of the country.

Emigration to North America followed along different lines. Religious struggles in Britain, the institution of the Anglican Church as the Established Church of England in the first half of the 17th century led religious dissenters – Puritans, Catholics, and various sects – to emigrate from Britain. They sought **refuge in the New World**, where they would not be persecuted for their faith. The Pilgrim Fathers (→ pp. 59, 66, 149) settled at Plymouth (Massachusetts) in 1620, William Penn and the Quakers founded Pennsylvania (1681), and Catholics settled in Maryland (1634).

The **First British Empire** (1607–1776) consisted of scattered possessions

- in the West Indian archipelago, e.g. Jamaica, the Bahamas, the Bermudas;
- in Canada, e.g. Newfoundland, the Hudson Bay territory, and Nova Scotia;
- in India: Bengal;
- in Europe: Gibraltar.

The **First British Empire** mainly consisted of colonies in North America settled by religious groups from Britain.

These colonies were conquered in wars with France (Canada, India) and Spain (West Indies, Gibraltar) and reflect Britain's rise to maritime and commercial supremacy. The principal part of the First Empire was formed by the North American colonies, stretching along the east coast from the Canadian border to the Caribbean. The two million colonists lived in three kinds of territories that were politically disunited:

- **The New England Colonies**, the territory around Boston, were populated by strict Protestants from England.
- **The Middle Colonies**, centred around New York (a former Dutch colony), attracted all kinds of European immigrants, because religious and political freedom were practised.
- **The Southern Colonies** were settled by merchants who profited from tobacco- and later from cotton-culture. The agricultural system was supported by the introduction of slave-labour. During the English Civil War (1642–1646) a great number of noblemen fled to Virginia having a strong impact on the Southern way of thinking (Aristocratic South).

to levy a tax: to charge a tax, to demand a tax

During the Seven Years' War (1756–1763), France lost all its Canadian possessions to England, but the war left England strongly indebted. Therefore, taxes had to be levied. The English colonists in America, however, did not need the protection of the mother country any more after the French were defeated. Therefore, in 1767, the colonists answered England's attempt to impose taxation on tea with the slogan "no taxation without representation" as they were not represented in Parliament. **The Boston Tea Party** in 1773 was a protest against the tea tax and led to the American War of Independence. In 1783, the Independence of the United States was acknowledged by the Treaty of Versailles and resulted in the disruption of the First British Empire.

The so-called Boston Tea Party (1773), a protest against tax, levied on the American colonists by the British mother country, led to the American **War of Independence** (1776–1783) and the break-up of the First British Empire.

After the loss of the American colonies, Britain turned towards the establishment of a new empire. The existing colonial possessions in Canada, the West Indies, and India were enlarged, and a policy of securing the sea route to India, which was to become the second pillar of the **Second British Empire** (the **Victorian Empire**), was pursued. India and the Far East exported cotton, spice, tea, and imported cloth and cotton goods, and were therefore vital for mercantile England. In the heyday of imperialism, in 1876, Queen Victoria was crowned Empress of India, just 100 years after the American Revolution. Through the acquisition of a chain of islands and ports of strategical importance (Gibraltar – Malta – Cyprus – Aden) the sea way via the Suez Canal was protected, just as St Helena, the Cape Colony, and Mauritius guarded the route round the Cape of Good Hope.

pillar: important part *(Pfeiler)*

The loss of the American colonies was followed by the foundation of the **Second** or **Victorian Empire** in the 19th century.

Its main parts were India and the Far East.

In the **19th century**, British colonialist policies, which were based on the idea that colonies were primarily markets for British goods and only of economic interest for the mother country, developed into the policy of **imperialism**. Important colonies of the **Second British Empire** were: Cape Colony (1795)/ Union of South Africa (1902), Malta (1800), Australia (1813), Singapore (1819), New Zealand (1839), Hong Kong (1841), Nigeria (1873), Suez Canal (shares) (1875), Rhodesia (1890). Statesmen like **Cecil Rhodes** or **Joseph Chamberlain** no longer saw the Empire only in terms of economic, but also of political, military and strategical advantages and as an extension of British rule over large territories. By means of conquests, diplomacy, discovery, purchase, and commerce, Britain enlarged its Empire within a century to such an extent that more than a third of Africa, the whole Indian subcontinent, and the Fifth Continent (Australia) formed part of it, or at least became spheres of British influence. Canada, Australia and New Zealand became Britain's main colonies of settlement, with an almost entirely European civilization. In Africa and Asia, merchants, administrators, generals, and Christian missionaries tried to impose Western values on the native population. The British rulers spoke of "the **white man's burden**" and mission to bring civilization to the "backward natives". Thus imperialism was also linked to the concept of racial and moral superiority of the Whites.

In the **19th century** Britain developed a policy of aggressive imperialism. It was marked by strategic territorial expansion and the doctrine of racial superiority of white people.

From Empire to Commonwealth

The decline of the British Empire was the result of a long internal evolution in the colonial territories. In Britain's colonies of settlement the change from colonial to **independent status** was in most cases achieved peacefully. In the colonies with large indigenous populations this shift was often a painful process, accompanied by conflict and rebellion.
The main causes of the disintegration of the Empire were demands for self-government and sovereignty, due to dissatisfaction with British rule, growing nationalism, and inter-racial tensions. Development of independent status proceeded generally in three major stages:

Independence of "white" colonies was, in general, peacefully achieved; in colonies with non-white populations it often caused bloodshed.

indigenous: native

The main reasons for the decline of the Empire were demands for self-government of the white settlers.

crown colony →	self-governing colony →	dominion
internal and external dependence →	internal sovereignty →	equal status, but often recognition of the Queen as Head of State

Originally all colonial possessions had the status of **"crown colonies"** that were governed by the Colonial Office in London, a department of the Foreign Office. It appointed a Governor who, assisted by an executive council, administered the colony. The Governor's power was gradually restricted by the institution of a legislative assembly that was first partly and later entirely elected by the settlers. A local government was created, parties were admitted, and responsibility was gradually handed over to the native government. The "crown colony" developed into a **"self-governing colony"** with internal sovereignty, while defence and foreign affairs were still reserved for the mother country. This type of colony finally acquired **"dominion"** status, a dominion being a completely free nation that owes loyalty to the Crown alone. First the "white colonies" (settlement colonies) were granted dominion status: Canada (1867),

The status of the "white" colonies developed in three stages:

1. crown colony,
2. self-governing colony,
3. dominion.

Australia (1900), New Zealand (1907), South Africa (1910), Ireland (1922). Today the term "Dominions" has been replaced by "Commonwealth nations" or "Commonwealth countries".

to lag behind: to develop more slowly

Development of independent status in the African and Asian colonies only started after WW II, sometimes after a long struggle.

As a result of imperialist thinking, the development towards sovereignty in colonies with a coloured population lagged behind. As the natives were only gradually initiated into British systems of democratic local government and no coloured élite had been trained to take over, the process towards self-government was delayed. Large-scale decolonization started only after World War II, when Europe lay in ruins and a wave of nationalism in the non-European world hastened national independence. This often took place before social and economic progress could provide stability for the new nations. The first Asian and African colonies to become independent were India (1947) and Ghana (1957). Since that time almost all the colonies which had formerly belonged to the British Empire have become sovereign states.

The legacy of the British Empire are 15 overseas territories which enjoy a special status.

The **remains of the British Empire** consist of a number of possessions, now commonly called **"British Overseas Territories"**. Many of them enjoy self-government, but Britain remains responsible for **defence** and **foreign affairs**. Since 2002, the inhabitants enjoy full British citizenship, with the right of abode in the UK.

Out of the 15 existing dependencies the chief ones are: Bermudas, British Antarctic Territory, Falkland Islands, Gibraltar, and St Helena. In 1997, Hong Kong, the most prosperous colony of the Second Empire, was handed back to China.

The Commonwealth (→ pp. 11, 51, 71, 171 f)

After WW I the Commonwealth countries signed the peace treaty of Versailles (1919) separately.

World War I hastened the development of the British possessions towards autonomous states. In 1914, Britain declared war on Germany for itself and the British Empire, whereas, in 1919, the Dominions signed the peace treaty of Versailles separately and achieved individual representation in the League of Nations. The **Imperial Conference** of 1926 defined the future status of the Dominions within a new union of countries:

"The Dominions are **autonomous communities** within the British Empire **equal in status**, in no way subordinate one to another in any respect of their domestic or external affairs though united by a common allegiance to the Crown, and **freely associated** as members of the British Commonwealth of Nations."

The Statute of Westminster (1931) established the independence of the Dominions.

The **Statute of Westminster** (1931) became the charter of the Dominions. It replaced the term "Empire" by "The British Commonwealth of Nations". In 1951, the word "British" was dropped and the organization's official name became the **"Commonwealth of Nations"**. This document defined the autonomy of the Dominions regarding foreign affairs and defence. Instead of Parliament the Crown became the unifying force of the different members. Later, countries which did not recognize the British Sovereign as Head of State (republics) also joined the Commonwealth. Instead they recognize the monarch as the Commonwealth's symbolic head. India set the precedent by becoming a republic. Today, all forms of government from military dictatorships to left-wing governments are part of the Commonwealth. In the Dominions of Canada, Australia and New Zealand the Queen as Head of State is represented by a Governor-General, who is appointed by the Queen on the advice of the Prime Minister of the respective country.

Since 1932, strong economic ties between Britain and the Commonwealth countries have been established, particularly through preferential tariffs for goods sold within the community. The fact that Britain managed to maintain good relations with most of her former colonies after their independence and that it replaced the Empire by a Commonwealth is generally acknowledged as a triumph of British diplomacy and foreign policy.

The economic links between Britain and the CW countries were strengthened through preferential tariffs.

The Commonwealth today is a **voluntary association** of 52 independent countries including Britain, with a combined population of almost a third of the world total, and ranging from tiny islands to a whole continent. The most important **members** are: Australia, Bangladesh, Canada, India, Kenya, Malaysia, New Zealand, Pakistan, South Africa, the UK. Zimbabwe left the Commonwealth in 2003. In 2007 Pakistan was suspended from the Commonwealth because of General Musharraf's undemocratic rule of the country.

The Commonwealth today is a voluntary association of independent states.

Of the original (1926) members, Australia, Britain, Canada, and New Zealand have been members throughout; South Africa was expelled in 1961 over apartheid, but rejoined in 1994; the Irish Republic withdrew on gaining independence in 1949; and Newfoundland became part of Canada. Pakistan joined in 1947, withdrew in 1972 when it was partitioned and Bangladesh was created, then rejoined in 1989. In 1999 and 2000 respectively Pakistan and Fiji Islands were suspended from the councils of the Commonwealth following military coups. Cameroon (mainly French-speaking) and Mozambique (Portuguese-speaking) are the only members that are not former British colonies.

to partition: to divide

to suspend: *zeitweilig ausschließen*

The **principles** underlying the Commonwealth are laid down in the **Harare Commonwealth Declaration** (1991), and include:

- democracy based on the British parliamentary system;
- the rule of law based on English Common Law;
- good government based on a civil service free of corruption;
- human rights and social justice;
- economic links, including aid for developing countries;
- common language, culture and traditions;
- sporting links such as the Commonwealth Games and cricket.

The Harare CW Declaration (1991) committed the CW to the principles of e.g. democracy, law, human rights and economic development.

The CW Secretariat in London is the central institution of the Commonwealth of Nations.

The **Commonwealth Secretariat** in London financed by the member states is the centre of coordination and communication. It prepares the meetings of the member states that take place every two years, and administers the Commonwealth Fund for Technical Cooperation.

Politically the CW has not always come up to expectations. In a number of international conflicts it has proved to be powerless.

Since the end of World War II, the Commonwealth has been involved in helping to smooth the path of the former British colonies towards independence (e. g. Zimbabwe 1980) and to promote racial equality (South Africa). In several important conflicts it has, however, been powerless to make its intervention effective; the civil-war nature of such conflicts makes them difficult to prevent or solve:

- 1947 Indian subcontinent partitioned, India-Pakistan wars
- 1967 Civil war in Nigeria (Biafra)
- 1967 Kenya drives out its Asian minority
- 1971 Partition of Pakistan, creation of Bangladesh
- 1975 Partition of Cyprus

About a century after the process of decolonization started in the British Empire it is almost completed, but much remains to be done to deepen and strengthen the principles of the Harare Declaration as applied in these diverse parts of the world. The ultimate test of the **effectiveness** of the Commonwealth lies ahead, in the 21st century, as the young independent states of the former British Empire mature.

British Empire and the Commonwealth

The British Empire

- was the largest colonial empire in history; at its peak it comprised ⅕ of the land surface and ¼ of the world's population. The making of the Empire proceeded in three major stages: discovery → trading posts → settlement.
- British colonialism pursued economic interests.

The First Empire (1607–1776)

- consisted of possessions in the West Indies, Canada, India, and especially of the North American colonies along the east coast;
- came to an end with the American War of Independence (1776–1783).

The Victorian Empire (The Second British Empire)

- consisted mainly of the Indian subcontinent, of more than a third of Africa, Australia, and many scattered possessions of strategic importance.
- British colonialist policies changed into a policy of imperialism as political and military advantages became more important than economic ones.

From Empire to Commonwealth

- Development of independent status in three stages: crown colony → self-governing colony → dominion (autonomous, but Queen often remains Head of State);
- demands for self-government by settlers of European descent (Canada, Australia, New Zealand);
- dissatisfaction with British rule (India);
- growing nationalism (black African colonies).

The Statute of Westminster (1931) became the charter of the Dominions replacing the term "Empire" by "British Commonwealth of Nations".

The Commonwealth Today

- is a voluntary association of 52 independent countries with a a population of almost ⅓ of the world's total.
- Its principles are: democracy based on the British parliamentary system, recognition of human rights and social justice, economic and sporting links.
- The Queen is recognized as the symbolic Head of the Commonwealth whereas 16 countries recognize the Queen as their Head of State.

The Overseas Territories

The remains of the British Empire consist of a number of overseas possessions. Its most important territories are the Falklands and Gibraltar; in 1997, Hong Kong was handed back to China.

OVERVIEW

1951 — Foundation of the **ECSC** (European Coal and Steel Community); member states: France, Germany, Italy, Benelux countries

1957 — Foundation of the **EEC** (European Economic Community) by the above mentioned six member states; creation of a common market for a free exchange of goods

1961 — **Britain's first application** for membership **vetoed** by the French President de Gaulle

1967 — Creation of the **EC** (European Community

1973 — Accession of **Denmark**, **Ireland** and the **United Kingdom** to the European Community

1975 — UK referendum on **membership of the EC confirmed** by a two- thirds majority

1981 — Accession of **Greece** as the tenth mem- ber state

1986 — Accession of **Portugal** and **Spain** to the EC

1992 — Signing of the **Maastricht Treaty** on the European Union (EU) as a single market

9 Britain and Europe

1995 – Accession of **Austria**, **Sweden** and **Finland** (15 member states)

1999 – Introduction of the single currency, the **Euro**, in 11 of 15 member states for financial transactions. Britain does not join the Euro area.

2002 – Replacement of national currencies by **Euro banknotes and coins**

2004 – Enlargement of the EU by 10 new member states: **Cyprus, the Czech Republic, Estonia, Hungary, Latvia, Lithuania, Malta, Poland, Slovakia, Slovenia**

2005 – **Failure** of ratifiying a **European Constitution**

2007 – Accession of **Bulgaria** and **Romania**. The EU consists of 27 member-states with a total population of about 487 million.

2009 – **Lisbon Treaty:** foundation of a more democratic and efficient EU

2010 – **European debt crisis**

2016 – **Brexit**

IN BRIEF

9 Britain and Europe

- Traditionally Britain's foreign policy was based on the principles of the "balance of power" and "splendid isolation".
- After World War II Britain had to redefine its political, military and economic role in the world.
- In the post-war years European statesmen embarked on a policy of reconciliation which, in 1957, led to the creation of the European Economic Community (EEC).
- Because of its close ties with the Commonwealth countries Britain did not join the EEC in the beginning.
- However, when trade with the CW countries declined, Britain became a member in 1973.
- The EEC has developed into the European Union (EU) of today, consisting of 28 member states with a population of over 500 million (2014).
- Britain has turned out to be a difficult EU member supporting the concept of economic cooperation of independent nations rather than the idea of a political union.

Guidelines of British Foreign Policy up to 1945

For many centuries Britain pursued a policy of the **"balance of power"** with regard to its European rivals in order to protect the sea ways to its overseas possessions.

A second principle was that of the **"splendid isolation"**, a policy of non-interference in European affairs.

aloofness: If a person stays aloof from something, he / she does not get involved in it.

to be at stake: *auf dem Spiel stehen*

After its vain attempts to conquer France in the 15th century, Britain gave up its continental ambitions and established new guidelines for foreign affairs.

In the face of the great continental forces of Spain and France Britain adopted the **"balance of power"**, both for its own security and for the protection of the sea ways to its new overseas possessions. The concept of the "balance of power" describes a state of equilibrium in which no nation is able to dominate others. Therefore, it was of vital importance for Britain to prevent any European nation from dominating the European mainland, in particular the Channel. Britain thus fought against Spain in the 17th century, against the France of Louis XIV and Napoleon in the 18th and 19th centuries, and against the German Empire and Nazi Germany in the 20th century.

On the other hand, Britain pursued a policy of detachment and aloofness from European affairs, as long as its own interests were not at stake. This **"splendid isolation"** regarding the European mainland simultaneously helped to strengthen Britain's links with the United States, and secured Britain US support in the two World Wars (→ p. 186).

One of the fundamental principles of British policy was to prevent the rise of any seapower equal or superior to its own. Therefore, when at the end of the 19th century the German Empire built up a rival fleet, the policy of European isolationism was abandoned regarding new systems of far-reaching arms, of aircraft and submarines and was replaced by a **system of alliances** with France and Russia. In doing so Britain created an equilibrium (a "balance of power") against Germany, the strongest military power on the Continent. Again in 1940, when Britain faced a possible German invasion, danger was averted with the help of powerful allies (e.g. the United States, the Dominions, the USSR) and the "Third Reich" defeated. But World War II meant the end of Britain's dominant position in the world and of its traditional foreign policy.

In the 20th century this principle was replaced by a **system of alliances** with regard to a strong rival (Germany) that threatened Britain's naval supremacy.

to avert: *abwenden*

Results of World War II

For many centuries Europe had dominated the world. It had been the political, economic and cultural centre of the Western hemisphere, and major scientific and technological revolutions had originated there. Moreover, various European nations had created colonial empires, so that, in 1939, the Europeans were in possession of more than a third of the world's land and sea area.
World War II, however, put an end to this supremacy:

- The war caused Europe's total breakdown.
- Millions of people died.
- A high percentage of Europe's economic power was destroyed.
- Europe lost its important position in the world.
- 1945 marked the end of the colonial empires.

At the same time, the post-war period saw the rise of the two superpowers, the United States and the USSR. The most important result of World War II was the **ideological and political partition of the "Old Continent"** into an eastern and a western part, divided by the "Iron Curtain". The Soviets established a communist Eastern bloc and the US promoted political stability in the Western European countries through substantial economic aid.

World War II put an end to European dominance in the world and left Europe a destroyed continent.

Political power shifted to the USA and the USSR, which divided Europe into an eastern and a western bloc.

Post-war Britain

In the same way Britain found itself in a completely new position after World War II. For centuries it had been the leading nation of the world. It had created the greatest empire the world had ever seen, and its navy had "ruled the seas". However, the war put an end to all this:

- Britain had lost its leading position as a world power to the United States and the USSR.
- Post-war Britain was war-ravaged, economically weak, and deeply indebted to the United States. The Americans had supported Britain with substantial economic aid and war-material during the war.
- From 1947 onwards the British Empire (→ pp. 158 ff) dissolved, as more and more dependent territories claimed their right to self-determination. This further diminished Britain's influence in the world.

After WW II Britain lost its dominant position in the world.

to ravage: to ruin, to destroy

Britain was economically weak and indebted, and the British Empire broke up.

- Britain's navy was only third in rank among the world's navies.
- In the age of long-distance weapons, Britain's position as an island was no longer an advantage. Britain had become as vulnerable to attacks as any other country. Within a short period Britain had lost economic, political and military leadership of the world.

Britain's Post-War Foreign Policy

In the post-war years European statesmen started a new policy of reconciliation in order to establish lasting peace in Europe.

hereditary enmity: *Erbfeindschaft*

In the post-war years, European statesmen started to reconsider their traditional nationalist policies, and seek new supranational institutions to overcome the hereditary enmity among many European peoples. They wished to create lasting peace in Europe. As a result various military, political and economic organizations were forged to promote European integration.

Britain and the Military Integration of Europe

In 1949, **NATO** was founded to deter potential Soviet aggression. Britain joined this military pact.

to deter: to discourage *(abschrecken, abhalten)*

In 1949, the **North Atlantic Treaty Organization** (NATO) was founded, consisting of the United States, Canada and most Western European states, among them Great Britain. This Atlantic military alliance was created in the days of the Cold War and aimed to deter potential Soviet aggression by providing collective defence for its member states. A remarkable fact was that this defensive alliance included the USA and Canada, two non-European states, to maintain or to restore the balance of military power against the Soviet Union and its allies. From that time on, Western Europe was militarily dependent on the US. Britain, too, realized that it could not refrain from any new alliance to keep up the "balance of power". Britain's own weakened military power and the rise of the USSR as the strongest continental power made it abandon its policy of non-interference in European affairs. It was even prepared to station troops on the Continent, a hitherto unparalleled British military commitment in Europe.

Britain and the Political Integration of Europe

In 1949 the Council of Europe (the forerunner of the European Parliament) was created by Western European states including Britain.

to foster: to promote

deliberative: consultative

Likewise in 1949, the Council of Europe was founded by ten Western European states, including Great Britain, to promote political integration in Europe. In 1950, however, British national reservations prevented the creation of a "European Union" favoured by the "federalists". Britain preferred the ideal of an alliance of independent nations. In 1958, the Council developed into the European Parliament (EP). The assembly discusses social, educational, environmental and legal problems, and fosters inter-governmental cooperation. It tries to give new impulses to a European Union, but so far the EP has only a deliberative function. The decisions made in Strasbourg have no binding force on the member states and are therefore only of symbolic value.

The European Parliament is directly elected every five years by the people in member states. The result of the European Parliament elections in 2014, in which about 34% of the British electorate voted, reflected the sceptical attitude of the British people. The Eurosceptic UK Independence Party (UKIP), which supports the withdrawal of Britain from the EU, made big gains with 24 MEPs.

The result of the 2014 elections for the European Parliament reflected Britain's Eurosceptic attitude.

Britain's Economic Development

Although geographically a European country, Britain had economically refrained from European affairs for more than three centuries. Instead it had steered its own course and established close transatlantic trading links, at first with its colonial possessions and later, when the colonies were transformed into dominions, with the Commonwealth. Therefore, Britain's attitude towards economic integration in Western Europe was completely negative. It would not and could not contract out of its responsibilities and therefore refused to join a new supranational economic organization in Europe in the 1950s.

In the post-war years Britain did not take part in the economic integration of Western Europe, but strengthened its trading links with other Commonwealth countries.

to contract out of sth.: *sich einer Sache entziehen*

Even after World War II, Britain pursued its traditional policy and established the **"New Commonwealth"** (→ p. 157) (1948), which now also included African and Asian members. The creation of this new multi-ethnic community, which was supposed to compensate for the loss of the Second Empire, was met with high hopes for it seemed attractive to develop the existing Commonwealth markets by introducing a system of preferential tariffs.

Economically, the Commonwealth did not live up to British expectations. Between the 1950s and 1970s the member states drifted apart and trade stagnated or even diminished. The traditional principle of economic complementarity, which had been the basis of British trade with the Commonwealth for so long, disappeared:

complementarity: *gegenseitige Ergänzung*

- The Commonwealth countries found new trading partners like the United States and Japan, who were technologically more advanced than Britain.
- After the war, Britain did not modernize its industries (→ p. 96), so with its outdated industrial plants it could not compete with other industrial nations.
- The long distances between the member states proved to be a handicap, especially at a time of increasing energy problems and rising oil prices.

Between 1960 and 1970, the import and export rates of British trade with Commonwealth countries declined sharply. Simultaneously, trade with European countries (EC and EFTA) rose considerably. Thus, by 1970, **Britain's membership of the EC** seemed the only logical consequence of this reorientation of Commonwealth trade.

As the trading links with the CW countries declined in the 1950s and 60s, Britain finally joined the EC in 1973.

Major steps towards economic integration	
1950	The French foreign minister Robert Schuman outlined the aims of a plan to join the coal and steel industries of France and Germany to overcome the traditional antagonism of these two countries.
1952	Foundation of the European Coal and Steel Community (ECSC) by France, Germany, Italy, and the Benelux countries.
1957	Foundation of the European Economic Community by the above-mentioned six member states. The EEC aimed at creating a common market which should provide for the free exchange of industrial and agricultural goods. The idea of the EEC was to bring the member states more closely together through cooperation, and eventually to form a political union.
1961	Britain applied for membership to the EEC, but was refused admission by the French President de Gaulle who feared that American influence in Europe would increase through Britain's entry, and who opposed special conditions for Britain's Commonwealth trade.
1967	The European Community (EC) was created, consisting of e.g. the EEC, the ECSC, the European Parliament, and the Council of Ministers.
1973	After three years of negotiations, Britain, together with Denmark and Ireland, joined the EC.
1975	A nationwide referendum confirmed British membership with a two-thirds majority.
1992	Signing of the Treaty on European Union in Maastricht.
1994	Acknowledgement of the European Economic Area.
1999	Introduction of the Euro in 11 of the 15 member states of the EU. Britain did not join. The European Central Bank (ECB) in Frankfurt assumed responsibility for the monetary policy of the Euro area.
2002	Euro banknotes and coins were put into circulation.
2009	The Treaty of Lisbon, ratified by each of the EU's 27 members, introduced new powers for the European Parliament, a European Council President and the removal of national vetoes in many policy areas.
2010 onw.	European debt crisis due to rising government deficits in the so-called PIIGS states (Portugal, Italy, Ireland, Greece, Spain). The economic troubles of these nations have led to doubts about the long-term future of the Euro.
2015	Greek debt crisis and the risk of a „Grexit" (Greek exit) from the eurozone.
2016	In a nation-wide referendum the majority of British voters decide to leave the EU ("Brexit").

The European Union Today

The present-day European Union consists of 28 member states. It is the world's largest trading power, covering about a third of world trade. The extension of the EU to the East marks the end of the Cold-War division in Europe into military and economic camps.
Since its entry Britain has proved to be a **difficult EU-member**. In the 1980s, the British Prime Minister, Margaret Thatcher, repeatedly made clear that her party's objective was a European Community "of independent, sovereign states working together in cooperation". In the same way the Labour Government (1997–2010) supported this idea of a Europe consisting of independent states.

Britain has proved to be a reluctant member of the EU. British politicians have always made it clear that they prefer a community consisting of independent nations to a political union.

Brexit

Sixteen years into the 21st century, with a majority Conservative government and a nation representing every shade of opinion on the subject of the EU, from extreme eurosceptics to extreme eurofanatics, the British people were given the opportunity to make their voice heard (→ pp. 173 f).
After the 2014 European Parliament election, in which UKIP made big gains, the Conservatives became worried that they would lose the 2015 General Election if they did not make concessions to the eurosceptics. Thus Prime Minister David Cameron announced that he would seek to renegotiate the UK's relationship with the EU, followed by a referendum on Britain's membership.

An increase in anti-EU opinion in the UK led Cameron to offer a referendum with a simple In or Out choice, as a concession to eurosceptics. The government expected a clear result to stay in, and made no plans for Brexit.

The referendum was held in June 2016. A very high turnout of voters brought **a majority of 52% to 48%** in favour of leaving, with more than 17 million UK citizens rejecting EU membership.
Prime Minister Cameron immediately stepped down. The new UK government led by **Theresa May** sought to stay as close to the EU as possible while accepting the result of the referendum. Such a deal was finally agreed by the negotiators on both sides, in spite of unresolved issues such as the **Northern Irish border**, Gibraltar and fishing rights, but it seemed unlikely that the UK Parliament would ratify it. The PM reacted promptly by postponing the parliamentary vote, but then suddenly saw herself faced with a vote of no confidence by her own party, the Conservatives. May won the leadership contest, but her authority suffered as a third of her own party, who did not support her deal with the EU, voted against her (200:117).

In June 2016, more than 17 million voters formed a clear majority to leave the EU, in a show of disapproval for politics in general and Brussels in particular. Cameron resigned, and was replaced by Theresa May.

In late 2018 Prime Minister Theresa May, who did not have an overall majority in Parliament, was forced to put her draft agreement for withdrawal from the EU to a vote. With very minor amendments she tried three times to get the deal approved, and three times it was rejected.
The proposed date for the exit from the EU was postponed, with the approval of the EU but with no concessions on issues such as the Northern Ireland border

Two and a half years after the referendum there was no agreement on the Brexit question. The UK parliament and public were split three ways; the Prime Minister did not have a majority for her agreed deal with the EU negotiators, who used the Irish border problem to make things as difficult as possible for the British.

arrangements, Gibraltar and fishing rights. With a clear majority of Members of Parliament rejecting every attempt at progress, Theresa May had no choice but to resign, which she so did in July 2019. A selection of a new Prime Minister was determined by a vote amongst of all members of the Conservative party nationwide, not just by Members of Parliament.
Boris Johnson was the public's favourite, and was thus duly elected. He still did not have a majority in Parliament and he set out work very quickly in trying to meet the deadline of October 31st, 2019 for withdrawal from the EU. Proposed changes in Northern Ireland, which were seen by some MPs as risking the break-up of the UK, and a timetable for passage through Parliament not giving members enough time for debate led to a further delay, and it became clear that the only solution was a general election.
This third general election in five years, and the first in winter just before Christmas, practically amounted to another referendum on Brexit. The Conservatives were seeking to leave the EU while most of the other parties – Liberal Democrats, Scottish Nationalists, Democratic Unionists (Northern Irish), Welsh Nationalists, Greens and Independents were in favour of remaining in the EU.
In 2016 Labour had voted in Parliament to accept the result of the referendum ("leave"). Then, during the next three years, they simply opposed whatever the Conservatives supported, using the policy of "remain" as a means of stopping May and Johnson. As the previous referendum had a percentage result of 52 for leave and 48 for remain, the result might have gone either way. However, with his slogan "Get Brexit done", Boris Johnson had a much better campaign than his main rival Jeremy Corbyn, who took Labour far to the left of the political spectrum, so that Johnson's risky undertaking paid off with an overall majority of 80 seats.
The pressure was now on to fulfil Johnson's promise to the electorate to meet the latest deadline of January 31st, 2020 for withdrawal from the EU – only seven weeks after the election, but three and a half years after the referendum which started the whole process. Within days the withdrawal agreement was again put to a vote in Parliament, and this time it was accepted with a majority of 124. The withdrawal meant that, after 47 years, the UK once again became an independent sovereign state, as it had been for centuries before it joined the EC in 1973.
Britain and the EU agreed on a transition period until the end of 2020, in which all European laws would still apply. Apart from the unsolved problem of the Irish border separating Britain from the EU, the question of **fishing quota** in the North Sea and different **social and environmental standards** form further, severe obstacles in the negotiation process. Both sides blamed the other for not willing to compromise. Although the talks seemed to be at a dead end, Boris Johnson categorically excluded the option of prolonging the transition period. Instead, he began to prepare the British public for a hard **"No-deal-Brexit"**, i.e. no treaty at all between Britain and the EU, with disastrous consequences for traffic, the delivery of fresh food and medical goods oder medicine on both sides of the Channel.

We offer this page as an update pdf on our homepage, depending on political developments in GB.

Britain and Europe

Britain and Europe up to 1945

General concepts: "balance of power", "splendid isolation", and a system of alliances.

Post-war Europe

- Loss of its important position in the world;
- loss of colonial empires;
- destruction of its economic force;
- split into two parts, divided by the "Iron Curtain";
- wish for reconstruction and unity.

Post-war Britain

- had lost her leading position as a world power to the USA and the USSR;
- was economically weak and deeply indebted to the USA.
- The British Empire dissolved.

Britain's Post-war Foreign Policy

- In 1949 Britain became a member of the newly founded North Atlantic Treaty Organization (NATO) and joined the Council of Europe, but prevented the creation of a "European Union" in 1950.
- Britain did not join the EEC in 1957, but preferred her traditional economic policy with the Commonwealth countries.

Britain and the EC / EU

- In the 1960s Britain's trade with the Commonwealth countries declined sharply.
- Britain applied for membership in the EEC, but was refused admission by the French President de Gaulle who feared American influence through Britain's entry.
- It became a member of the EC in 1973, which in 1975 was confirmed by a nationwide referendum with a two-thirds majority.
- In the following decades, Britain proved to be a difficult member of the EU, fearing for the loss of its sovereignty.
- In the 1980s the British Government repeatedly made clear that Britain's aim was a European community of independent states and not a United States of Europe, as expressed by the founders of the EU.
- In 1999, Britain did not join the Euro area.

Britain and the EU Today

- The Labour Government of Tony Blair accepted the "social charter" of the EU in 1997.
- With regard to Europe Britain pursues the aim of a European Union consisting of sovereign states.
- The Government accepts that the UK will not adopt the Euro in the foreseeable future.
- In a referendum on Britain's membership in the EU in 2016 the British decided to leave the European Union.
- After very difficult negotiations Britain formally cut the ties with its European partners on 31 January 2019.

OVERVIEW

1606 – 1783 Colonial Period
1775 – 83 War of Independence

1899 "Open Door Policy" (China)

1898 – 1917 Overseas Expansion (Hawaii, Philippines, Panama, Haiti)

1904 Roosevelt Corollary to the Monroe Doctrine

1790 – 1890 Age of Isolationism

1890 – 1945 Rise to World Power

1823 Monroe Doctrine

1861 – 65 Civil War

1917 – 18 World War I

1919 League of Nations

The Apollo 11 mission was the first manned mission to land on the moon. On July 20, 1969 Neil Armstrong took "a giant leap for mankind"

1919 – 39
Between the Wars
1919 Membership of the League of Nations rejected
1930s Depression
1933 – 38 New Deal

10 The United States and the World

1941 – 45 World War II

1949 – 89 "Cold War" period

1947 Truman Doctrine

1948 Marshall Plan

1949 NATO

Europe
1990 German reunification
1991 End of the Warsaw Pact
1991 Break-up of the USSR

1945 – 1990 Leadership of the Western World

1990 → Leadership of the World

1950 – 53 Korean War

1964 – 73 Vietnam War

Middle East
1990/91 Gulf War
2001 September 11 terrorist attacks
2001 → Afghanistan War
2003 → Iraq War

The **White House** is the residence of the President of the United States (Washington D.C.)

The **Pentagon** is the headquarters of the United States Department of Defense (Virginia)

10 The United States and the World

IN BRIEF

- From independence (1783) up to 1890 the United States pursued a policy of isolation, as the young republic was concerned with domestic affairs.
- The Monroe Doctrine (1823) stated that the USA would not interfere in European affairs, but would not tolerate any new European influence in the Americas.
- Entering upon a new phase of intervention policy, the country developed between 1890 and 1945 into a world power.
- From 1945 to 1990 the USA as the leading power of the Western world and the Soviet Union, which sought to spread communism, were opposed in the "Cold War" period.
- The Truman Doctrine (1947) declared that the USA would accept its responsibility for the whole world and that it would protect the Western world against the threat of communism.
- Since the dissolution of the Warsaw Pact (1991) and the USSR (1991) the United States has been the only remaining world power.
- From the 1990s onwards the "Cold War" period has been replaced by a phase of international terrorism threatening the world.
- Present-day transatlantic relations between Europeans and Americans are not always free from political, military and economic disagreements.
- Anglo-American relations have always been "special" due to a common language, shared democratic values and mutual support in military and political affairs.

The Age of Isolationism (1790 – 1890)

In the 19th century the USA was preoccupied with domestic issues.

For about a hundred years, from the founding of the new state to the end of the 19th century, the attention of the young American republic basically centred around domestic affairs. Some important aspects were:

- the geographical expansion of the American domain; the conquest and settlement of new territories in the South and West;
- the formation of an American nation of immigrants and American identity;
- the development of political institutions;
- the slavery issue (→ p. 66) and the "War between the States" (→ pp. 32, 66);
- the economic and political reconstruction of the South;
- from the 1870s onwards, the beginning of the Industrial Revolution and large-scale exploitation of mineral resources;
- the opening up of the whole territory by means of a comprehensive railroad system.

Foreign Policy

Developments in the Spanish colonies in South America made the young American republic establish guiding principles in foreign policy. From 1811 to 1825 Spanish America fought for independence. When rumours spread that France and Spain would send troops to the New World to suppress the revolts, the American government intervened and announced the **Monroe Doctrine** (1823) as a warning to all European powers:

- no involvement or interference in European problems or wars (isolationism);
- recognition of the existing colonies in America, but no further extension of the colonial system in the New World would be tolerated;
- any attempt of a European nation to establish a monarchy in the Americas would be regarded as an unfriendly act toward the United States.

The **Monroe Doctrine** (1823) rejected mutual interference between the USA and European states.

Rise to World Power (1890–1945)

In the late 19th century, the United States began a policy of **spreading American civilization, of economic imperialism and of overseas expansion.**
Some Americans held that the American republic had the mission to spread law and order, American civilization and democracy to other parts of the world. The **Roosevelt Corollary** to the Monroe Doctrine (1904) even justified US interference in the internal affairs of Western Hemisphere nations to stop "chronic wrong-doing" (intervention policy).
By 1890, a single American market was created. Its enormous productivity demanded new markets. Thus, in 1899, the US Government announced the "Open Door Policy", i.e. the opening of China's markets to the trade of all foreign nations. Regarding the countries bordering the Caribbean, America pursued the "Big-Stick-Policy" (also called "dollar diplomacy"), i.e. political and economic influence through massive US capital investment.
In the 1860s, the United States reached its natural geographical limits. Not much later American ideas about imperialism changed and the acquisition of new lands overseas or the creation of spheres of influence became an important objective of US foreign policy.

In the late 19th century the USA began a policy of economic imperialism and overseas expansion.

Seeking new markets in the Far East, the USA announced the "Open Door Policy".

After the Spanish American War (1898) the USA acquired territories in Central America and the Pacific.

1898	Annexation of the Hawaiian Islands, a bridge to the market in the Far East. After the US victory in the Spanish-American War, Cuba became an American protectorate, and the Philippines, Puerto Rico, and Guam were annexed.
1903	US support of the independence of Panama from Colombia; the Americans were given the right to build the Panama Canal (opened in 1914) and to control the Panama Canal Zone.
1915/16	Haiti, the Dominican Republic, and Nicaragua became virtual protectorates.
1917	The USA purchased the Virgin Islands from Denmark.

In order to defend these widely separated territories a new, modern fleet of powerful warships was built up and naval bases in the Caribbean and the Pacific were established.

Within a few decades the USA developed into a world power.

Within a period of thirty years the United States developed into a world power and an empire-building nation. South Americans, in particular, mistrusted this development, accusing the "Colossus of the North" of imperialistic methods. Even US politicians held the view that the "land of the free" should not rule other people. Expansionists, on the other hand, maintained that the USA only interfered to maintain order, to advance democracy or to protect natives against other imperialist nations.

The USA in World War I (1914–1918)

During WW I the USA avoided conflict at first. In 1917, however, the country declared war on Germany.

In 1919, US President Wilson established a "League of Nations", but the US Senate rejected membership.

1914	Policy of neutrality, but sympathizes with the Western European democracies of England and France; support of the Allies with loans, food and war supplies because of US economic interests.
1917	Declaration of war on the **Central Powers** after Germany's announcement of unlimited warfare and the sinking of US merchant and passenger ships.
1918	Germany's surrender; President Wilson's fourteen-point programme for a peace based on justice: e.g. freedom of the seas, disarmament, self-government, and a "league of nations" to protect peace. The League of Nations became a forerunner of the United Nations founded in 1945.
1919	Paris Peace Conference: Wilson's idea of a "peace without victory" fails, as he is outvoted by the other allies, but he succeeds in the creation of the League of Nations. The United States Senate rejects membership of the League for fear of further involvement in international, especially European conflicts. America's aim to bring about a "democratic world revolution" seems to have been realized in Europe, as various monarchies are replaced by republics.

Between the Wars (1919–1939)

During the inter-war period the USA returned to its isolation policy.

These two decades saw a return to the United States' traditional isolation policy from world affairs and concentration on home affairs: Prohibition (→ p. 150), Depression (1930s) (→ pp. 87, 103), New Deal (1933–1938) (→ pp. 32, 87).
Main issues of American foreign policy were:

- Announcement of a "good neighbour policy" with Latin America (1933); military retreat from Central America (end of imperialist phase), but continuation of financial control;
- Neutrality Acts (1935–1937): prohibition of the sale of arms and of loans to belligerents to prevent involvement in international conflicts like in 1917.

belligerent: nation waging war *(Krieg führende Nation)*

World War II (1939–1945)

US neutrality at the beginning of WW II ended with the Japanese attack on Pearl Harbor (1941).

Regarding the rise of dictatorships in Europe, the American period of isolation came to an end in the late 1930s.
During the war the United States rose to the status of a major world power, a position that was no longer rejected. It was the only nation in possession of the atomic bomb and, in 1945, it was at the height of its power.

1939	Cash and Carry Act repealed the arms embargo of the Neutrality Acts allowing the sale of munitions to belligerents.
1941	Lend-Lease Act authorized the President to send war equipment to countries without payment (Britain).
1941	Japanese air attack on Pearl Harbor (Hawaii) and US entry into war (end of isolationism).
1942–1945	Involvement in a European War with the Axis Powers (Germany, Italy, and later Japan) and a Pacific War with Japan. With the help of the biggest war-machine the world had ever known the US forces brought about the fall of Germany and Japan.
1945	Surrender of Germany and Japan.

Leadership of the Western World (1945–1990)

The Post-war Period

WW II left Europe divided between two spheres of influence – an American democratic alliance (NATO) in the west and a Russian communist bloc in the east.

In the post-war years the Allies' common political aims became increasingly antagonistic over the reorganization of the conquered states in Europe. The United States started to arrange world policy according to the Western democratic principles of freedom of speech, opinion and worship, and freedom from fear and want (**Roosevelt**'s four principles 1941). The USSR sought to establish communist governments in the occupied Eastern European states, and to spread communism to non-communist countries as well. The spread of world communism was accompanied by continuous Soviet armament, and, in 1953, the USSR became the second atomic superpower.

The foundation of the United Nations Organization (UNO) in 1945 to secure world peace and to protect human rights proved to be an inefficient instrument for influencing the opposing powers.

The **Truman Doctrine** (1947) declared that the USA would support countries threatened by communism.

The Americans' answer to the Iron Curtain in Europe and the Cold-War years was the **Truman** Doctrine (1947). It stressed the responsibility of the USA for the whole world. The Americans were not going to turn away from world affairs, as they had done in 1918, but were determined to use their power and wealth to bring about a peaceful world. These were the principles of the Truman Doctrine:

- acceptance of leadership role in the world;
- spread of democratic values to other countries;
- military and economic aid for countries threatened by communism.

renunciation: *Verzicht*

The Truman Doctrine marked the renunciation of American isolationism as stated in the Monroe Doctrine.

The **Marshall Plan** (1948) offered financial help to rebuild European countries.

The **Marshall** Plan (1948), also known as the European Recovery Programme (ERP), offered raw materials, goods and loans to the war-ravaged countries of Europe to stop the march of communism. Sixteen states responded to this offer, the USSR and its satellites rejected it as "dollar imperialism". A second answer to communism was the foundation of a system of military treaties:

Military treaties like NATO and SEATO were founded to stop the spread of communism in Europe, Asia and Central America.

1949	NATO (→ pp. 170, 184)
1951	ANZUS: treaty between Australia, New Zealand, and the USA for mutual support in the Pacific
1954	SEATO: South-East Asian treaty between the USA, Great Britain, France, Australia, New Zealand, Pakistan, the Philippines, and Thailand

Post-war US foreign policy became known as "containment policy": its main objective was to prevent the spread or infiltration of communism in the world. Americans came to regard the peace of the whole world as a US responsibility. After the **Berlin Airlift** (1948/49) a status quo was reached in Europe, and US involvements in international conflicts shifted to:

containment: *Eindämmung*

- Asia: Korean War (1950–1953), Vietnam War (1964–1973);
- Central America: Cuban Missile Crisis (1961), El Salvador (1982), Nicaragua (1983), Grenada (1984), Panama (1989);
- the Middle East: Egyptian-Israeli peace treaty at Camp David (1979); Iranian Revolution and US hostage affair (1980); PLO terrorism and US air raid on PLO-headquarters in Tripoli, Libya (1986); protection of the Persian Gulf against Iranian missile-attacks on tankers (1988); Iraqi invasion of Kuwait (1990).

The Vietnam War (1964–1975)

The USA aimed to keep communism out of South East Asia, but was defeated by the Vietcong.

The Vietnam War, a conflict between the United States and communist revolutionaries in South-East Asia which lasted nearly 20 years, ended in 1973 with a victory for the communist guerilla forces, the Vietcong. It signified the first important military defeat of a US government.

The effect of the unpopular war on the US was great:

- Some 50,000 Americans were killed.
- The war had a deeply unsettling effect on the economy of the country.
- Among Americans there was a strong feeling of humiliation after the defeat by the guerilla forces of a peasant people.
- Americans became disillusioned and distrustful of their government after Vietnam and Watergate.
- The Vietnam War had a profound impact on US foreign policy. It resulted in US disillusionment about its role as the "world police" and revived the wish to keep the country free of long-term world-wide commitments.

The "Arms Race" and Détente

After the Cold-War period, relations between the Soviet Union and the United States appeared to improve in spite of many setbacks. Phases of friction and confrontation alternated with periods of peaceful co-existence and détente. The "arms race" and the "balance of terror" led to the development of destructive weapons on an apocalyptic scale on both sides. The realization that a nuclear war might eventually cause the destruction of the entire globe resulted in direct negotiations between the two superpowers (**SALT** I, 1972). Disarmament talks continued after the fall of the "Iron Curtain" and the Berlin Wall in 1989 and were completed with the first (1991) and second (1993) **START**-Treaty.

friction: conflict

détente: *Entspannung*

In the 1970s, fear of global destruction led to successful arms limitation talks between the USA and the USSR.

The only Superpower (since 1990)

The **Cold War** ended in the late 1980s when Soviet leader Gorbachev introduced the glasnost reforms. This led to the dissolution of the Soviet Union (1991).

In the 1980s the Cold-War period came to an end, when Gorbachev came to power in the Soviet Union and declared a policy of glasnost (political openness). Communist governments began to dissolve throughout Eastern Europe with the effect that the United States moved into the role of the only remaining superpower. This historic phase saw German reunification (1990), the dissolution of the Warsaw Pact (1991), and the breakup of the USSR (1991). In 1993, NATO offered former Warsaw Pact members limited associations with NATO (Partnership for Peace).

With the end of the Cold War, world attention shifted to the Middle East. Especially the 9/11 terrorist attacks drew the USA in a long war on international terrorism.

Due to the new political situation in the East, there was a change in America's Eastern European policy. US policy was supportive of Yeltsin and of his successor Putin in their efforts to bring democracy and the free market system to Russia. The USA supported a reunited Germany and at the same time guaranteed that Germany would respect European borders and all security treaties. Although the USA was no longer engaged in the Cold War, the Clinton Administration (1993–2001) decided that the USA as a superpower had a role to play in the ethnic and religious wars in the world: Bosnia 1995, Kosovo 1999, Middle East 1990s, Iraq 1998/99. Then, in early 2014, the shadow of the Cold War unexpectedly reappeared when Russia seized the Crimea region of Ukraine.

Also throughout the 1980s and 1990s, and into the 21st century the United States faced the worldwide threat of terrorism. During the 90s terrorist attacks of Muslim fundamentalists on e.g. the World Trade Center in New York City (1993) and American embassies in Africa (1998) alarmed the country. The most devastating attack came in 2001, when hijackers crashed three commercial jets into US landmarks, the twin towers of the World Trade Center and the Pentagon, the symbol of US military power. The attacks shattered the nation's sense of security and threatened to involve the United States in a long war on international terrorism.

rogue nations: *Schurkenstaaten*

warheads: *Sprengköpfe*

Due to globalization the United States faces constant challenges in the world. In the new world order of the 1990s and the 21st century, the threat to the USA and the world no longer comes from Russia but from "rogue nations" with nuclear weapons and from a terrorist network, including nuclear and bio terrorism. Therefore, in 2002 and again in 2010, the USA and Russia signed treaties on the reduction of nuclear arms (nuclear warheads) to counteract global threats and challenges. The arms pact reduces both nations' nuclear warheads by two-thirds.

Present-day US-Western European Relations

In the post-war years the United States appeared as the rescuer of Western civilization and democratic values, as a guarantor of new economic strength and as a shield against Soviet expansionism. The post-war generation of Europeans was therefore totally committed and grateful to the United States.

By the 1960s and 70s, however, a new Western European generation had grown up that did not share the experiences of the war and post-war generation and was therefore less committed to America. They were more rebellious about political and cultural authority and also more critical about US domestic and foreign policy. Moreover, they showed a new and growing self-confidence, leading to profound rifts and serious mistrust.

Since the 1990s a fundamental shift in world power, politics and trade has taken place, symbolized by the fall of the Berlin Wall. The perceived military threat from the Soviet Union has been removed, the EU has been enlarged from the original six member states to 28, Islamic militancy is widely seen as a menace (9/11), and the rise of economic power in Asia, notably India and China, is revolutionizing world trade. All of these factors have made the US-Western European relationship much more complex than the simple "Cold War" period (1945–1989).

Post-war Western Europeans were very grateful to the USA for restoring democracy and protecting them against communism. Younger Europeans, however, were more critical about America.

rift: serious disagreement *(Unstimmigkeit)*

The US Opinion of Europeans

- Young Europeans do not fully appreciate the principles of democracy.
- Europeans are not willing to commit themselves to defending Western civilization, especially Europe; growing European criticism of the United States is interpreted as anti-Americanism and increases readiness of the US to withdraw from Europe.
- They are not willing to support common action against international terrorism.
- Americans fear growing European neutrality.
- Europe is seen as economically irrelevant compared with Asia and the Middle East.

Americans often criticize the lack of commitment Europeans show to defend Western values. Criticism is interpreted as anti-Americanism.

The Europeans' Opinion of America

Since the 1960s, America has no longer appeared to be the symbol of liberty and equality, but has lost prestige and shown a lack of leadership. The following events in particular made Europeans adopt a more critical attitude towards the United States:

- racial inequality and the Civil Rights Movement (1960s);
- US commitment in the Vietnam War (1964–1973);
- the Watergate affair (1972–1974);
- the assassination of J.F. Kennedy (1963), Martin Luther King (1968), Robert Kennedy (1968);
- the role of the CIA in the overthrow of socialist regimes in South and Central America (e.g. Chile).

Many Western Europeans have developed a more critical attitude towards the USA with regard to foreign, domestic, cultural and environmental issues.

In more recent times, a growing hostility has been felt by some Europeans about:

- the Americanization of European culture;
- the USA as the Western superpower and corporate giant;
- the role of the USA in the Gulf War (1991) and the Iraq War (2003), including torture and abuse of prisoners held at Abu Ghraib Prison, Bagdad;
- since 2002 long-term imprisonment of 600 terror suspects at Guantánamo Bay, Cuba, most of them without any meaningful connection to Al Quaeda or the Taliban;
- the refusal of the USA, responsible for a quarter of all greenhouse gas emissions, to sign the Warming Act of 2001, the biggest global effort against the greenhouse effect.

New problems between most European states and the USA arose when, in 2013, it was revealed that the US government had used the **NSA (National Security Agency)**, the biggest of the US' intelligence organisations, for years for broad surveillance programmes at home and abroad. This controversial agency intercepts telephone and internet communications worldwide, seeking information on terrorism, foreign policy and economic advantages. It even spies on the EU member states, including allies and trading partners. In retrospect, though, Obama's foreign policy, especially his reluctance regarding the use of military force, was greatly appreciated by most European countries. Donald Trump forced Nato's European member states to take over more international responsibility and to press on the allies' defence spending. He seriously questioned the post-war system of security guaranteed by Nato with his position "America first".

to intercept: *abhören*

However, the continuation of the alliance lies in the interest of both Europeans and Americans. The geographical, military, political and economic differences of the two partners must be overcome again under the Biden administration. It definitely needs a balance of influence in the alliance, an equal share of responsibility and more mutual consultation.

Anglo-American Relations

The special relations of Britain and the United States, two English-speaking countries, are deeply rooted in their common interests.

Even today, British people tend to lean more to America than to Europe. These special relations between the two countries are historic. Their roots are:

- a long history of parliamentary democracy;
- the use of the same language;
- the fact that Britain was the mother country of the American colonies;
- multiple cultural ties.

Moreover, the special Anglo-American relations are based on mutual support in international conflicts in the 20th century:

- US support of Britain in the two World Wars;
- British support of the United States in the Korean and Vietnam War;
- US support of Britain in the Falklands conflict with Argentina (1982), against United States' interest in South America;
- British permission for the use of US planes stationed in Britain for the bombing of Tripoli (1986);
- military cooperation during the Gulf War (1991), the Iraq conflict (1998/99), the fight against international terrorism and the Taleban regime in Afghanistan 2001/02, and the Iraq War 2003.

On the other hand, Britain did not hesitate to criticize US military intervention in the Middle East and Libya or to support EU economic policy against US interests. The most outstanding example of a clash of British and American interests was the US invasion in Grenada in 1983. This took place without the consultation of the British Government, although Grenada is part of the Commonwealth.

In spite of these strong ties Anglo-American relations have not always been free of tensions.

Some observers argue that the special relationship with the USA has prevented Britain from becoming a committed European member state.

These examples show that transatlantic relations are not always free of tension and that Britain takes its own stand, if necessary. British critics of the special Anglo-American relationship have pointed out that it had, and to a certain extent still has, a crippling effect on Britain's relations with its European neighbours. They maintain that Europe will be Britain's real special relationship for the coming century. Notwithstanding these considerations, Britain has continued to be America's closest ally up to the present day. In 2013 it turned out that UK spy agencies had supported the USA for years in their worldwide surveillance programmes against terrorist threats. They had collected people's personal data from email accounts for American intelligence agencies like the **NSA** or **CIA**.

crippling: harmful, paralyzing

Under Donald Trump and Boris Johnson, two politicians with a similar populist style, the relation between the US and Britain was closer than ever. Trump publicly supported Johnson's way out of the European Union.

The United States and the World

The Age of Isolationism (1790 – 1890)

For about the first 100 years the young republic centred around domestic affairs:

- conquest of the West, formation of an immigrant nation, development of political institutions, slavery issue, and Civil War.
- In the Monroe Doctrine, 1823, the US Government announced no involvement in European problems or wars (isolationism) and no toleration of a further expansion of the colonial system in America.

Rise to World Power (1890 – 1945)

- From 1890 onwards a phase of economic imperialism and overseas expansion: "Open Door Policy" (China) and "dollar diplomacy" (Central America);
- World War I (1914 – 1918): after Germany's announcement of unlimited warfare declaration of war on Germany in 1917;
- 1918 President Wilson's fourteen-point programme and the creation of a "league of nations";
- between the wars a return to the US' traditional isolation policy;
- World War II (1939 – 1945): in 1941, after the Japanese attack on Pearl Harbor US entry into war; surrender of Germany and Japan in 1945.

Leadership of the Western World (1945 – 1990)

- Cold-War period: USA (spread of western democratic principles) – USSR (spread of communism);
- Truman Doctrine (1947): responsibility of the USA to accept its leadership role of the world, spread of democratic values, and support of countries threatened by communism (Korea 1950 – 1953; Vietnam 1965 – 1969);
- Marshall Plan (1948): aid to rebuild European countries, rejected by the Soviet Union and other eastern European states (split of Europe into East and West; "Iron Curtain");
- system of military treaties between the USA and other countries: NATO, ANZUS, SEATO;
- "Arms race" and "détente" (limitation of nuclear weapons) in the 1970s and 80s;
- end of the Cold War: fall of the "Iron Curtain" and the Berlin Wall in 1989.

The only Superpower (since 1990)

- Change in America's Eastern European policy as a reaction to Gorbachev's policy of glasnost;
- new world order: German reunification (1990), dissolution of the Warsaw Pact (1991), and breakup of the USSR (1991);
- US commitment in the Gulf War (1991), Bosnia (1995), Serbia/Kosovo (1999);
- after September 11, 2001, fight against international terrorism, intervention in Afghanistan (2002), and new US doctrine of pre-emptive strikes with regard to "rogue nations" (Iraq, 2003).

US-Western European Relations

- Post-war generation of Western Europeans: feeling of gratitude to the USA (→ democratic values, economic strength, protection against communism);
- the next European generation is more critical: economic disagreements (trade war, protectionism), military differences of opinion (deployment of US missiles in Europe, Vietnam War, Gulf War, Iraq War), US domestic policy (Civil Rights Movement, situation of US minorities, role of the CIA), environmental issues (Warming Act of Kyoto), growing Americanization of European culture.

Anglo-American Relations

Centuries-old "special relations" due to:

- history, parliamentary democracy, use of language, Anglo-Saxon culture, mutual military support (US support: WW I and II, Falklands conflict; British support: Korean War, Vietnam War, Gulf War, intervention in Afghanistan, Iraq War);
- negative effect of special relationship on Britain's attitude to Europe and the European Union; today Britain has closer economic ties with Europe, but politically ties to the USA remain dominant.
- Trump supported Britain's way out of the European Union (Brexit).

Federal Hall, New York City, with the statue of George Washington

OVERVIEW

1171 – **Henry II** of England declares himself Lord of Ireland **(origin of Anglo-Irish conflict)**

1536 – **Henry VIII** tries to impose Reformation on Ireland **(origin of religious conflict)**

1601 – **Flight of the Earls** (The O'Neills, Irish chieftains, flee to the Continent)

1602 – **"Ulster plantation"** with Protestant settlers **(origin of Northern Irish conflict)**

1649 – **1649 – 1652 Oliver Cromwell** conquers the whole of Ireland

1690 – **Battle of the Boyne** (Protestant William of Orange defeats Catholic James II)

1695 – Introduction of **Penal Laws** to discriminate against Roman Catholics

1801 – **Act of Union** (Irish Parliament is abolished and Ireland becomes part of the "United Kingdom of Great Britain and Ireland")

1829 – **Catholic Emancipation Act** (Anti-Catholic Penal Laws are abolished)

1845 – **1845 – 1849 Great Irish Potato Famine** (causes mass starvation and emigration to America)

1858 – The **Fenian Movement**, predecessor of the later IRA, is founded

Ireland 2009

11 Anglo-Irish Relations

1914
Home Rule Bill is passed, but suspended until the end of WW I

1915
Easter Rising fails

1919
1919 – 1921 Irish War of Independence

1921
Anglo-Irish Treaty: Partition of Ireland into two states: a Catholic Irish Free State and Northern Ireland (Ulster) with a Protestant majority **(origin of a divided country)**

1937
Irish Free State is renamed **Eire**

1949
Eire leaves the Commonwealth

1969
Beginning of the Northern Irish **Civil Rights Movement**

1969 – 1998
The **Troubles** (a period of riots, bombing, violence between the IRA and British troops; more than 3 000 people are killed)

1973
Ireland joins the **European Community** along with Britain and Denmark

1998
Belfast Agreement (a peace deal about Northern Ireland's future)

2007
Home Rule (devolved Irish Assembly in Belfast restored)

Bono and The Edge (left) of the Irish rock band "U 2".

In their song "Sunday, Bloody Sunday" the band criticizes the warlike religious conflict in Ireland:

"And the battle's just begun,
There's many lost, but tell me who has won?"

11 Anglo-Irish Relations

IN BRIEF

- In the 16th century Henry VIII attempted to spread Protestantism in Catholic Ireland.
- Under Oliver Cromwell (1599 – 1658) Protestants settled in Ulster (Northern Ireland).
- The Protestant victory at the Battle of the Boyne (1690) led to anti-Catholic laws.
- In the Act of Union (1801) Ireland became part of the "United Kingdom of Great Britain and Ireland".
- In 1829 the Penal Laws oppressing Catholics in Ireland were abolished.
- In 1858 the Fenian Movement (forerunner of the Irish Republican Army) was founded with the goal of Home Rule (self-government).
- The Anglo-Irish Treaty of 1921 partitioned Ireland into a Catholic Irish Free State and a predominantly Protestant Northern Ireland (Ulster).
- Between 1969 and 1998 the "Troubles", a period of conflict and bloodshed between Northern Irish Catholics and Protestants, took place.
- In 2007, after a decade of peace talks, Home Rule for Northern Ireland was re-established.

History of Ireland up to 1920

(Ireland → pp. 12–15, 99 ff, 144, 147, 162, 172)

For five centuries (1171 – 1690), the English struggled to conquer Ireland.

The history of the British occupation of Ireland began about a century after the Norman conquest of Britain in 1066. In 1171, the Anglo-Norman Henry II invaded Ireland, gained control over most of the country and declared himself King of Ireland. In reality, however, a long period of time passed before the country was systematically conquered and colonized.

The origins of the present-day conflict in Ireland started in the 16th century with Henry VIII's attempt to spread Reformation among the Catholic Irish. The Anglican Church was established, but on the whole Ireland remained a Catholic (→ pp. 15, 144 ff) country. The Irish state was based on a clan system and, consequently, was not well organized. Therefore, various Irish rebellions were easily suppressed by the British. In the same way, the most determined resistance of the Gaelic chieftains of Ulster, that of the clan of the O'Neills, was doomed to fail. When the O'Neills left for the Continent in 1601, in the "Flight of the Earls", their lands were confiscated, and Protestants (Scottish Presbyterians) settled in Ulster ("Ulster plantation"). This development accounts for the present political division of Ireland into a pro-English Protestant North and the Celtic Catholic South. It was especially under Cromwell that Irish land was given to English landlords and soldiers, while the original inhabitants cultivated the soil as mere tenants.

Tenants pay rent for land or buildings that they use.

In the fight between King and Parliament in the 17th century, the Irish supported the Jacobites, but James II, after landing in Ireland with French troops, was decisively defeated by the Protestant William of Orange at the Battle of the Boyne in 1690. After that, rigorous Penal Laws oppressing Irish Catholics were introduced. Catholics were, for example, excluded from schools and public offices.

After Catholic resistance was broken, Penal Laws against Irish Catholics were enacted.

The year 1801 marked the end of Irish independence. In the **Act of Union**, Ireland officially became part of the "United Kingdom of Great Britain and Ireland". The Irish Parliament was dissolved, and from then on, Irish interests were represented in the British Parliament at Westminster by a small number of Protestant Members of Parliament, who could easily be outvoted by the English majority.

In 1801 the whole of Ireland became part of the United Kingdom.

At the beginning of the 19th century, discrimination against Catholics came under pressure. Catholics were admitted to universities, and in the **"Catholic Emancipation Act"** of 1829, the Penal Laws were repealed. Catholics were granted the right to become MPs and were admitted to nearly all public offices.

to repeal a law: to end a law officially

Around 1840, the failure of the potato crop for several successive years led to mass starvation and, finally, to mass emigration to Britain and later to the United States. Within a few decades, the Irish population fell from about eight to four million. According to the US census of 2000, the Irish constitute, after the Germans, the second largest group of immigrants to the United States, the English ranking third.

In 1848 the country was struck by a disastrous famine.

Towards the end of the 19th century, the growth of Irish nationalism became apparent. In 1858 the Fenian Movement was founded with the aim of **Home Rule** (self-government), land reform, and, ultimately, political freedom. This secret revolutionary society was supported by Irish-Americans, who had served in the American Civil War.

In the middle of the 19th century an Irish nationalist movement was founded to overthrow British rule in Ireland.

After three vain attempts, the Irish party in the House of Commons finally forced the enactment of a Home Rule Bill at the outbreak of World War I. The law was suspended until the end of the war, but provoked the foundation of the "Protestant Ulster Volunteers" fighting for the Union with Great Britain. This was answered by the foundation of the "Catholic National Volunteers", and violence broke out. In 1914 the country was on the brink of civil war. Irish nationalists, helped by Germany, attempted to revolt against British rule, but the famous **"Easter Rising"** of 1916 failed. The rebellion was brutally crushed by the British, and resulted in the **Irish War of Independence (1919–1921)**, a guerilla war between the Fenians (now called the Irish Republican Army) and the British military police. This situation ultimately forced a solution on the Westminster government in the **"Government of Ireland Act"** of 1920, which foresaw the first official division between the North and the South.

Demands for self-government led to the **Irish War of Independence** (1919–1921).

to suspend: to put off for a period of time

on the brink of: *am Rande*

Partition of Ireland

In 1921 Ireland was partitioned into two states:

- the "Irish Free State" with a large Catholic majority
- the mainly Protestant province of Northern Ireland as part of the UK.

The division of the country, as projected in the "Ireland Act" of 1920, was accepted by moderate Irish nationalists, but rejected by the extremist party under **Simon de Valera**. This controversy led to the Irish Civil War, in which the Fenian extremists were defeated.

The **Anglo-Irish Treaty of 1921** established the three historical provinces of Leinster (Dublin), Munster and Connacht with an overwhelming Catholic majority of 95% and a population of 3,5 million as the "Irish Free State" with its own government in Dublin. It remained, as a Dominion, a member of the British Commonwealth. In 1937 the new State adopted the name of **Eire**. It remained neutral during World War II. In 1949 it left the Commonwealth and became the "Republic of Ireland". In 1955 it entered the United Nations, and in 1973 the EC.

As a result of the general election of 1918, six of the nine counties of the former Irish province of Ulster were kept within the United Kingdom. They became the Protestant-dominated British province of Northern Ireland with a government of its own in Belfast. The population rose to 1,5 million. Three counties with an 80% majority of Catholic nationalists were added to the Irish Free State. In the remaining six counties Protestants had a majority of 66%, but the two counties of Tyrone and Fermanagh with a 55% Catholic majority were included. This meant that a substantial Catholic minority of 33% was part of the Northern Irish population.

Nearly 100 years later, in the 2010s, only 48% of Northern Irish residents described themselves as Protestants (2001: 53%) whereas the number of Catholics rose slightly to 45% (2001: 44%).

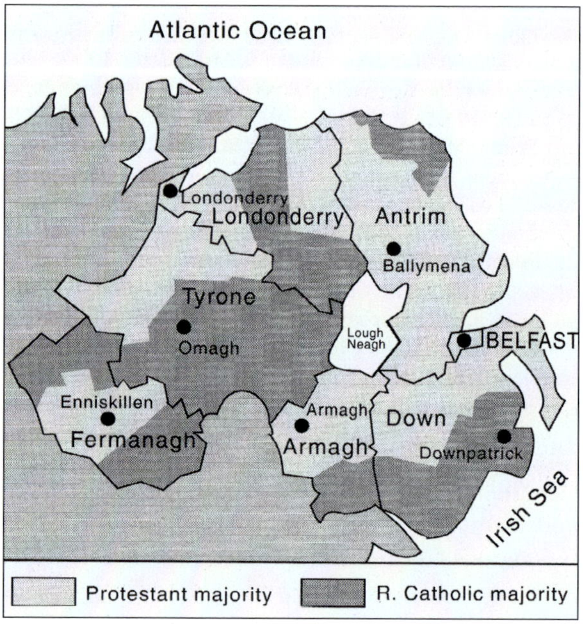

In the following decades up to the 1960s, different methods were introduced by the Protestants in order to guarantee the Unionist majority in Parliament, in the local councils such as in Londonderry and in the counties with a Catholic majority. The following are examples of such methods:

- the practice of **gerrymandering**;
- use of "**property qualification**" for local government elections;
- **disfranchisement** or restricted franchise.

The process of this political injustice and discrimination continued up to 1967, when a new forceful movement began to demonstrate for the rights of the underprivileged Catholics in Northern Ireland.

Discriminatory methods were practised to guarantee Protestant dominance in Northern Ireland.

gerrymandering: *willkürliche Verschiebung von Wahlbezirken, um einer politischen Partei Vorteile zu verschaffen*

The "Troubles" in Northern Ireland (since 1969–1998)

The **Northern Irish Civil Rights Movement** was inspired by the comparative success of the Civil Rights Movement of the American Blacks. It began in the late 60s with peaceful demonstrations in Ulster, and demanded opportunities for Catholics and the end of discrimination and sectarianism. It met a hostile reaction from the Protestants, who considered it to be infiltrated by the IRA. Riots in Londonderry and Belfast forced the Northern Irish Government to request British troops to restore peace and order (1969).

The decision of the Northern Irish Prime Minister in 1971 to intern IRA suspects without trial (Special Powers Act of 1971) led to a further polarization of the two population groups and increasing violence. Finally, in 1972, **"Direct Rule"** from Westminster was introduced. The formation of a special wing of the IRA, the Provisionals, a paramilitary terrorist organization, made attempts to reconcile the two populations groups impossible. The Civil Rights Movement failed, as did the Peace Movement that was awarded the Nobel Peace Prize in 1977. Bombs exploded in Ulster and Britain, and killing became a part of everyday life.

Demands for equal opportunities and justice for Catholics resulted in the "Troubles", a period marked by violence and terrorism.

Survey of political and military groups in Ulster

	Protestants	Catholics
Parties	• Ulster Unionist Party, conservative, 1921–72 in power; favours complete union with Britain	• **Sinn Fein**, political wing of the IRA; aim: a united Ireland
	• Democratic Unionist Party (leader: Ian Paisley), extreme right wing; aim: union with Westminster, but with local law-making and administrative powers	• SDLP (Social Democratic and Labour Party, moderate; aim: a united Ireland

Main Protestant and Catholic groupings

	Protestants	Catholics
Militant organizations	Ulster Defence Association (UDA), a paramilitary group; aim: to counter IRA	Provisional Irish Republican Army (IRA); aim: a united socialist Ireland; favours military action to destroy Ulster; terrorist activities
Religious organizations	Orange Order, a group of leading Ulster Protestants with the aim of perpetuating Protestant domination	Irish National Foresters

Three decades of violence

Ulster's History of Violence	
1972	"Bloody Sunday" in Londonderry; 13 inhabitants were shot by British troops.
1972	"Bloody Friday" in Belfast; the IRA set off 26 bombs which killed 11 people.
1974	Bombs exploded inside two Birmingham pubs killing 21 people.
1978	A napalm bomb killed 12 guests at a restaurant near Belfast.
1979	**Lord Mountbatten** was murdered on his yacht, whilst visiting Ireland. 18 British soldiers were killed in Northern Ireland.
1981	IRA prisoners went on a hunger strike in Maze Prison (Belfast) to achieve the status of political prisoners. Ten of them died before the strike ended.
1982	In Regents Park, London, a bomb exploded and killed eight people.
1983	A bomb exploded at Harrods, London, and killed five people.
1984	Attempted assassination of Margaret Thatcher and members of the Government at the Conservative Party Conference at Brighton.
1987	An IRA bomb went off in Enniskillen (Fermanagh), killing 11 people and injuring 60.
1989	Ten marine band members were killed and 22 injured in one of the worst IRA attacks on the British mainland, when the IRA bombed a Music School in Kent.
1991	Attempt to kill John Major and his Cabinet during a meeting at No. 10 Downing Street.
1993	An IRA bombing of an English shopping mall left two children dead. A Dublin peace march drew 20,000 people.
1993	The IRA bombing of a Shankill Road fish shop in Belfast killed seven people. Within days, Protestants retaliated, spraying a pub with bullets. Seven were killed.
1998	A car bomb killed 29 and injured 220 people in Omagh, Northern Ireland. Responsible for the bombing was Real IRA, a Republican paramilitary splinter group. The explosion threatened to destroy the peace process in Northern Ireland.

to retaliate: *Vergeltung üben*

In 30 years more than 3,300 people have been killed.

The Northern Irish Conflict

If we want to describe the true nature of the Northern Irish conflict, we have to distinguish the different roots of the **complicated situation** of today.

The Northern Irish conflict has historic, religious, cultural and economic reasons.

- It is, first of all, a centuries-old colonial conflict between colonists or conquerors and natives. Nationalists like to point out the similarity between the Irish Catholics and the US Blacks on the one hand, and between the Protestants in Ulster and the Whites in the United States on the other. One need not go as far as that, but one aspect seems to be important, and that is that the two population groups do not consider themselves to be part of one and the same nation. Instead there is deep resentment and hatred of each other, which prevents any development of cooperation and reconciliation.
- The lack of identification with each other has a second origin in the difference of denominations, and the fact that the English conquerors tried to impose their faith on the original inhabitants, who were fervent Catholics. This religious aspect seems to have become less significant, as the unrest does not derive from theological questions or attempts to convert each other. On the contrary, religion has come to serve the interests of political groups. Schoolchildren of the Protestant state schools and private church-supported Catholic schools are influenced at an early age by the respective church authorities, and politico-religious organizations play a decisive part in everyday life in Ulster.
- Furthermore, it is a national and cultural conflict, a conflict of different nations originally speaking different languages and disposing of their own cultural heritage.
- Above all, the conflict is economic, as financially underprivileged Catholics confront the more affluent Protestants in Northern Ireland.

affluent: prosperous; if you are affluent you have a lot of money and a high standard of living.

In 1985 Margaret Thatcher and the Irish President signed an Anglo-Irish agreement, recognizing the Irish Government's right to be consulted and to intervene in matters concerning Northern Ireland.

From the mid-1980s onwards the British and Irish governments tried to find a peaceful solution for the Northern Irish question.

John Major and the Irish Prime Minister Albert Reynolds continued Thatcher's initiative with the signing of "The Downing Street Declaration" in 1993. This is a statement of fundamental principles in the search for a settlement in Northern Ireland. The British Government stressed the need for the IRA to cease military action completely before any discussions with **Sinn Fein** could take place. In 1994, the Provisional IRA announced a complete cessation of military operations, and the "loyalist" paramilitaries responded with the announcement of a ceasefire. No talks ever took place, however, as Sinn Fein / the IRA was unwilling to disarm before talks, and the Government refused to talk while the armed threat remained.

In 1998 all the parties involved agreed on a peace deal.

After the electoral victory of 1997 the Labour Government under Tony Blair renewed the initiative to promote peace in Northern Ireland. In April 1998, all parties involved (the British and Irish Governments, Northern Irish Protestant Unionists, and Catholic Republicans) reached an agreement to end three decades of sectarian violence by altering constitutional arrangements for Ulster. Key points of the Belfast Agreement were:

- The agreement would be put to the people of Northern Ireland and the Southern Republic of Ireland.
- Irish Republican voters would be asked to amend their constitutional claim that the North was an integral part of the Republic.
- Northern Ireland would remain part of the United Kingdom until a majority in the North chose unity.
- A new political body of 108 members would administer Northern Ireland.
- A new North-South Irish ministerial council would deal with common issues such as roads and agriculture.
- The governments would speed up the release of political prisoners.
- Both sides would promise to use influence to bring about disarmament within two years at the latest.
- Britain would promise to make progress towards demilitarization of Northern Ireland to normal peacetime levels and remove all emergency powers.

All parts of the agreement except for disarmament had been put into practice by December 1999, when the power to govern the Province was handed back to Northern Irish politicians after 26 years of direct rule from London. The refusal of the terrorists to disarm was still causing serious problems as the new millennium dawned, however, with the Assembly being suspended in 2002 and dissolved in 2003. The Secretary of State assumed responsibility for the policies and administration of the Northern Irish Departments.

Because of the IRA's refusal to disarm, it took another 8 years until, in 2007, Home Rule was restored.

In 2007 the leaders of the Sinn Fein and the Democratic Unionist party agreed to set up a new power-sharing government, which meant the end of suspension and the restoration of the devolved (→ pp. 15, 17) Irish Assembly. The agreement was hailed as the beginning of a new era of politics in Northern Ireland.

Anglo-Irish Relations

History of Ireland

- Conquest of Ireland from about 1200;
- in the 16th century Henry VIII's attempt to spread the reformation in Ireland;
- settlement of Protestants (Scottish Presbyterians) in Ulster;
- defeat of the Catholic James II by the Protestant William of Orange in 1690;
- in 1801, Ireland officially part of the UK;
- in the 1840s large-scale emigration of Irish to America;
- towards the end of the 19th century growing Irish nationalism;
- in 1920 partition of Ireland into a Catholic South (Eire) and a Protestant North (Province of Northern Ireland);
- discriminatory laws against the Catholic minority introduced in Northern Ireland by the Protestant two-thirds majority;
- in the late 60s, beginning of the "Troubles": for the following 30 years Protestants and Catholics engaged in a fierce civil war with more than 3,000 people being killed;
- Belfast Agreement (1998): renewal of peace talks and agreement to end three decades of violence;
- in 2007 a devolved Northern Irish Assembly restored.

Political and Military Groups in Ulster

- The Protestants' interests are represented by the conservative Ulster Unionist Party, the right wing Democratic Unionist Party, by militant organizations like the Ulster Defence Association and by the religious Orange Order.
- The Catholics are supported by political parties such as Sinn Fein (the political arm of the IRA) and the moderate SDLP, and by militant organizations like the Provisional Irish Republican Army (IRA).

Complexity of the Conflict

- A centuries-old colonial conflict between conquerors and natives;
- a religious conflict between Catholics and Protestants;
- a national and cultural conflict of different nations originally speaking different languages and having different cultures;
- an economic conflict of more affluent Protestants and poorer Catholics in Northern Ireland.

Glossary (erklärt alle im Text mit blauer Farbe markierten Begriffe.)

B

BERLIN AIRLIFT	in 1948, the Soviet Union violated the four-nation agreement on Berlin by closing the land routes to Berlin. The Allies' answer to the blockade was the Berlin Airlift. For over a year the allies flew tons of vital supplies into Berlin each day.

C

CENTRAL POWERS	military alliance of Germany and Austro-Hungary during World War I.
CHAMBERLAIN, JOSEPH (1836 – 1914)	British imperialist politician. As colonial secretary he worked for imperial expansion in Africa and closer ties within the British Empire. In 1897 he described the Empire as a territory where "the doors of the temple of Janus were never closed" and spoke of the British people's "strength to fulfil the mission (their) history and (their) national character had imposed on (them)".
CIA	short for Central Intelligence Agency (Abwehrdienst der Vereinigten Staaten).
CREATIONISM	theory that takes Genesis as a scientific explanation of how the earth came into being.
CROMWELL, OLIVER (1599 – 1658)	conquered the whole of Ireland between 1649 and 1652. He became the sole ruler of Britain and gave himself the title of Lord Protector (1654).

D

DE VALERA, SIMON (1882 – 1975)	leader of Sinn Fein, headed the Irish Government as Prime Minister 1932 – 1948, 1951 – 1954 and 1957 – 1959.
DEISM	belief in the existence of God, but rejection of revelation or religious dogma.
DISFRANCHISEMENT	action of taking away the right to vote. This applied to Northern Irish lodgers who were not householders, in practice mainly Catholics.

E

ECUMENISM	belief that all the different branches of the Christian Churches should cooperate and be united.

F

FENIAN MOVEMENT	(or Irish Republican Brotherhood): the predecessor of the Irish Republican Army (IRA).

G

GERRYMANDERING method of manipulating the boundaries of a constituency to give advantage to a political party.

H

HEARST, WILLIAM RANDOLPH (1863 – 1951) a representative of sensational, yellow journalism, built up a media empire (the Hearst Concern) consisting of newspapers, broadcasting stations and news services.

I

ISLAMIC STATE (IS) a militant Islamist group fighting in Syria and Iraq. Its aim is to establish an Islamic emirate.

J

JACOBITES they were adherents of James II and his descendants, especially in Scotland. James II tried to re-establish Catholicism, until he was forced to flee to France.

M

MARSHALL, GEORGE US Secretary of State from 1947 to 1949.

MAYFLOWER COMPACT first document on the rules of a democratic system in America drawn up by the Pilgrim Fathers who agreed to be governed by the will of the majority, and not by the divine right of a king.

MONROE, JAMES US President from 1817 to 1825.

MOUNTBATTEN, LORD (1900 – 1979) naval commander and member of the Royal Family who distinguished himself during World War II as supreme Allied commander in South-East Asia.

MURDOCH, RUPERT Australian businessman, rules over a media empire which includes newspapers in Britain, Australia, the US, Hong Kong and New Zealand as well as television broadcasting companies in Britain and the United States.

O

OXFORD MOVEMENT Anglo-Catholic high-church movement which restored many ritual practices such as High Mass.

P

PROPERTY QUALIFICATION owners of a business in Northern Ireland could be given up to 6 votes for each business.

R

RASTAFARIANS adherents of Rastafarianism, a religious African cult popular among West Indian youth. Reggae music is associated with the movement. Rastafarians stress black separatism.

RHODES, CECIL (1853–1902) British imperialist and statesman helped to establish British rule in southern Africa (Rhodesia) and to promote the dream of a British Empire from the "Cape to Cairo".

ROOSEVELT, FRANKLIN D. US President from 1933 to 1945.

ROOSEVELT COROLLARY extension of the Monroe Doctrine by Theodore Roosevelt, US President from 1901 to 1909.

S

SALT = Strategic Arms Limitation Talks: limited nuclear arms and deployment of antiballistic missiles (Stationierung von Abwehrraketen).

SEPARATIST PILGRIMS unlike the Puritans, who only intended to "purify" the Church, the Separatists wanted to separate from the Church of England and set up their own churches. They left England in 1607 and settled in the Netherlands for some time before crossing the Atlantic.

SINN FEIN extreme Irish nationalist party, founded in 1905, aiming at political independence and revival of Irish culture and language; the Gaelic name means "ourselves alone".

SOAP OPERA a popular television drama serial about the daily lives and problems of a group of people; this type of programme was originally sponsored by a corporation which chiefly produced "soap".

SPUTNIK SHOCK the launching of Sputnik I, the first man-made satellite, in 1957 by the Soviet Union was a shock to the USA, because it demonstrated Russian superiority in space technology. As a result the US Department of Education developed new science curricula.

START = Strategic Arms Reduction Talks

T

TRUMAN, HARRY US President from 1945 to 1953.

W

"WHITE MAN'S BURDEN" is the title of a poem by Rudyard Kipling (1865–1936), British writer who glorified the magnificence of the British Empire in his work.

Index

Abbildungsnachweis:
S. 8 o li Queen Elizabeth II: Shutterstock, New York (Featureflash Photo Agency); S. 8 o re Houses of Parliament: Shutterstock, New York (r.nagy); S. 8 u li Gordon Brown: Shutterstock, New York (36b); S. 8 u 2. vl David Cameron: Shutterstock, New York (landmarkmedia); S. 8 u 3. vl Theresa May: Shutterstock, New York (Twocoms); S. 8 u re Boris Johnson: Shutterstock, New York (Bart Lenoir); S. 9 o Washington Capitol: iStockphoto, Calgary, Alberta (zrfphoto); S. 9 M Supreme Court, Washington, D.C.: iStockphoto, Calgary, Alberta (sframephoto); S. 9 u li Barack Obama: Shutterstock, New York (Everett Collection); S. 9 2. vl Donald Trump: Shutterstock, New York (Evan El-Amin); S. 9 u re Joe Biden: Shutterstock, New York (Pix_Arena); S. 41 US Wahlergebnisse 2020: Wikimedia Commons – Public Domain by Kingofthedead, https://commons.wikimedia.org/w/index.php?curid=95785583; S. 44 o li Queen Elizabeth II und Prinz Phillip: Shutterstock, New York (Lorna Roberts); S. 44 o re Demonstration: Shutterstock, New York (1 Words); S. 44 u Menschen verschiedener Herkunft: iStockphoto, Calgary, Alberta (FatCamera); S. 45 o Freiheitsstatue: Fotolia, New York (romanslavik.com); S. 45 u Ellis Island Dollar, 1986: Klett-Archiv, Stuttgart; S. 57 o Sikhs: Shutterstock, New York (Elena Rostunova); S. 57 u Obdachloser: iStockphoto, Calgary, Alberta (andrearoad); S. 62 Weg nach Westen: Klett-Archiv, Stuttgart; S. 64 o The World seen by an Indian: Klett-Archiv, Stuttgart; S. 64 u The World seen by a white man: Klett-Archiv, Stuttgart; S. 80 o li Florence Nightingale: Shutterstock, New York (Tony Baggett); S. 80 o re NHS Krankenwagen: Shutterstock, New York (VanderWolf Images); S. 80 u NHS March 201727.06.2017 Shutterstock, New York (John Gomez); S. 81 o Obdachloser: Shutterstock, New York (meunierd); S. 81 M Medikamente, Geld: Shutterstock, New York (AVN Photo Lab); S. 81 u Schild Obamacare: Shutterstock, New York (Kelly vanDellen); S. 92 o Fabrik in Birmingham 1851: Thinkstock, München (Photos.com); S. 92 M Stahlfabrik, England Thinkstock, München (Kapook2981); S. 92 u Finance Distict, London: Shutterstock, New York (Zoltan Gabor); S. 93 o Freihandel, Schiff: Thinkstock, München (AmyLaughinghouse); S. 93 u Silicon Valley, USA: Shutterstock, New York (soulgems); S. 94 Erzvorkommen und Minen, GB: Klett-Archiv, Stuttgart; S. 107 Industrieregionen USA: Klett-Archiv, Stuttgart; S. 112 Schüler in England: Thinkstock, München (DGLimages); S. 113 o Schüler beim Sport, USA: Thinkstock, München (monkeybusinessimages); S. 113 u College-Abschluss, USA: Thinkstock, München (Rawpixel Ltd); S. 13 o BBC Broadcasting House London Thinkstock, München (Nickos); S. 13 u Zeitungsleser: Thinkstock, München (Stockbyte); S. 131 o Interview: Thinkstock, München (Picsfive); S. 131 u Antenne und Satellitenschüssel: Thinkstock, München (moodboard); S. 142 St. Paul's Cathedral, London: Thinkstock, München (Paul_Knight); S. 143 Gospelchor, USA: Thinkstock, München (Digital Vision.); S. 154 Westminster Abbey, Eng-land: Shutterstock, New York (holbox); S. 166 britische Pfund: Shutterstock, New York (Pigprox); S. 167 Euro-Scheine: iStockphoto, Calgary, Alberta (Christopher-Oliver); S. 176 Fußabdruck auf dem Mond, Apollo 11, 1969: Thinkstock, München (Purestock); S. 177 re Pentagon, USA: Thinkstock, München (Mlucas); S. 177 li Weißes Haus, USA: Shutterstock, New York (Andrea Izzotti); S. 189 Federal Hall, New York City, mit Statue von George Washington: Thinkstock, München (MBPROJEKT_Maciej_Bledowski); S. 190 politische Karte Irlands: Thinkstock, München (PeterHermesFurian); S. 191 Bono, Sänger von U2: getty images, München; S. 194 Teilung Irlands: Lay Martin, Freiburg;

Nicht in allen Fällen war es uns möglich, den Rechteinhaber ausfindig zu machen. Berechtigte Ansprüche werden selbstverständlich im Rahmen der üblichen Vereinbarungen abgegolten.